Praise for

COLLABORATIVE HARDBALL

"This book is pure feminine fire. Susan Coleman doesn't just teach negotiation—she reclaims it. *Collaborative Hardball* is a pleasure-fueled, truth-telling, system-shaking call for women to stop settling for crumbs and start leading from radiance, desire, and unapologetic power. Read it, rise with it, and remember who the hell you are."

Regena Thomashauer, aka Mama Gena, founder of the School of Womanly Arts; author, *Pussy: A Reclamation*

"In *Collaborative Hardball,* Susan Coleman offers a vital next chapter in the evolution of negotiation. Building on the foundations of *Getting to Yes,* she shows how women—standing in both strength and empathy—can lead us toward more just, collaborative, and lasting agreements. At a time of global conflict and deep division, this book reminds us that real power lies not in domination but in grounded clarity, deep listening, and the courage to change the rules. A powerful guide for a world that urgently needs new ways forward."

William Ury, author, *Possible: How We Survive (and Thrive) in an Age of Conflict*; co-author, *Getting to Yes*

"*Collaborative Hardball* is a book for everyone who wants to know how to negotiate, including negotiating with those still stuck in a domination worldview. It is a practical and important tool for cultural transformation from domination to partnership."

Riane Eisler, author, *The Chalice and the Blade, The Real Wealth of Nations,* and *Nurturing Our Humanity*

"In *Collaborative Hardball* Susan Coleman asks us to reimagine tough negotiations as thrilling activism. Powered by cutting-edge research, unforgettable stories, and step-by-step tactics, Coleman offers us the essential playbook for toppling stale hierarchies as we advance gender equity, make climate progress, and get you that raise you totally deserve."

Zoe Chance, PhD, professor, Yale School of Management, and bestselling author, *Influence Is Your Superpower*

"In *Collaborative Hardball,* Susan Coleman offers more than a new way to negotiate—she offers a call to evolve. Her compelling framework challenges outdated systems of power and charts a path toward inclusive leadership rooted in strength, empathy, and gender equity. Coleman's 'New Negotiation' approach reclaims voice, rebalances power, and pushes us to create a more inclusive and collaborative world. This book is essential reading for anyone ready to lead with both courage and conscience."

John Barkat, PhD, mediator, International Monetary Fund, and former UN assistant secretary-general

"After decades as a mediator and coach, Susan Coleman consolidates her wisdom and vast understanding of best practices in negotiation, conflict resolution, and large-scale systemic change into a tour de force, *Collaborative Hardball.* Her contribution is a call for women, and all who champion a new way forward, to lead with clarity, courage, and mutual collaboration. Coleman calls us to higher levels of healing and integrity and invites us into the struggle for justice and peace with ferocity and pragmatism. I believe Susan's voice will resonate far and wide as people look for practical guidance on how to serve life at this urgent time."

Amy Elizabeth Fox, CEO, Mobius Executive Leadership

"If you're ready to stop giving your power away and rewrite the rules, *Collaborative Hardball* is your guide. Susan Coleman shows us that true power comes from knowing who you are and negotiating from that place."

Barbara Stanny, author, *Secrets of Six-Figure Women* and *Overcoming Underearning*

"Filled with practical guidance and inspiring stories, Susan Coleman offers a powerful roadmap for women ready to lead with clarity, courage, and compassion. Her AEIOU model is both practical and profound—inviting us to negotiate not through 'power over' but through authentic connection and shared purpose. *Collaborative Hardball* is a vital guide for women—and anyone—committed to transforming systems and stepping into leadership that truly serves."

Peggy Holman, author, *Engaging Emergence*; co-author, *The Change Handbook*

"In *Collaborative Hardball,* Susan Coleman offers a bold, necessary invitation to reshape how we lead, negotiate, and connect—especially as women. With clarity and conviction, she shows that reclaiming power is not about domination but about deep relational engagement and authentic presence. This is more than a book on negotiation; it's a guide to transforming systems from the inside out, grounded in the values of empathy, equity, and collective wisdom."

Nadine B. Hack, CEO, beCause Global Consulting; author, *The Power of Connectedness*

www.amplifypublishinggroup.com

Collaborative Hardball: Using the Power of a New Negotiation as Women to Change the World

For more information, please contact:
Amplify Publishing, an imprint of Amplify Publishing Group
620 Herndon Parkway, Suite 220
Herndon, VA 20170
info@amplifypublishing.com

Library of Congress Control Number: 2025915559

CPSIA Code: PRV1025A

ISBN-13: 979-8-89138-454-5

Printed in the United States

To my two beautiful children, Ava and Jack: May you bring your gifts to the future.

Also, in the last few years as I have been writing this book, I have mentioned it to the many women (and others) I have encountered along the way—of all ages, and from many countries. You have all had a similar response: "Move forward, and write this book; this is important." I have heard this from Maneesha, Manvi, and Tarana from India, and from Bibi, who is high up in the UN and could speak volumes about the need for gender equality and more collaborative systems. I have heard it from my two beautiful millennial children who are shaping a more nonbinary worldview; from Beatrice, a performance artist in Portugal who was stoned when presenting in Greece, not because of her content but just because she was a single woman daring to step out into the public square. I heard the call from Shatai, a local Uber driver and Black single mother of three who was shoved down the stairs by her ex while trying to comfort her one-year-old child. I have heard it from savvy Belle in the Philippines who is navigating her business, children, and husband with an authoritarian dictator nipping at her heels, and from Jing from China who wants desperately to negotiate but must do what she is told. I heard it from women engineers at NASA navigating a complex system with male colleagues and from the most senior women leaders I worked with in Afghanistan who are brave and powerful and now, as I write this, have either escaped or been largely silenced in their own country by the Taliban. I have also heard the call from myself and the ghost of my very talented mom so bounded by patriarchy. This book is dedicated to you.

COLLABORATIVE HARDBALL

Using the Power of a New Negotiation as Women to Change the World

SUSAN COLEMAN

CONTENTS

INTRODUCTION

Our Collective Landscape

The world is on fire.

For many of us, it can be hard to turn on the news. It is often too overwhelming, exhausting, and frightening. The planet is smoking, flooding, and too hot, and it's getting worse. Long-fought-for gains for women's liberty and freedom like access to abortion in the United States are under attack. The rainforest in the Amazon upon which life on the planet depends is being cut down for profit. Sexual assault is pervasive in India, little girls in Afghanistan are forbidden to laugh, there is virginity testing in Mongolia, and authoritarianism, sexism, racism, homophobia, and transphobia are rising across the globe.

My mountain guide son has to wear a face mask at 10,000 feet (about 3,048 meters), where the air should be pristine, because there is so much smoke from climate-related forest fires.

Many young people, including both of my children, are hesitant to have a family because the future to them is looking too bleak and uncertain. In spite of decades of global negotiations to tackle the climate crisis, carbon emissions and planetary temperatures continue to rise. My country, the United States, is teetering on fascism, and with the support of Big Oil and billionaires has elected a convicted felon who has bragged about sexually assaulting women to the presidency.

Scan the planet. What are the biggest challenges that you see?

To me, there are four, and they are all related:

- The rapidly heating planet,
- The Doomsday clock hovering at eighty-nine seconds to midnight, the closest it has ever been to catastrophe,[1]
- The struggle between authoritarianism and democracy,
- The persistent and widening gender, racial, and income imbalance.[2]

A small percentage of people, with various economic ideologies (mostly male but with many women in supporting roles), are working hard and together all over the planet to ensure that wealth, resources, and power go to a small few and that the rest are left to support and serve. A stuck consciousness and narrative of white, male, and human supremacy prevails. This is a human problem at the heart of which is a patriarchal world culture ("PWC"). It is not serving the planet, women, the collective, or the larger whole, and it needs to be dismantled.

You cannot talk about negotiation for women without talking about patriarchy. Patriarchy promotes "power-over" versus "power-with" which has big implications for women when we negotiate and lead. Power-over versus power-with is reflected in the two basic strategies in negotiation, competition and collaboration (win-lose/win-win). The building blocks of patriarchy are found in the details of how we negotiate and resolve our differences as people.

All negotiation happens in a bigger picture context. No human interaction ever happens in isolation. Women's ability to walk away from a negotiation or conflict, the essence of what gives us power in negotiation, has been severely weakened by patriarchy. This diminished power affects us on every level—sovereignty over our bodies, freedom from sexual assault or domestic violence, our ability to care for our children, to partner if and how we wish, to make a living and bring our voices into the world, and to evolve into the human beings that we want and are meant to be.

But what is patriarchy exactly, and how do we dismantle it?

Patriarchy is masculinity writ large, the supremacy of male over female, the masculine over the feminine.

It is a worldview of dominion and control as opposed to partnership and collaboration.

It is driven by a sense of needing to be "better than" and to "own more than." It is greed as opposed to living together creatively and interdependently on this planet with each other and with nature.

It is about a one-up, one-down way of thinking: win-lose versus win-win. It is about individualism, an incessant race to the top, winning at all costs.

At its most predatory, it is rape culture.

It is a system of arrogance that puts humanity above all other life on the planet—men over women, White people over Black and Brown people, rich people over poor people, heteronormative people over the gender-fluid.

It is ego versus eco-consciousness.

Patriarchy is closely linked to a system of competition, violence, and militarism and the trillions of dollars humans spend on war each year, as well as the climate catastrophe which is threatening all life on earth. It shows up in many different social systems—capitalism, authoritarianism, socialism, liberal democracy—and is least present in human systems with more gender equality. Even if not explicitly stated by their own constitutions and laws, most contemporary societies are still, in practice, patriarchal.

Yet while patriarchy has been here for seemingly all of humanity, it has actually been the dominant paradigm for only a nanosecond of the total amount of time humans have been on earth. Indeed, for 99 percent of human history, anthropologists tell us that women and men have lived in partnership, and that patriarchy is more of a "modern" invention, designed for profit and production.

While patriarchy was a reality in the twentieth and now the twenty-first centuries, many women and people (in parallel with a transition to more renewable energy) have made tremendous strides toward a more gender-equal world. Women's move out of the home and into more public spheres has been one of the largest transformations of recent human evolution. Women are everywhere—voting, speaking, leading, growing our strength and influence. We have gone through first-wave, second-wave, third-wave feminism—and now a fourth wave.[3] While this evolution is exciting and transformational for many, it is a great concern for the PWC. Democracy likes gender equality; patriarchy prefers authoritarianism. As women rise, so too does authoritarianism and patriarchal dictatorships, probably in equal measure and as a direct consequence. Patriarchy is dying, but it is not going quietly.

I am not calling out patriarchy to antagonize men but rather to name our current reality. Calling things what they are in order to see them clearly is always the first and most important step in changing them. Many men have suffered a lot under patriarchy. They've been molded into little soldiers at tender ages with all the sweetness kicked out of them so they can fight wars and protect the patriarchal hierarchy. Also, there are many women who zealously protect patriarchy and are happy to defer to a male authority. For gender nonconforming people, patriarchy has been an impossible mold to fit into, but in many ways, their increasing visibility in our modern world is leading the way to a world beyond patriarchy.

A few men are running the world, and it's not going that well. This is not to say that women are perfect, far from it, but it is time for true gender equality and a balancing of the qualities of the masculine and feminine on our planet and in all of our dispute systems. With the climate clock ticking, time is of the essence. It is time for women to fully step into our leadership, stand firmly, and say enough! Negotiation can give us that power.

A New Negotiation

One of the greatest ways to turn the wheel and move forward toward gender equality and democracy is with a New Negotiation for women, who are the largest untapped resource on the planet.

To many, negotiation is a narrow concept, and has something to do with buying, selling, or bargaining. But negotiation is much broader than that. Rather, it is the key skill of influence and conflict resolution, the key skill of shifting the balance of power and building a peaceful and sustainable planet.

In 1981, Roger Fisher and William Ury, members of the Harvard Negotiation Project, published *Getting to Yes: Negotiating Agreement Without Giving In* and started an interest-based revolution that spanned the globe and changed many people's lives, including mine. I was introduced to their ideas in 1986 when I attended Harvard's Kennedy School. Shortly thereafter, I began partnering with Ellen Raider, and we (along with many others) strengthened this movement, both through our work at Columbia University and as independent practitioners. Though Ellen and I didn't frame it like this at the time, I now see, looking back, that in essence our aim was no less than creating a more feminine-infused model for negotiation.

Fast-forward to the present day; these ideas and methods have evolved into what I now call "a New Negotiation." The style is collaborative, as Ellen and I taught in our earlier years, but it now brings a significant attitude shift, awareness, and knowledge of our not being secondary in any way. When women employ a New Negotiation, we are:

- firm, fierce, fair, and unapologetic;
- in our sovereignty;
- free (not codependent, not owned);
- speaking the language of needs;
- honoring our emotional intelligence;
- transcending tribalism and supporting a global sisterhood;
- balancing the feminine and masculine, and renouncing the toxic extremes;
- developing strong walk-away alternatives;
- saying a collective no to violence and dominion;
- thinking systemically, from the intimate to the global and in alignment with nature;
- and working to manifest a deeper, more true global democracy.

Patriarchy exists only because women are complicit with it. When we as half of humanity decolonize ourselves of patriarchy, we are saying "enough" to violence and planetary destruction, "yes" to nature, creation, and life, and not taking no for an answer. This is Collaborative Hardball, a force large enough to take on the PWC and create a world that works for all. Granted, this is a big lift, but, in the words of Halla Tómasdóttir, president of Iceland, "We don't need realistic goals; we need courageous goals now, ambitious goals. We are facing massive challenges the world over, and empowering women, closing the gender gap, is a big part of solving them—if not the key to solving them."[4]

The goal of this book is to give you the tools, techniques, insights, and ideas for a way forward in each and every conflict and negotiation in which you engage. The goal is to "grow our bench," so to speak, to empower all of us. The feminine is rising and women are not going back.

About Me

Who am I, what do I want, and how am I going to get it? These are three orienting questions that I have asked myself at regular intervals throughout my life, and they are the questions I ask when I first meet many of my clients—from individuals up to large organizational systems.

I am a deep lover of the wilderness and the diversity of nature and humanity, who has been working most of my life to create a more just and equal world. For close to four decades, I have had the privilege of working with people all over the world as a teacher—and always a student—of negotiation. I have worked from war zones to boardrooms to inner city public schools, and with people and organizations from every continent. Engaging with diverse groups of people when they are either in conflict or trying to learn how to handle differences better is an amazing lens through which you can see what's really going on in the world. Whether in real time or in role-play, people reveal themselves quickly, even if they are coming from vastly different "tribes."

I have learned that *how* we resolve our differences has everything to do with how successful we are at reaching positive outcomes. Process, or the how, is the stuff of the feminine. In organizational circles you often hear, "the soft stuff is the hard stuff." That's simply because the "feminine" is often missing in how we resolve differences, in our legal systems and governments, our workplaces, our communities, and even in our families. It is time to reclaim it. The feminine is also at the core of collaboration—and collaboration is foundational for the deeper multicultural democracy that is struggling to be birthed in so many places.

My early partner in this work, Ellen Raider, had so much chutzpah and smarts. When we were in Germany working for a large pharmaceutical company to help them revisit an intercultural negotiation gone awry, Ellen put together a group of five consultants from different countries, all women, which made me very nervous. As we walked into the training room, one of the participants (who were all men) mumbled under his breath, "All ladies?" My stomach clenched, but Ellen was unfazed. We went on to deliver an amazing program, and everyone was happy. These successes encouraged me on. Everywhere I went, people were clearly receptive and hungry for the work of the collaborative and multicultural feminine.

Later on in my career, with Ellen's support, I bid on and

won a contract to deliver intercultural negotiation and mediation training to the United Nations Secretariat worldwide. This work, as it unfolded either though me or others, ended up being one of the largest peacebuilding initiatives worldwide and rippled to many large, multilateral organizations.

As my work evolved, I was drawn to taking a more "whole-systems approach," with increased focus on the group of stakeholders of which individuals were just a part and addressing conflict more "upstream" at its source to build more collaboration. I also then launched the *Peacebuilding Podcast* and began interviewing people about the best processes to build common ground in complex systems. What became super obvious to me, as to so many others, is that the most impactful "peacebuilding intervention" we could undertake on the planet is to empower women and achieve true gender equality. From there, more fair and democratic systems that could address other issues of exploitation, including the rapid destruction of our planet and discrimination of Black and Brown people, would follow.

In 2014, I stumbled into Mama Gena's School of Womanly Arts, a school founded in 1998 by Regena Thomashauer.[5] At first, I was resistant because, as I said to my friend who was dragging me along, "Oh, I have read her books, I've been a feminist forever and, if you ask me, way too much pink." But when I entered that auditorium, I was immediately blown away. I had never experienced that much raw joy, emotion, and aliveness among women, women of all skin colors and nationalities who were in their power, connected to their life force energy, and elevated together. For the next six years, while I actively participated in Mama Gena's programs, "Mastery" and "Creation," and most often as part of the volunteer crew "Team Pleasure," I reflected on the work I had been doing in the peace and conflict field. It was through these intense experiences with women that it really landed: The processes I was advocating for and supporting my clients with were much more based on what I think of now as feminine principles—collaborative, celebrating diversity, feelings, needs-based, holistic, creative, and transformational. My commitment to the feminine propelled me away from the power struggle of litigation, toward dialogue, relationality, and the growth and innovation that comes from using conflict well.

On a more personal front, I come from one of the oldest colonial American families—Anglo Saxon, affluent, and yes, patriarchal. I was well fed, well clothed, well educated, but second class and worth "less" from the moment I was born because I was a girl. Throughout my childhood my brother, five years my elder, was given license to dominate me in ways that the animal of my body still remembers. It was part of the culture, part of the neighborhood. In my childhood surroundings, I was also aware of other forms of domination: the apartheid-like private beach club with the "colored" help relegated to the far side of the beach, the rampant antisemitism, and later the Vietnam/American War. Throughout my life, especially in the earlier part of it, I have had a front row seat to the irony of privilege and power. People who celebrate money and stuff often don't have a lot of tolerance for that irony.

While I have included many women's stories in this book, I use my own because it parallels both the glories of my country, the United States of America, and my nation's darker tendencies. And true to feminist form, I wanted to make this book personal, as well as professional and political. I use my own story to communicate many of the themes I seek to convey. My aim is to inspire you to reflect on your own story and the world you would like now to manifest. See what you relate to; the feelings are more important than the facts.

As a young person, I could see from my bird's-eye view from the top of the social hierarchy. At one moment decades later, when I was working with senior women leaders in Afghanistan, we kicked out the (very lovely) male translators who were working with us and held a women's-only circle in a private interior space of the hotel in Kabul where we were working. One by one, we told our stories of how a male-dominated world had impacted us. I started. My Afghan sisters were stunned by my story, that a privileged American woman could have experienced the domestic violence and insult that I had experienced in my family of origin and my marriage. They thought that only happened in Afghanistan. It reminded me how powerful it is for us to share our stories. When we listen to and share with one another, we can see the world more clearly, spot the global patterns, and identify what is needed to move forward.

About the Book

There has been a lot written on the topic of negotiation and conflict resolution. Some of it addresses women and conflict resolution specifically. None have placed the topic of negotiation for women clearly with the backdrop of patriarchy. This book does.

I've written this book for women—but no matter how you identify, if you have picked the book up and read this far, this book is for you. "Woman" is how I have identified throughout my life and the gender I feel I have the most authority to speak to and for. It's important to draw a boundary around us (women and women-identified) so we keep the focus on ourselves when we reflect on and discuss the ideas in this book. It helps to create a container so that we aren't distracted by male confidence or experience, or the call to do any male caretaking. To create the rapid change that our planet and world requires, we need to keep ourselves on the hotseat of opportunity, leadership, mutual support, and transformation.

Having said that, I welcome all male and non-women-identified readers. Your voices and support are invaluable. We are all in this together, and when men or nonbinary people partner with women to negotiate in a new way, we are most likely to positively coevolve quickly.

My hope is that this book will be useful to a wide range of us—from seasoned professionals to amateurs, from home-makers to organizational consultants, lawyers, government folks, diplomats, educators, changemakers, dispute resolution practitioners, peacebuilders, artists, musicians, and more. I am especially hopeful this book will reach and support younger people. We have left you with daunting challenges but also a world that is pregnant with possibility.

Here is what follows. In chapter 1, I introduce you to what negotiation is and why it is critical for women to learn the skills of a New Negotiation. Negotiation is power, and whether we are consciously aware of it or not, we are negotiating all the time, every single day. In order to amplify our negotiation power, it is important to understand at the outset that negotiation has been deeply affected by a PWC. This affects how we think about negotiation, what is "good" negotiation or "bad," who has the authority to negotiate, and whose voices get heard.

In chapter 2, "The Patriarchy Hex," I first bring you back to the time before patriarchy took hold (about seven thousand to ten thousand years ago), to show that the "power-over" paradigm has not always been the dominant worldview of humans. There is no evidence of war during that time, and it appears that men and women lived together as equals subservient to the natural world. Reverence to a preeminent female Goddess or Goddesses was quite common in some ancient cultures. Revisiting this in order to know and sense our innate divinity and majesty as women supports our ability to hold on to our power when we negotiate and endeavor to resolve conflict. In this chapter, I then unpack how patriarchy has shaped concepts of "the feminine," "the masculine," and "the patriarchal," negotiation dynamics, expectations of us as women, and violence and war. Finally, I address trauma and codependency (a form of trauma), because trauma has had an impact on our negotiating brains and clearing this makes us ready to embrace a New Negotiation, one that is free of patriarchal narrative or structures.

In chapters 3 to 9, I detail what I mean by a "New Negotiation." In chapter 3, "Get Comfortable with Conflict," I explore basics about conflict, the "thing" we are trying to address through negotiation. Conflict is a reality of life, and we need to get comfortable with it because how we deal with it matters. We need to stop compromising or avoiding and become the conflict "maestras." Over the millennia, the violence of patriarchy has spooked us into deference, but it's time now to say no to violence and lead the way to a more collaborative and high-functioning world order.

In chapter 4, separating negotiation Positions from underlying Needs and Interests is central to the idea of "Getting to Yes," but speaking the language of needs, giving them priority instead of the language of power or coercion, is fundamental to a New Negotiation. Clearly stating our needs sets in motion their fulfillment. Fulfilling needs is not zero-sum as is maintained by a PWC.[6] There is, indeed, enough to go around on this planet. But as women, we need to build strength with stating what we want, "our position," which is sometimes simply, "No."

In chapter 5, "Use AEIOU to Guide Your Communication," we get into the nitty-gritty of mastering "I want, I need, I feel" through "Informing" behavior, listening with "Opening" behavior, and "Uniting" to reframe, highlight common ground, and more. We also learn to parry the predicable "Attack/Evade" styles of a PWC. Conventional wisdom has it that Attack/defend, fight/flight is how humans behave, but research on women shows that we are much more likely to prefer "tend and befriend." The AEIOU model helps us isolate the best negotiation tactics to use for a New Negotiation.

Chapter 6 guides us to "Own and Honor Your Emotional Intelligence." The language of emotion is the language of the feminine and one which humanity is crying out to recognize in conflict, negotiation, and leadership. Women need to embrace our full range of emotional intelligence and model it. Emotions are energy—and reveal needs that are either satisfied or frustrated. They are a clear window into what is really at the heart of the matter. Anger is a most important emotion for women. To a large extent, men have been allowed anger, women fear, sadness, and shame.

In chapter 7, "Celebrate Worldview Differences and Build Sisterhood across Cultures," I first help you understand key cultural variables that can impact negotiation. Then, I go on to explain how competition, the adversary system, and patriarchy predictably polarize us by identity group. Dismantling patriarchy, still, the largest "culture" on the planet, is key to dismantling intercultural or identity group polarization. We are much more alike than we are different. Women are the group that can truly model global sisterhood and transcend tribalism.

In chapter 8, we pause and integrate what we have talked about so far. I introduce two tools. The first helps you plan for or analyze a conflict as it's progressing, using concepts we have addressed. I use an example of a conflict that was mediated by a colleague in Medellín, Colombia, around the time of Pablo Escobar. The second tool brings together all the steps and stages of a collaborative negotiation in a "Bare Bones," or rather the skeletal structure of a collaborative negotiation. My example here is a conflict between intimate partners.

In "Stand Up to the Domination System" (chapter 9), I explain how negotiation is only useful if the other side is willing to negotiate. Women need to get good at supporting ourselves and each other to stand up to the domination system even when it's dangerous. This is true both in the intimate confines of our homes and at the global negotiation table. We need to be clear about when to use negotiation, and when to quit and move into more "rights-based" processes like litigation or power-based activism.

In the last two chapters, "Fire Up Your Money Power" and "Reclaim Your Body," I go deeper into two critical realms for our skills with negotiation. Money (chapter 10) is a means to an end, and it is also a metaphor for power. We don't need to replicate the extreme financial inequalities of a PWC but we do need to get relaxed and comfortable with managing our own money for our own pleasure, the power that comes from being able to walk away, and to have an equal say in how we spend planetary resources.

Chapter 11, "Reclaim Your Body," focuses on our physical selves, where it all begins. Fundamentally, powerful negotiation comes down to the body and how we show up in it. Powerful negotiation is ultimately powerful presence, and powerful presence comes from clearing trauma from our bodies and knowing our deep power and right to be present, persuade, and influence.

I end the book with where I have arrived in my own journey with negotiation and conflict—thinking systems and circles. I spent a good deal of time teaching individuals the skill sets of negotiation but my most powerful work happened when I got the whole system[7] into the room to sit in a circle and work things out. Here, I share with you a few key stories from some of what I think of as my best work, and a vision of where this work might take you and us.

Throughout every chapter, I offer some reflection questions and prompts to help you put things into practice. I recommend using a journal, a place where you can respond to the reflection questions I have posed and write about your practical experiences with the ideas in the book.

Feel free to read the book in any way that makes most sense to you. Read it straight through or read the part that feels most pressing in your life now. Read it by yourself or with a group so you can talk about it together.

Use the book to deepen your skill with negotiation. Reflect on what it might look like to balance the masculine and the feminine in your negotiations with others as well as to stand up for the feminine in your own life and in the world.

Learning anything new requires an openness to new skill sets, narratives, knowledge, and attitudes. I hope this book will support you on all these fronts.

I encourage you to read the book as "whole bodied" as you can. Tune in not just with your head—but all the parts of you that give you intelligence.

May a New Negotiation ignite the power of the feminine in all of the conflicts in which we find ourselves, diminish hierarchy, and strengthen the power of the circle, the original form of healing. In spite of some very scary stuff—climate catastrophe, nuclear annihilation, fascism, maybe AI, I choose to believe that we can restore and rewild our planet, move beyond armed conflict, and create a beautiful world for all living creatures. Nothing is impossible. While there are big obstacles, we are on track and moving ahead, despite the voices that try to distract us by creating chaos, division, and polarization. It is my hope that this book will support you in realizing more fully what you want individually and contribute to our collective power as women to lead our planet forward in positive and life-affirming ways that dismantle patriarchy one negotiation at a time.

CHAPTER 1

Negotiation Is Power!

> *A powerful woman knows who she is, what she wants, and stands for it unapologetically.*
> —Barbara Stanny, "Becoming Your Own Prince Charming", 2019

It was 2019. I was in Saint Bartholomew's Cathedral in the heart of New York City with one thousand other women of every color, every age, and from just about every country on earth. It was the start of Mastery, the School of Womanly Arts's signature empowerment program for women, and I was on "Team Pleasure," the sexy, badass volunteer crew. The church was Episcopal, the religion of the dominant class in the United States and the religion I was raised in. On the church walls, portraits of the industrial and patriarchal benefactors (99 percent male) stared down at us from all corners.

As was typical of how "Mama Gena" (Regena Thomashauer), the leader of the program, magically worked the crowd in those days, within minutes of getting underway, she asked one woman in the audience why she was there. As the woman's story unfolded, it quickly became apparent that it was the story of all women and the trials and tribulations of living in a PWC. In a whisper at first, she said, "I didn't want to accept crumbs." Then she said it a bit bolder and louder, "I was sick of accepting crumbs." Then louder still. Before you knew it, the entire cathedral, surrounded by the glittering stained-glass windows of the Christian stations of the Cross, had erupted into a resounding chant of *"No more crumbs, no more crumbs!"* All of us went wild. We started to dance, scream, pound our fists, and roar. The chant had hit a nerve and released raw, intoxicating enthusiasm, rage, commitment, and resolve. Together we were like a genie that was unlikely to go back into the bottle.

Something magical happens when you get large groups of women together. Profound healing can occur. One person's story is quickly recognized as theme and variation of most everyone's story. In this group of women, everyone was recognizing how we had agreed to our role as "lesser than" and we were agreeing to it no longer. We were now willing to do the work to put that behind us.

But how?

First and foremost, we need to get very good at negotiation, specifically, the firm, collaborative, and feminine-infused New Negotiation that is free from the patriarchal constructs that have held us back for so long.

Negotiation Defined

Think to yourself quietly for a moment and complete this sentence:

Negotiation is ________.

What comes to mind?

What images?

What stories?

How would you explain negotiation to someone who had never heard the word?

Here's my definition: Negotiation refers to any time a person or a party is trying to directly influence or persuade another person or party.[1]

By this definition, negotiation is happening everywhere all the time. Many of us women negotiate a lot, or would like to.

Negotiation can be about anything—where to go for dinner, who is going to take the kids, how to budget or spend money, who is doing the housework, how to make love. Negotiation occurs in discussions between families, spouses, neighbors, and work colleagues, and between countries. It occurs over matters of war and peace, our climate and the survival of our planet, and much more.

Sometimes it's obvious we are negotiating because the conversation is formal and specific, like when we negotiate over the purchase and sale of a home, but most negotiations are not formal; they are ongoing, unresolved "issues" about money in a household, for example, or who keeps getting the juicy assignments at work. Many happen over time, sometimes even over a lifetime. They can be ad hoc, informal, and even unplanned.

The more aware we are of how frequently we are negotiating, or trying to negotiate, the more we can consciously apply the concepts and skills of a New Negotiation to those interactions and get better outcomes as a result. Our awareness will also help us gain insight into why things don't always go the way we want. We will begin to see where we are not actually negotiating at all and are just deferring or being compliant because that's what the culture has so often taught us to do.

Substance/Relationship Tension

There are two types of negotiations—conflict and exchange. Exchange negotiations happen when we make a trade: I'll give you this for that. Conflict negotiations are discussions or transactions where we disagree about the preferred solution to a problem and a simple outcome isn't obvious.

This book focuses on conflict negotiations because they are far more difficult. This is true because, for most humans, conflict is difficult. Conflict requires us to balance the two major subsets of a negotiation that matter to us: the substance and the relationship. The substance part is the "what-we-want" part, whether it is help with childcare, money, more time for ourselves, help with the dishes, or regular full-bodied orgasms during sex. The relationship part involves the rapport and connection between the parties—whether that's between family members, spouses, countries, or adversaries. It's about our desire and willingness to continue dealing with each other, either personally or professionally, as a result of the negotiation.

In order to understand the substance/relationship tension, let's start by imagining a purely substance-oriented negotiator.

What would a person who is focused entirely on what they want, without consideration for the relationship, sound like? What behaviors or tactics would they use? Typical answers I have heard in my workshops are:

Tough
Focused
Blunt
Brutal
Self-focused
Strong

Now pause for a second and think—what is the likely impact of this substance-focused approach on the outcome?

It is likely to generate high substance for the negotiator (a win) but with an obvious downside. Those who rely on just substance are tough, push hard to get their way, refuse to concede, and use personal attacks and hard-nosed tactics. The ends justify the means—at all costs. But when we behave this way over time, the relationship suffers and people are not likely to want to negotiate with us in good faith in the future. So, an exclusively substance-oriented style is probably not sustainable over time. Agreed?

Now imagine a purely relationship-oriented negotiator. How would this person behave? What tactics would they use? Typical responses I have heard from folks in my programs include:

Flexible
Accommodating
Giving
Pushover
Deferential
Soft

In my courses, I have even heard people call relationship-oriented negotiators "pussies" (under their breath).

What's the likely impact of this style on outcomes?

In a purely relationship-oriented approach, we are more likely to preserve the relationship, but we very well might end up empty-handed.

When we want to maintain or strengthen the relationship side of things, we tend to be accommodating, flexible, and willing to find a way to say yes to meet their other's needs, but if we do this over time, we neglect our own substantive needs. An exclusively relationship-oriented strategy is not sustainable over time either. Also agreed?

This is the key tension when people negotiate. Do I pursue substance at the expense of the relationship, or do I nurture the relationship at the expense of the substance?

The goal is to find a way that allows us to do both.[2]

Key Tension

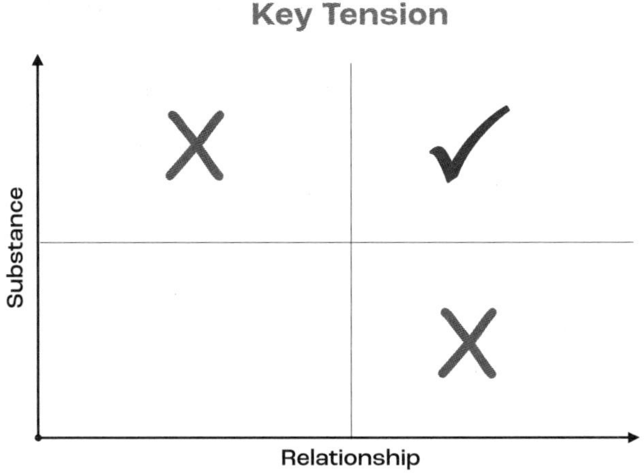

When I first heard my colleague Zach Metz, a wonderful negotiation trainer, explaining these distinctions, a smile came across my face. I wondered if participants were noticing the gender component in these two distinct negotiation styles. Do you?

It's hard to look at the descriptions and not see stereotypical gender.

Traditionally, humanity has mostly put substance in the male camp and relationship in the female camp. Men go out and conquer, and women smooth things over and clean up the collateral damage. Because of this, women have deferred, accommodated, or avoided to preserve the relationship, and men have been asked to conquer and be strong, macho, commando, or hypermasculine. On a global scale, women have been acculturated to "lump it," just accept something they don't like. It's time, sisters, to stop. Ultimately, life on the planet will improve if both men and women, all humans, balance substance and relationship in negotiation. We need both.

Because we live in a world where substance is prioritized over relationship, many popular negotiation techniques promote winning and beating one's counterpart. In other words, the patriarchal approach breeds strategies and techniques where the needs and feelings of one's counterpart are ignored. Many negotiation strategies have been developed to help a party gain advantage over or beat their counterpart. The message we must muscle up in a conflict is pervasive, and new theme and variation of win/lose strategies keep coming. I call the promoters of these strategies the "red-meat" negotiators: They are addicted to coercion and deeply influenced by patriarchy.

One could argue that win/lose strategies are effective in short-term relationships, where the parties are not likely to see each other again, or where there isn't any interdependence. A stereotypical example of one of these short-term relationships might be between a buyer and a seller when buying a used car. Since we don't expect to see the other person again and we sell the car "as is," we can afford to be more tough and uncompromising, but even in that situation, we may see the person again, or may care about the relationship. Indeed, this was exactly the case for me when I sold my old Prius to a neighbor who responded to my advertisement. I was transparent with him about the pros and cons of the car and, knowing that his young daughter was going to be driving it, felt good about doing so. I also got a fair and good price for the car. It was a win-win.

While there are certainly moments for taking a win-lose approach, is there really such a thing in today's world that is all "I" and no "we"? Through a lens of enlightened consciousness, how many of these situations do you actually know where we can assume no connection with a stranger? As women, is this the world we want to shape?

I believe negotiation should include strategies that will support people over time. Exclusively focusing on winning at all costs is not good for long-term relationships, and focusing solely on the relationship is not good for long-term substance either.

Process Choice

Negotiation is a process. When conflict arises between two or more people, there are different ways to respond. If we are among the lucky sisters on the planet, we have the power to choose which response or process is best for our purposes. Skillful negotiation includes skillful process choice. It might sound biblical, but "there's a time for every season."

When we are in a conflict we can:

- Avoid—walk away
- Negotiate—work it out directly with the other side (either competitively or collaboratively)
- Mediate—have a neutral, non-decision-maker facilitate the negotiation
- Arbitrate or grieve—have a neutral third-party expert decide the outcome by applying established rights, rules, and regulations

- Litigate—have a judge decide the outcome based on law
- Fight—use physical force or coercive power to win

For those situations that matter to us, where we want to address the issue and not simply avoid it, negotiation (and its close cousin mediation) is generally the best process choice because: (1) it gives us the most control over the outcome; (2) we can create tailor-made solutions; (3) it is more relational; and (4) we are not handing the outcome over to a third party.

Culture and Negotiation

While all of these processes show up around the globe, different language is used to describe them. For instance, some countries might use the word "arbitration," and others use "conciliation" to refer to very similar processes. In some countries or cultures, the word "mediation" might have a connotation more like meddling or interference and might not be seen as a positive option. In some countries, there isn't even a word for negotiation, though it is practiced nonetheless.

Some cultural groups think of negotiation like a sports game. Some think of it as relationship-building over time. Many associate it with bargaining like in an Arab bazaar. I include in its definition (somewhat unconventionally but justified) a much "wider" process of getting all stakeholders, or the whole system, in the room to work through differences (often with the support of a neutral facilitator/mediator.)

Based on where we sit on the planet, our gender, and our economic situation, the concept of negotiation may vary along a spectrum of cultural values. Some human groups will emphasize the "I," and others the "we." Some are much more comfortable with risk. Some are loose with time (i.e., "Whenever we get to it is fine"), while others demand strict punctuality. Some are more deferential to hierarchy (i.e., "Do what the top dog says"), and others will question authority.

Generally, the "culture" of women is more collaborative, relational, and communal, and whatever we may call it, most women are trying to negotiate everywhere on the planet to get our needs and the needs of our families met.[3] Globally, there is a "culture" of gender that either highly respects women or does not, which makes negotiation more easy or more difficult. For example, women who live in in a highly authoritarian environment—be it the culture of her country or the culture of her work or home—has limited power to negotiate. She is much more likely to be following the directives of a higher, mostly male, authority even if she would prefer to have a voice and negotiate.

Negotiation requires democracy—at home, at work, and in the world. By its very definition, democracy allows us to participate in the decisions that affect us. In a more authoritarian dynamic, it is "Do what I say"—it is power-over. In a more democratic dynamic, there is room for voice, debate, and collective decision-making.

When people can participate in the decisions that affect them, they are more likely to accept the outcomes and abide by them. This is why negotiation is the essential process for resolving conflict and for building peace on our planet. It is also why women, as half of humanity, need to have great negotiation skills and meaningful opportunities to use them.

Reflections on Negotiation

- *How was negotiation modeled in your family of origin? Were you able to negotiate on your own behalf?*
- *What was your mother's style of negotiation? Your father's? Other important caregivers?*
- *What were the predominant messages from your culture about negotiation for women?*
- *What has been your life story with negotiation?*
- *How much do you negotiate in your daily life now? At home? At work or school?*
- *Do you believe that negotiation requires democracy?*

Power Defined

> *Power is the greatest taboo for women.*
> —Kasia Urbaniak, *Unbound*, 2021

In recent years, there has been a lot of conversation about power in women's circles because as women, we haven't had a lot of it. Either it hasn't been conferred, we haven't taken it back, or we haven't stepped into it.

For most of human time on earth, women have been considered powerful among humans. Our bodies mysteriously created life, which was revered and seen as a great source of power. That power is also the thing that a PWC has most tried to control in us.

Over time and with the rise of patriarchy, women's power declined rapidly, and we were largely controlled by men and male-designed institutions. Since then, our power has been curtailed by roles prescribed by patriarchy: relegated to being just mothers, housewives, supportive partners, nurses, caregivers, property of men, providers of sex.

Perhaps whatever part of the world you hail from, you have watched old American Westerns and are familiar with the big old Hollywood patriarchal archetype John Wayne. One of his old Western movies, *Stagecoach*, depicts the stereotypical roles available for American women as we moved westward on the continent in the 1800s. The passengers in the coach were a mother/wife and a prostitute, women's two options at the time—mother/wife or whore, both defined by men, not by us.[4] While musty and outdated, these limitations continue to reverberate around the world.

As we allow ourselves to step into a wider range of roles and shake off these constraints, we also reclaim our power in negotiation.

So, what does it look like to reclaim our power?

- Knowing that we are not secondary in any way
- Believing in our deep divinity
- Manifesting our voices and leadership
- Knowing what we are here to do, our purpose, and being aligned with it
- Taking action to create the world we want to create

In the words of Martin Luther King Jr., "Power properly understood is nothing but the ability to achieve purpose. It is the strength required to bring about social, political, and economic change . . . power without love is reckless and abusive, and love without power is sentimental and anemic."[5]

When it comes to women, power and voice are just about tantamount to the same thing. In her seminal work, *In a Different Voice*, Harvard psychologist Carol Gilligan famously conveyed the idea that patriarchy has created violence in men and silence in women.[6] The fundamental problem of patriarchy, she says, is that it has taken away women's power and voice. So many of us have been taught that we are victims or helpless damsels in distress, a surefire message that usurps our power and voice and teaches us that we should be OK with just being ignored and not getting our needs met. But, as poet Alice Walker has conveyed, the most common way people give up their power is by thinking they don't have any.[7]

Learning how to cast off these muzzles, to get out of the traditional roles that limit us, to change the narrative about who we are via the skill set of negotiation is hugely empowering. This, of course, can terrify both the more traditional men and women alike and create a lot of pushback, often in the form of antidemocratic movements.

Like race, gender has been a caste system set up in service of a certain hierarchy. Breaking this is both exciting and challenging. My family of origin installed powerlessness in me from the beginning. The kind of power that would truly put me in the driver's seat was not taught or modeled for me or my sisters. We were taught that the "feminine" way to derive our power was from men—find one, and have him exert it on our behalf. My mother, from her gilded generational cage, gave me many subtle and not-so-subtle messages to not get caught in this bind. She lived empathically through me, and steadfastly cheered me on with my various academic or professional achievements that weren't available to her in her day.

A scene from when I was twelve comes to mind that makes me both grimace and chuckle. We lived near a golf course—and I somehow got the idea to organize the girls from my grade and challenge the boys "to a rumble" (a fight). I'm not sure exactly what my motivation was, but I suspect a certain amount of sexual tension as well as frustration over the inherent power imbalance already seeping into my awareness compelled me. I was physically strong, attractive, and growing into my fullness—and I wasn't having it with what I now see as the binary rigid roles of the PWC and the way it was limiting who and what I could be. I understand now that I held that rumble to defy the traditional norms that were beginning to envelope and strangle me.

As I continue to challenge the patriarchal thinking in my own family of origin, I continue to receive pushback from family members who remain stuck in or continue to benefit from the patriarchal hierarchy. I am sad about the estrangement and hopeful that one day it will shift.

Throughout my life, what has most undermined my success and blooming is the way I had internalized the patriarchy's messages to dim myself down. Indeed, my ambivalence about power has cost me a lot. There was a distinct pattern: Each time I reached another height in my business success, I would undermine myself—sometimes by "falling in love" and cycling into what I call "love addiction," where I obsessed over some undeserving guy. Many women have shared with me that they have seen a similar pattern in themselves. As women, we have become skilled at hiding and finding ways to undermine ourselves and not rock the boat.

Reflections on Power

- *What were the messages you received about power growing up? Who had power? Where did they get it?*
- *Have you accepted crumbs in your life? In what way?*

- *What's your definition of power now? What makes you feel powerful?*

Putting into Practice

- *Pay attention to when and where you are negotiating today. How is it going? Are you getting what you want?*
- *Pay attention to what makes you feel most powerful. Write about it in your journal.*

Negotiation Is Power

As I wrote in the introduction, you cannot talk about negotiation without talking about power, and you cannot talk about negotiation for women without talking about patriarchy. Patriarchy, which upholds a power-over dynamic, has big implications for women in negotiation.

"Power-over," domination, is the essence of our current patriarchal, macho, world culture. "Power-with," win-win, is much more evolutionary, sustainable, and, I might add, fun.

Negotiation power allows us to articulate what we want in life toward a world that works for us, our families, and the global community.

Have you ever noticed that traditionally dominant men, especially the powerful ones, prefer compliant wives? Donald Trump once commented that what he likes about his wife, Melania, is that she does what he tells her to do.[8]

In the United States, there are men who order brides from Asia, assuming they will be compliant. What does this mean exactly? It means they want a wife who won't talk back. In other words, she will not try to negotiate. She will "accept followership," a term my ex often used as our marriage was breaking up and I refused to do as he asked.

In negotiation, the party who has the most power is the party who is least dependent on the outcome of the negotiation to meet their objectives.

So how do you get power in negotiation?

There are three things.

When we have the ability to meet or satisfy the needs/interests of the other we have power. For instance, if we are negotiating with someone who is hungry and we have food to offer, we have power to influence the situation and might be able to strike a deal. Or it might be that simply our presence, the way we show up, moves them and inspires them to follow our lead.

When we have the ability to thwart or frustrate the other side's needs or interests, we also have power. In 2020, when the famous basketball player LeBron James threatened to refuse to play ball to protest racially motivated police shootings of unarmed Black people, that gave him big power to possibly shut down the National Basketball Association and frustrate fans that were waiting to see the game.[9]

Finally, when we have a strong BATNA, we also have power. "BATNA," a term coined by the Harvard Negotiation Project and featured in the Fisher and Ury book *Getting to Yes,* is your "Best Alternative to a Negotiated Agreement." In other words, BATNA refers to the most advantageous alternative course of action a party can take if negotiations fail and an agreement cannot be reached.[10]

Here's an example. You are looking for a job, and you get a few offers all of which you like and you are negotiating the terms of employment beyond base salary. In this situation, you have power: You have options to choose from. In other words, you have a strong BATNA. You can negotiate for the strongest package knowing that you have two other offers to back you up if one doesn't work out; you can walk away from one to the best possible alternative.

A BATNA is a simple idea yet very important for women.

Long ago, a beloved therapist of mine said, "Susan, you can't really negotiate unless you are willing to walk away." She was so right. I have thought about her comment a lot and repeated it many times in negotiation programs. When we are preparing for an upcoming negotiation (or difficult conversation), we need to think about what happens if it doesn't work out the way we want. We could settle for something we don't want—or we could walk away, which might be the far better option. This is key to assessing our power to influence the situation.

As women we need to be clear-eyed about our alternatives, our walk-away positions, our BATNAs, in any negotiation or conflict, personal or professional. This is often not so easy—first and foremost because of the tenacity of the PWC, which seeks to limit our options and keep us controlled.

A story that might sound familiar to you comes to mind that exemplifies this. I run an Airbnb out of my home, from which I get a welcome second source of income and a lot of interesting guests. One of them was an adorable twenty-four-year-old Indian man and graduate student in New York City. A self-described feminist, he shared openly about his parents' divorce. Apparently, in the negotiation of his parents' marriage (and yes, marriage is a negotiation—all the principles apply), it was OK for his dad to be abusive to his mom and to have affairs with other women. His mom, in contrast, was a dutiful mother and wife and, while a professional herself, supported her husband as the main breadwinner. His dad walked away from the marriage and was able, through his greater economic power and the Indian laws that privilege men, to have custody of the kids—which was super painful to my guest, and I'm sure to his mom as well. In other words, my guest's mother lived in a context with fewer walk-away options and thus far less negotiating power.

Patriarchy is a system, it is global, and while it's not so great for men either, it generally strengthens men's options, or BATNAs, in the negotiations or conflicts they have with women.

Building Our Negotiation Power as Women

> *Women will change the nature of power, rather than power changing the nature of women.*
> —Bella Abzug, keynote, National Women's Conference, 1977

At the beginning of this chapter, I encouraged you to explore what comes to mind when you hear the word "negotiation." I could also have asked *who* comes to mind.

Be honest with yourself. Exploring who comes to mind will give you some idea about the unconscious bias imprinted in your brain about negotiation, about leadership, about power.

Are they male or female?

How old are they?

What are they wearing?

What color is their skin?

What language do they speak?

In spite of our tremendous strides, there continues to be a hidden—or not so hidden—bias that negotiators are male, sixty-ish, more powerful if White, and dressed in a navy suit.

During the 2020 pandemic, I spotted a moving post on Facebook with powerful images and music that brought tears to my eyes: It showcased all the women that had stepped into leadership roles in recent years. It said something like "While the world has been distracted by the noise of all those resistant to change, change has been happening anyway." And then it showed face after diverse face of women leaders around the world: Angela Merkel, chancellor of Germany; Sheikh Hasina Wazed, prime minister of Bangladesh; Erna Solberg, prime minister of Norway; Nicola Sturgeon, first minister of Scotland . . . It was followed by about twenty-three more women leaders.[11] These women got where they are because they know how to, and are willing to, negotiate. Women are building our negotiation power in all spheres. There are examples everywhere. But we have a long way to go.[12]

In my negotiation trainings with women, I have observed that many women at some point realize that they carry the key skill sets for negotiation within them. We all do. We just need to transcend our tendency to defer and accommodate and any fear we may hold toward negotiation itself.

Negotiation is a "power" word, and power is taboo for so many women.

We must challenge the narratives we have absorbed about our powerlessness and clear out our unconscious bias about who has the privilege to negotiate.

Clearing out these narratives can take work and compassion for ourselves. Katrina, one of my clients doing powerful peacebuilding work in Africa, finds that words get stuck in her throat when she tries to set limits and negotiate on her own behalf. When I asked her about this, she told me that she still carries the template in her brain of her violent father who kept her mother in line. It takes work to combat the silence her mother was forced to carry.

Far too many women will get slapped, reprimanded, sexually harassed, or worse if they try to advocate on their own behalf or on behalf of their kids or other interests. We need to firmly and collectively say *no* to what is not acceptable behavior.

Strong men like Donald Trump have crafted their image, with books like *The Art of the Deal*, as being the essence of the good negotiator.[13] They use coercion, threats, authoritarianism, and grandiosity to get their way. And these patriarchal models have left us believing that negotiation is an adversarial power struggle where the winner takes all. Many women who have lived with this paradigm believe that, at the very least, they must compromise or settle for less. It is essential that we look inside of ourselves and get honest with how much of this myth we have swallowed.

I often think about Nelson Mandela's capacity to negotiate on Robben Island. Even in solitary confinement, he was able to influence guards to get more of what he wanted. He had tremendous personal power, confidence, and a constituency who believed in him. He had enormous moral authority because he simply stood unwaveringly for equality, fairness, and the importance of relationships.[14]

Sisters, we can do the same.

Reflections on Your Walk-Away Alternatives (BATNA)

- *Think about some of the conflicts in your life.*
- *Are you able to walk away from situations in your life that no longer serve you? What would it take?*

- *What steps do you need to take to make your walk-away options stronger?*

Reflections on Unconscious Bias in Negotiation

- *What narratives have you absorbed about who negotiates?*
- *How does unconscious bias impact you in advocating for yourself? In advocating for other women?*
- *How has the PWC impacted you in negotiation?*

Putting into Practice

Notice who is "negotiating" around you today—at home, out in the world, and in the news.

Bring to mind a negotiation or conflict situation that you are in or are facing soon. Think of two to three ways that you could lessen your dependency on its outcome to achieve your objectives. Does this increase your power to influence the situation? Write about this in your journal.

CHAPTER 2

The Patriarchy Hex

> *A big part of our problem is ignorance of what older cultures have to teach us.*
> —Gloria Steinem, *The Full Circle*, 2020

I think I was eleven. I had on my Sunday best, a knit wool coat tight at the waist with nice buttons, and I was sitting in a pew of the Episcopal church that my mom and I attended every Sunday. "Trinity" Church was its name—the trinity being the Father, the Son, and the Holy Ghost. It was hard to see my beautiful girl self in that lineup.

We were listening to the tall, White, older male minister, Mr. Moody, tell the story of Adam and Eve. Mr. Moody lived up to his name. I remember asking him once, in all sincerity, "Are you God?" He was not at all amused.

A rib, he said, was taken from Adam to create Eve. Adam had wanted companionship and asked God for it. This was God's—a man's—solution. I remember slowly realizing that according to this teaching, I, a girl, was somehow an afterthought. Girls came second, were second best, and there for the comfort of Adam.

My trips to church ended shortly afterward. My mother and I decided together that the minister was way too stuffy, and this wasn't really in our best interest. Good riddance! We didn't have the language of patriarchy then—but we felt it that day. We didn't feel included in our power, beauty, and ability to lead and influence in the world. My mom had good instincts; she knew when she was being sold a bill of goods.

The ubiquitous story of Adam and Eve is completely opposite of what I now understand to be a closer version of the truth: Humans evolved from the female XX, and the male XY came after. This well-known biblical narrative goes right to the core of the dominant messaging about the relationship between men and women, which teaches that men have primacy and women are there to serve them. To many men, this myth has communicated a certain dose of impunity and false empowerment to their detriment, and to us women a sense of inferiority and shame.

At about sixty, post-divorce, when I first became aware of the "upside-downness" of the Adam and Eve story, I was dating a guy to whom I had yet again given away too much of my power. Learning this truth, about our origins as women and the falseness of this narrative, immediately shifted my more baked-in deferential stance, subtly, but definitively. I didn't need to find power outside of myself in a guy. The divinity, the source energy, was in me.

As Gloria Steinem so accurately said, "I think we can't understand what it means that divinity is one sex, what it means that males are the same sex as God. This is a very deep lesson that children pick up on and it stays with us from cradle to grave."[1] Whether you are a woman who believes in a higher power or not, the idea of a male God is an enormous all-encompassing cultural imprint that has affected many of us and has profound implications for our negotiation power. The stories that we've learned have a big impact on how we see the world and how we see ourselves. They affect our sense of self-esteem and our ability to advocate for what we want through negotiation and leadership. In *Cassandra Speaks*, Elizabeth Lesser writes, "Stories created only by men are really stories about men . . . They were not created to help women respect their bodies, intelligence, and legitimacy. They were told and are still told to bury the truth of our equality, values and voice."[2]

Negotiation is the key skill set of influence, conflict resolution, and building peace in our homes, communities, and world. These stories influence so much about the process itself—how we should approach a conflict, who should be at the table, what we should wear, who should speak, who should listen, and who should serve the coffee. There is arguably not a single aspect of the process of negotiation that isn't influenced by these narratives in ways that undermine our power and voice as women.

The Age of the Goddess and Our Collaborative Past

The Adam and Eve story, of course, is just a myth—and there is evidence that in our evolution as humans, the female form came first. It also appears that, for a vast majority of our time on this planet, human beings have lived in harmony with each other without war and have a very long collaborative past.

Elizabeth Rabia Roberts, EdD, aka "Rabia," spent years researching the "HerStory" of women, which she describes as "a huge empowering story of the evolution of homo sapiens most especially from the perspective of women." Among her many eurekas, one that most stands out to me addresses the story of Adam and Eve head on:

> The beginning of mammals was cloning, two XX's. It's female for a long time, the females of the species of insects to the apes are females reproducing themselves. XY evolves later, perhaps even as a genetic mutation. Females were the first in our evolution—males came later. While maleness brought diversity in the gene pool it also brought a much greater tendency toward violence, which has been a challenge for humanity and other species.[3]

As Rabia describes in her research, dating back to forty thousand years ago, our ancestors survived two major ice ages, food shortages, natural disasters, and so much more. One of the key reasons for their resilience was the "working mom," "one of the most skilled creatures that ever existed on the planet." As Rabia points out, women were deeply revered: "The oldest grave that is known about with decorations and shells all around, it was a little girl. It wasn't a big Chief. It doesn't seem like male chiefs were any more decorated than the females that were found."[4]

I remember reading an article that showed that, contrary to long-standing conventional wisdom, archaeologists now have evidence that young women were big game hunters.[5] This certainly bursts my bubble in terms of what I thought was truth and influences how I view my own sense of physical capacity and courage.

Why is it important to consider these new narratives of our past in a book on negotiation? Because when we come to terms with our innate divinity, strength, and value, we are less likely to accept crumbs and more likely to claim our true worth, step into leadership, and take charge through the skill of negotiation. Knowing our inherent worth makes us stronger and empowers us to negotiate. It's not our lot in life to be secondary to men or to serve a patriarchal culture. What if you had heard, as you were growing up, more of what now appears to be true about our earliest beginnings as women on this planet? How might that have impacted you and what you thought you were capable of?

Contrary to conventional wisdom, humans have not always been violent and there has not always been war. When I was in my twenties, I read the life-changing book *The Chalice and the Blade*, by Riane Eisler, in which Eisler examines how societies constructed the roles and relations between the female and male halves of humanity throughout time. It was such a eureka moment to learn that humans have not always been in a state of war and violence. In fact, the vast majority of human existence is characterized by what Eisler calls "models of partnership versus domination" or what anthropologist and negotiation expert William Ury articulated as "2,500,000 years of possible coexistence to 10,000 years of coercion."[6] Warfare, it turns out, is a relatively modern invention.

In his book *Getting to Peace*, Ury tells a great story about an anthropologist who, because of his own worldview, assumed humans were always bloodthirsty. When he found a skull, he assumed the crack in it came from a blow from another human. But on deeper examination, others concluded it was the result of rock pressure and an attack from a leopard. "There turns out to be little conclusive evidence in the archeological record for the story of pandemic human violence during the first ninety-nine percent of human evolution," writes Ury.[7] So much for the conclusions we draw and how they create the stories that we live by!

It is, of course, hard to know exactly what happened in the past. As Ury writes, "It remains possible that archeologists will find evidence of warfare pre–8000 years ago, but to date they have not."[8] Many of us have always believed that there has always been war, that humans have always been violent, and that competition, violence, and domination are at the core of our very nature. But there is plenty of alternative evidence that long ago humans lived together as equals where they collaborated with one another and, in many of these societies, the Divine was often a revered Goddess and, god forbid, a super sexy one with the power to create life.[9]

In my early days of teaching negotiation skills at Columbia University, I came across the Film Board of Canada's *Goddess Remembered: The Spiritual Journey of Earth's Peoples,* a film that told the tale of early humans celebrating a Goddess called the Great Mother who embodied the primal power of the female to give and nurture life. The narrator pointed out that "only recently, for six thousand years ago is recent in the age of humankind, has the earth and the female perspective been ignored." Later, in an interview I conducted with anthropologist Douglas Fry, Fry supported this view and expressed his surprise when he realized that there is no evidence of war and his observation that "you get cultural beliefs and cultural narratives that just evolve . . . [and that] are just incredibly important in shaping how we will view the world . . . These types of domination societies come in very late, or another way to put it, very recently . . ."[10]

In 2024, I took a trip to Crete, the cradle of the Minoans, an ancient civilization that thrived in the second millennium BCE and that embraced nature, art, athletics, music, pleasure, and—most noticeably—did not appear to pursue war. Their religious belief was expressed in the worship of the Great Goddess, protector of nature, and also multiple Goddesses, including my favorite, the "Snake Goddess." It was a moving experience to walk through the archeological museums on Crete with so many images and references to a powerful female divine, so different from the thousands of impressions that had been fed to me throughout my life from Michelangelo's *David* to other images of the Father, the Son, and the Holy Ghost.

The Minoan civilization lasted for a couple of thousand years and then met its demise. First, a major earthquake happened on the nearby island of Thera, now Santorini, with an accompanying tidal wave that probably didn't immediately destroy life on Crete but led to gradual destruction and starvation, which likely led to a loss of faith in the Goddesses that protected the harvest among other things. A boy statue—perhaps a young Zeus—was discovered from around the time of the demise of the Minoans, signaling a turning away from the Goddess toward the preeminence of the masculine. The statue was found in many pieces, and anthropologists have speculated that it was thrown across the room by someone in great anger.[11] We can only wonder who tossed the statue to the ground and why. Had the Goddess forsaken? Was the thrower angry about just their current moment, or were they foreseeing further out—a future of perpetual warfare, power struggles, the rise of a PWC, and the destruction of nature?

History, of course, is "his" story and written by the victors, not the vanquished.

Reflections on Our Stories, Myths, and Collaborative Past

- *What have been your assumptions about our human "her" story? What did you learn at school, at home, from religion, from culture?*
- *Were you aware that females were probably first in human evolution? How does that awareness impact you—your sense of agency, worthiness, power?*
- *Assuming you are familiar with it, how do you feel about the story of Adam and Eve likely being the reverse of how humans actually evolved?*
- *Is it possible that our true nature is to be collaborative and to revere women?*

The Emergence of Patriarchy

> *Then God said, "Let us make humankind in our image, according to our likeness; and let them have dominion over the fish of the sea, and over the birds of the air, and over the cattle, and over all the wild animals of the earth, and over every creeping thing that creeps upon the earth."*
> —Genesis, chapter 1, verse 26,
> New Revised Standard Version

These words, from the first book of the Bible, are at the heart of a dominator and coercive worldview and are at the core of gender inequality, our environmental crisis, and how we conceive of the process of negotiation and dispute resolution.

When I read the book *The Mists of Avalon* by Marion Zimmer Bradley (1983), I had an uncanny feeling that the story lived in my bones like a very ancient memory. The novel tells the story of the acclaimed King Arthur and the kingdom of Camelot through the perspective of the women as they feel their power fading into the mist as Christianity takes over the pagan world. Weirdly, my mother and daughter, who each read the novel independently of each other, reported feeling a similar sense of a majesty we once knew. Perhaps you think me "woo-woo," but I believe we had accessed an epigenetic knowing in our genes of an earlier time when the feminine was revered, a time that we only receive whispers of in our current consciousness.

Eisler's *The Chalice and the Blade* talks about a cataclysmic turning point in human history from partnership to domination, coercion, and war, "worshipping the lethal power of the blade, the power to take rather than give life . . . to establish and enforce domination."[12]

As patriarchy gained power, it systematically suppressed and erased the worship of the Goddess, as well as the notion that women could be spiritual, holy, or practice sacred arts like midwifery. In Europe, Christian sites were often constructed atop ancient, sacred locations associated with the Divine Feminine. For example, the Chartres Cathedral in France was built over a revered pagan site dedicated to the Divine Mother.[13] Similarly, the global celebration of Christmas was strategically placed over the pagan winter solstice, marking the darkest point of the year in the western hemisphere.[14] In Ireland, however, where Catholicism fused with the pagan traditions rather than attempting to eradicate them, "Sheela na Gig" figures—depictions of a woman's vulva—still adorn ancient structures as a symbol of fertility and the Sacred Feminine.[15]

And what does pagan even mean? The Church used to kill people for being called a pagan, then a derogatory word to mean an unrefined non-Christian. I consider myself "pagan," which to me simply means "of the earth," which, as a naturalist, I consider myself to be.

How did we shift from a gender-equal, collaborative past to patriarchy and celebrating models of coercion and warfare some six thousand or so years ago? For early humans, babies appeared magically from women, one of the reasons we were revered. At some point, however, with the donning of agriculture and more settling down, humans began to understand paternity which became increasingly important. This corresponded with controlling property and correspondingly us, our sexuality, and a shift in ideas about "the Divine."

According to Rabia's research in *HerStory*, the first three commandments of the Bible say what no other god had ever said, "I am God. I am the Lord thy God, you shall have no other gods but me." This was such a break from the past, she notes, "and was not how humans had developed spiritually up to that point." This new God was now a faraway God—distant and all male. And, in everything that came after the Ten Commandments, a quarter of the stories are about how women should be treated and behave. "The most important thing about owning a woman is that she had to be chaste because a man's honor was dependent on a woman's behavior." If she had sex, he was dishonored. There was now no honor for women. Honor became the main thing that men had. Bravery was measured by going to war and wearing armor and killing a lot of other men. It was not the bravery required to carry a pregnancy and deliver a beautiful baby which had been revered for thousands of years from Spain to Indonesia. Rabia notes that, in the Code of Hammurabi, the longest and best-organized legal text from the ancient Near East, "one-third to one half of the code is about how to deal with women who have sex, who don't clean your house, who talk back."[16]

William Ury, in his book *Getting to Peace*, explained the big pendulum shift of human history from coexistence to coercion like this: With the dawn of agriculture, human population increased. Settling down into permanent homes had a powerful impact on how we related to one another, negotiated, and resolved conflict. Crowding created more tension and we shifted from a more cooperative to a more competitive way of relating. "For perhaps the first time in human evolution, it became useful to treat other humans in large numbers as slaves, servants, or subordinates."[17]

Essentially, the rise of coercion and getting other humans to do one's bidding was the beginning of sexism and slavery, the power of men over women. It was the beginning of "power-over" dominion thinking, where the needs of others became less important. It is not a huge leap to think that religion was used as justification to dominate and move away from earlier models of partnership. Recently, when I traveled through Europe, I could not help but notice how Christianity and its patriarchal roots have left such an enormous imprint.

In 1452, in the *Doctrine of Discovery*, Pope Nicholas the Fifth decreed:

> European explorers who come upon inhabited lands are instructed by the Pope to invade, search out, capture, vanquish and subdue all pagans whatsoever and to reduce their persons to perpetual slavery. These explorers must appropriate and give to the Pope and his successors all of the inhabitants (slaves) kingdoms,

> counties, dominions, possessions and goods and to convert these pagans to his use and profit.[18]

One of the most shocking manifestations of the emergence of patriarchy occurred during the Women's Holocaust when, over a period of three hundred years throughout Europe, millions of women, female healers, leaders, and gender non-conforming men were hunted down, shamed, tortured, and burned at the stake by the "holy" Inquisition, an institution founded by the Roman Catholic church to suppress heresy.[19]

A hallmark strategy that humans have used over time to dominate other humans is to make them somehow less human. This was used as the strategy to justify slavery and depictions of Africans brought in bondage to my country four hundred years ago, and it was used to justify the subjugation of women, half of humanity, as patriarchy took over. The narrative changed. Not only did the word "pagan" become disparaged and reason to burn someone at the stake, but words associated with reverence for female divinity also became some of the dirtiest words in our society. For instance, *wit* originally meant wise, so a witch was a wise woman, and *hag* meant holy, so a hag was a holy woman, and Hor was a priestess of Horace.[20]

References to witch burning continue to show up regularly in modern day but now have been appropriated by the likes of the US authoritarian Donald Trump. A master of the gaslighting tactic of the "pot calling the kettle black," Trump has chronically whined about being a victim of "witch hunts," a huge dishonor to the memory of those women who were burned alive.

Why did the feminine fall subject to the masculine after so many years of living in partnership? Why did partnership models get overwhelmed by domination? As I reflect on this, with twenty-first-century hindsight as propaganda is running rampant today to support authoritarians who wish to control people and resources, the word *hex* comes to mind. Here is its definition: "Verb, to cast a spell on; bewitch. Noun, a magic spell. A curse."[21] Could it be, ladies, that we have been hexed by false narrative, propaganda, fake news, the oldest political trick of the trade?

What was the motivation for this hex, this false narrative? I suspect it was inspired by the almighty dollar. Greed, the fear that there is not enough to go around, and the belief that those who have more are superior, allowed patriarchy to propagate and justify domination of people and the earth for cash. Injustice is profitable, at least in the short term, and grandiosity can feel so good. Hierarchies that justify raping and pillaging—of women, entire groups of people, or the earth—have been a cornerstone of a patriarchal world order.

It was not a coincidence that, around the same time that women in the United States lost their constitutional right to control their own bodies, right-wing politicians justified their support for the continued extraction of fossil fuels (in spite of our urgent need to stop burning them) with words from their Bible: "We were put on this earth as creatures of God to have dominion over the earth for our benefit, not for the earth's benefit."[22]

Reflections on the Emergence of Patriarchy

- *Have women been hexed into believing we are secondary to justify our domination and servitude? What are your thoughts?*

- *Have you allowed the PWC narrative to hex your sense of power? If yes, how so? How has this impacted your life?*
- *Why do you imagine so much evidence about the female divine has been crushed or erased since the dawn of patriarchy?*

The Feminine, the Masculine, the Patriarchal

It was 2006. Al Gore had just released his film *An Inconvenient Truth*, and I decided to show the documentary to my then nine-year-old son Jack because I wanted him to understand the threat the planet was under. Within minutes of watching the opening scenes of the film, which show glaciers melting and crashing into the sea, my son began to tear up. I looked over at his young face. He seemed crestfallen. "I can't watch this, Mom," he said, devastation in his voice. Such a sensitive, smart kid then, such a sensitive, smart human today as I write. Of course, it was not an age-appropriate choice, so I turned the TV off.

Fast-forward to 2023. We had just had one of the hottest heat waves ever in the Hudson Valley, where I live, just north of New York City. I escaped to the relative coolness of the woods and pitched a tent, but there really was no escape. The forest, the ground, the trees, the critters, all of us were just plain hot. My thoughts drifted to what life might be like for future generations—thirty, sixty, one hundred years from now. I cried and swore to the trees and then pulled myself together and refocused. We have work to do. The planet is on the brink. A quote from Mama Gena came to mind: "Violence is what happens when the feminine retreats." Violence is what happens when the masculine subsumes the feminine. The masculine and the feminine are severely out of balance on the planet, evidence of which is screaming at us in the form of the climate crisis, persistent gender inequality, and our brinksmanship with nuclear annihilation.

So, what do we mean by the feminine and the masculine? What are the values and qualities inherent in these terms? And how are these ideas shaped by patriarchy?

I look to nature first for guidance. Female, male, reproduction is everywhere. Nature is all about reproducing itself, whether it be flora or fauna, and the female is at the center of the drama. Humans make a lot of hoopla about gender, but nature appears relaxed and fluid when it comes to female and male, masculine and feminine. For example, avocado trees alternate their gender expression back and forth within a thirty-six-hour period, red squirrels are seasonally bisexual, the parrot fish's transsexuality is so common that species that don't change sex are considered highly unusual. The list goes on and on—red foxes, grizzly bears, fungi, and more.[23]

Because we are nature, gender in humans is fluid too. Women and men's genitals are formed from the same embryonic tissue. Female and male embryos start out the same, XX, and then diverge into male if the second X chromosome turns to Y. As sex educator and scientist, Emily Nagoski, PhD, tells us, our genitals are made of the same parts, just organized differently.[24] But, as Nagoski says, humans have inferred a lot of meaning from our biology about the meaning of masculine and feminine: "We are masters of metaphorizing anatomy."[25]

Yin and yang from ancient Chinese philosophy divide humans into yin, the receptive and more feminine, and yang, the active principle, more masculine. Joseph Campbell, now-deceased professor of comparative mythology and comparative religion, has said, "Woman is life and man is the protector of life."[26] I certainly know from my own experience how great it was to have a supportive husband when I was walking around with a baby weighing in at ten pounds (about 4.5 kilos) that I had to pass through my legs! It's a vulnerable feeling.

All humans embody masculine and feminine qualities to varying degrees, but patriarchy has been hell-bent on a mission to rigidify them. While there are no absolute definitions of the feminine, the masculine, the patriarchal, here is what I have deduced from various conversations, sources, presentations, and my own observations.[27]

The Feminine

Qualities of what humans describe as "feminine" stem from women's biological role as the originators and creators of life, the egg producers, mothers, the ones who carry and birth children. The feminine includes caring, nurturing, being empathic, relational, supportive, compassionate, kind, but also fierce (protection of young). It values love (Venus), connection, communication, beauty, vulnerability, intimacy, and pleasure. The feminine is closely aligned with nature; it is creation and life-force energy. It is circular, not hierarchical. When it comes to conflict and negotiation, the feminine values collaboration, listening for needs versus a power and rights-based focus, highlighting common ground, respect for difference and diversity (because that is like nature), inspiring creativity, long-term, holistic, systemic thinking that benefits future generations.

The Masculine

Qualities of what humans describe as masculine stem from men's biological role as the protector of life, the one who brings "home the meat." They include strength, speed, independence, assertiveness, action, leadership, resilience, task and goal-orientation. Values include logic, rationality, efficiency, practicality (building and fixing things), focused and linear, competitiveness, playfulness, protectiveness. Masculinity is hierarchical (pyramids) versus circular. When it comes to conflict and negotiation, the masculine values application of rights and rules to resolve differences and splitting the difference.

It is important to understand that the masculine and patriarchy are not the same thing. Nonetheless, the close connection between them has been confusing to many men and, in recent decades, either inspired an exploration of a healthier understanding of masculinity or a doubling-down on patriarchy.

The Patriarchal

Qualities of the patriarchal stem from the desire of some humans to dominate and make war, to differentiate between the masculine and the feminine, and to make the roles of male and female, men and women more rigid and more suitable for domination and war. Patriarchy shapes men into warriors so they can go off and fight and women to keep the home fires burning when they do. (Interestingly in Wikipedia, Mars, the God of War, and masculine are the same thing.)

Beliefs include "might makes right," the ends justify the means, the masculine is superior, women are the weaker sex, God is male, being homosexual or transgender is wrong.

Marriage is between a man and a woman. Men should dominate in the home, at work, and in the world and women should submit, be silent, "sugar and spice," codependent, sexually available as needed, and not confront men.

Values include "nose to the grindstone," work harder, faster and better, suck it up. Profit and individual gains are the goal, not the common good. Production is more important than relationships, connection, or intimacy.

Behaviors include heightened individualism, go it alone, aggression, emotionally walled-off, mean, selfish, extractive, predatory, "drill baby drill," rape.

When it comes to conflict and negotiation, while the feminine and the masculine might value partnership, the patriarchal is all about power-over, zero-sum, domination.

The Three Rings of Patriarchy and the Gender Binary

The rigid distinctions between the masculine and the feminine in the PWC is known as "the gender binary," which goes right to the core of an adversarial world in conflict. In the words of trans activist and author Alok Vaid-Menon:

> The gender binary is a cultural belief that there are only two distinct and opposite genders: man and woman. This belief is upheld by a system of power that exists to create conflict and division, not to celebrate creativity and diversity . . . This false choice of boy or girl, man or woman, male or female is not natural—it is political . . . Gender diversity is an integral part of our existence. It always has been, and it always will be.[28]

Family therapist Terry Real describes how the gender binary impacts our thinking by what he calls "the three rings of psychological (as opposed to political) patriarchy," in other words, what we believe.[29]

The "First Ring" is what Real calls "the great divide." Imagine taking a human and theoretically splitting them down the middle. All the qualities to the left are "masculine;" all the qualities to the right are "feminine." In Real's description, the feminine is expressive, nurturing, dependent, and weak; the masculine is strong, independent, logical, and unemotional, which, he points out, is intrinsically traumatic, because it forces us to disown qualities of our beings that may be essential to us.

The "Second Ring" is "the dance of contempt." The two halves of the human are not considered equal; rather, the masculine is exalted and the feminine is devalued. The essential relationship between the masculine and the feminine, Real says, is contempt, with the masculine holding the feminine in contempt.

The "Third Ring "is the "core collusion." Whoever inhabits the feminine side of the equation has a profound compulsion to protect whoever is on the masculine side, even if they are being hurt by that person. Colluding in this way can manifest as, for instance, "don't talk truth to power," "don't shake up the fragile male ego." This is codependent, women's traditional role, to manage men, and not confront them, Real says.[30]

Many women and men are perplexed by the behavior of some women in power who exhibit what they claim is just as much "toxic masculinity" as their male colleagues. Real's model sheds light by showing that a woman can uphold the masculine side of the split and a man can uphold the more traditionally feminine side.

Masculinity (i.e., the biology of being male) and the system of patriarchy are not the same thing. Patriarchy damages men and boys by putting them in a straightjacket and shaping them to be fighters from as early as the age of five. And women, says Real, can be "up to their eyeballs in upholding the system of patriarchy, whether it's mothers, tearfully and pridefully sending their sons off to war or women voting for Trump in the United States and places like that."[31] Indeed, it's my observation that it's often women who perpetuate misogyny and patriarchal beliefs most strongly on each other.

The acculturation to maleness, say some experts, is a negative—"not female" or "don't be a pussy."[32] My adult son reminded me recently of how many of the boys in his early teenage cohort ended virtually every sentence with "no homo," a manifestation of the serious anxiety they felt at being perceived as too feminine as they came of age.

Patriarchy is a system that supports violence, domination, and often ultimately war. In the United States and sometimes in other countries in recent years, we have had a series of horrific mass shootings. The vast majority of the shooters are male and White. In August of 2019, the *Washington Post* reported that all but 3 of the 165 mass shootings that have occurred have been committed by men. The article went on to say that most of these men carry a "triple cultural entitlement;" in other words, they are heterosexual, male, and White—and they are angry that they are losing their privileged status.[33]

The guns are designed for men, geared for male bodies. Gun advertising is completely consistent with the war system; it is geared toward veterans and asks them to be the guardians for the true American and the American flag. It appeals to men in their traditional role as the protector, the breadwinner, the one in charge in their households.

A study by Michael Kimmel, a scholar of masculinity studies, looked at four organizations that help deprogram men who have left hate groups like White supremacists and jihadists. He found that the ideas of traditional masculinity were alive in all of these men. The more rigid the vision of the traditional masculine, the more fervently the man held on to his rigid beliefs that aligned with hate and the more vulnerable he was to extremist politics and violence. Countering this vision of masculinity was key to the deprogramming. With this as our cultural norm, some experts have declared traditional masculinity a health hazard, not just to men, but to the families who live with them.[34]

Patriarchy teaches men to go it alone, be the hero, disconnect from feelings, all because that's what it takes to go to war. The code of invulnerability is essential to patriarchy. Patriarchy doesn't celebrate men for the softness or vulnerability, just for what they can do—which is detrimental to both men and society as a whole.

Beyond Stereotype and Toward Health and Wholeness When We Negotiate

How do these interpretations of the feminine and the masculine impact us in negotiation?

What are the messages we as women can take from this for ourselves as negotiators? As we rise in our power, we cannot afford to be straightjacketed by unhealthy stereotypes or projections of what is masculine and what is feminine and how we should behave as negotiators.

With any difference, like male or female, there can be descriptors of it, and then interpretations and judgments which you might also call projections, stereotypes, or social expectations. Let's say you are negotiating with Human A. Your description of that person might be six feet two (1.88 meters), light colored skin, blue eyes, hairy chest, deep voice, flat chest. Your interpretation or judgment of them, depending on who you are and your assumptions and experience about life, might be that Human A is commanding, smart, leadership material. Or, you also might judge them as overentitled, too much power, dominating, speaking too much, et cetera. You get the idea.

In a recent workshop, a female astrophysicist lamented, "I am so tired of having to fulfill what is considered a feminine stereotype—and I am tired of encountering a world where collaboration is considered weak." As women, we need to be aware of the big cultural noise on this subject and not let it run us or mess with our minds. We must decide who we want to be and how we want to be.

Timea, a participant in one of my courses, has been doing peacebuilding work in Francophone Africa, where she is referred to as an *homme ratte,* a French expression for "wasted man" or "missed man." They see her as somebody who was almost born a man but actually became a woman. "It cracks me up all the time," she said, "because as negative and mind-blowingly chauvinist as it sounds, they still don't realize there is anything wrong with it. Second, they think they are complimenting my strength, straightforward nature, and goal-orientedness. And third, not showing feminine traits, and being businesslike, makes me come across as tough even though I am very kind with everybody. So, I am probably confusing them."

In organization circles these days you might hear the phrase, "The future is female." Perhaps, but to me it is really about balancing the qualities of the feminine and the masculine. In negotiation and conflict, we need both; we need qualities across the spectrum, depending on what is needed in the moment. As negotiators, we need to allow ourselves to be strong, forceful, empathic, sensitive, hard-driving, logical, attracting, receptive, open, rational, competitive or collaborative, caring, nurturing, practical, individualistic, focused, linear, all of the above, a mixture of masculine and feminine qualities, a whole human. We can all stretch ourselves with new qualities that might not be our norm. Gender straight-jackets are detrimental to our own expansion.

But all of us need to move beyond patriarchy and the pathological behaviors it creates in both the feminine (codependency) and the masculine (toxic masculinity). It is killing us. All of us need to stop disparaging the feminine, or expect only males to act masculine and females to act feminine. And, we need to stop declaring the masculine superior. As acknowledged in Greta Gerwig's 2023 film *Barbie,* "Everyone hates women; even women hate women." Women and men alike can decide to no longer be complicit with this arrangement. We can choose to believe that it is more of the feminine that we need in today's world and take a stand for it as women leaders.

Reflections on the Masculine and the Feminine in How We Influence and Negotiate

- *How has the gender binary impacted you in negotiation?*
- *What does it mean to you to negotiate using more of "the feminine"?*

- *When you negotiate, influence, or lead, do you use more feminine or masculine qualities or do you rely equally on both?*
- *In the current state of our planet and world, many women and men alike believe that the qualities of the feminine—receptivity, beauty, intuition, long-term thinking—are the keys to creating a better future. Are these qualities valued enough? By others and ourselves? Do you agree that this is what is needed?*

Putting into Practice

In an interaction this week, intentionally choose to use more masculine traits. How did that feel? In a different interaction, intentionally choose to use more feminine traits. How did that feel? Journal about your experience.

Rewiring Our Brains to Rock a New Negotiation

It was 1975, and I was headed down to Mexico on a train. I was wearing a pink jersey sundress and matching bandana to keep my strawberry-blond hair tied back.

I was twenty.

My plan was to take the train from Nogales, Arizona, down to Mexico City, a two-night journey. My mother had asked her brother, my Uncle Peter, to drive me across the border from Arizona to Mexico's Nogales and to get me safely on the train.

My Uncle Peter, ironically the same name of the man I would ultimately marry, did not pay any attention to my needs but was focused entirely on his, a scenario that would also often be the case with my future husband. Like so many of us do, I followed a pattern (albeit unconsciously) that was familiar but that did not serve me by entering a marriage that mirrored the dynamics of power I had with men in my youth. I am grateful to report that this pattern is now largely healed.

Uncle Peter had a new product line of flashlights that he was very excited about selling to police departments. We made many spontaneous stops along the way so that he could talk to prospective buyers. He was ecstatic and it was all he talked about. I couldn't have cared less. I was anxious about catching my train.

Maybe you know Nogales, Arizona. It is a place where, at least at that time, the "first and third" worlds collided. The modern, new, rich homes and businesses of Arizona contrasted sharply with the dusty streets and shanty shacks of Mexico.

I was two years into my college education and majoring in Latin American Studies, so I had learned a lot about US imperialism and how my country had intervened militarily in Latin America hundreds of times in order to extend our economic dominance and extract profit. I knew that our CIA had undermined democratically elected leaders like Allende in a bloody coup in 1973. I knew my father, a senior partner at the prestigious Wall Street firm of Davis, Polk, and Wardwell, had represented ITT at the time of the coup in Chile and had inevitably profited from it. I felt responsible for the actions of my country and my family and I was ashamed. Though not conscious of this at the time, I was also drawn to Latin America because I empathized with it; I sensed a parallel between how countries in the global south and women are dominated.

As a result of my uncle's detours, we arrived to the train station within minutes of my train pulling out of the station. I did not have time to get a ticket for the sleeper car, which my mother had specifically requested of her brother because it would be much safer. With no time left, I got on the "cattle car." I sat in the back, battened down by a heavy suitcase stuffed with what I would need for my year in Mexico and then Colombia.

As I sat there, both freaked out and naively excited, Brown campesino faces, both male and female, turned around to look at me and stare. I will never forget holding their gaze. They clutched goats, chickens, and other purchases they had just made in Nogales. The look on their faces said: "What the hell are you doing on this train, señorita? Why are you in this car with all of us, *sola* (alone), with your blond hair and that pink dress?"

I don't remember exactly how it all went down.

It got later and darker as the train rumbled southward through the Sonoran desert. It stopped periodically, but I didn't dare get off and risk being left behind. My Spanish was not good, and I wasn't confident that I would understand how long each stop would be or where exactly I could hope to purchase a ticket for a sleeper car. Around eleven p.m. or so, a smooth-talking Mexican man of about forty came up to me. He wore a fedora and a white suit. I was grateful that he spoke a bit of English.

"Señorita," he said, pointing to the front of the train, "I have a car up there. You can come stay in my sleeper car. I promise you can trust me."

I was tired. I was scared. I was desperate. And I was naive. But it seemed like my best option, so I agreed. What happened next is both a very vague and sharp memory.

Of course, he got on top of me in his bunk. Of course, he tried to have intercourse with me. I remember struggling and then using my hand to make him climax so he would leave me alone. Finally, he rolled off me and went to sleep. I'm not sure how long I lay there. I don't think I dared move. I do remember, when I finally opened the cabin door the conductor, with his ear to the door, was waiting just outside and said to me in his broken English,

"Me next, señorita?"

I have no recollection of how I ultimately got a sleeper car ticket for the second night on the train, but I do know myself to be resourceful and a survivor. Thankfully I was able to feel safe enough to sleep the second night.

I haven't shared this story much until writing it now. In spite of the healing I have done to clear the trauma along with other sexual transgressions from my past, I still feel some shame around it. Healing takes a long time. So many of us survivors of sexual assault are healing and trying to put sunlight on this issue because it is such a pervasive aspect of the domination system for women. I know now that I did nothing wrong on that train except dare to venture out into a PWC that assumed that a single young woman in a pink sundress was free game.

I know now the statistics regarding the pervasiveness of sexual violence against women around the world. About one in three women is sexually assaulted in her lifetime, and the vast majority of us are constrained by the threat of it.

I know now that the odds were against me.

I also know now that my uncle was careless and failed to protect me perhaps unconsciously playing out a family pattern of predation (sexual and economic). My uncle, "Peter Stuyvesant Wainwright," and I are direct descendants of Peter Stuyvesant who was, in the best of lights, a global explorer and innovator, and, in the worst, a slave trader and dominator of the highest order.[35]

I know now that the guy who sexually assaulted me was also playing out a narrative that this was his right. He felt entitled to my body and spirit. Same with the conductor.

I know now that in a world of freedom, dignity, and deep and equal respect for women, none of this would be anywhere nearly as likely to happen. I would have been safe to be the bold, open, adventurous girl who dared to wander out into the world, self-advocate, and negotiate on my own behalf, equal to my brothers.

The trauma and codependency I have experienced (and mostly healed) was largely a result of living in a PWC, which was the culture of my country, my family of origin, and my marriage.

It showed up in various sexual transgressions of others done to me, and in my own skewed executive function that put myself in bad situations.

It affected my confidence and my self-image.

It affected my ability to make money and to feel that I was deserving to be paid well for my work. It affected my ability to get myself out of a relationship that turned toxic. And it affected my ability to negotiate.

In order to negotiate well and embody a New Negotiation, we need to heal our trauma and codependent behaviors.

Unfortunately, there aren't really any shortcuts to doing this work, decolonizing ourselves, growing ourselves free of the influence of patriarchy.

I have engaged in many modalities to heal trauma and evolve—some more conventional and studied like EMDR (eye movement desensitization and reprocessing) and some more "alternative."[36]

I engaged in the practice of "swamping" with the School of

Womanly Arts—which probably was some of the best trauma healing I have had and certainly not something my medical insurance would pay for. I was a different person after releasing so much crap and rage out of my body.

Because of the trauma healing I have undertaken, my physical health has improved, I look different, I have grown taller, I dress differently. I walk my talk, and I take no shit.

I have stopped giving my power away to men and am no longer a "love addict," my form of codependency, or at least it is in remission, a day at a time.

I am blessed to have had the resources to pursue my own healing, and I am proud of myself for taking advantage of them.

EMDR helped me take my brother off a pedestal. The very skilled therapist I worked with carefully reenacted some of the dysfunctional encounters I had had with him as a child, reworking them in my brain to help me regain control. My brother's imprint was such an archetype for me. How he lived in me kept showing up in different forms, in both the men I worked with and loved.

Life's challenges can be a blessing. I now truly understand what my excellent therapists were talking about by calling me "very codependent." I have learned. Now, instead of putting my energy into being a corporate wife—enabling a guy so he could presumably take care of me—enabling patriarchy and systems of domination, I am keeping the focus on myself and putting my energy into empowering women and dismantling patriarchy alongside the many humans working hard to build a deeper, more true global democracy.

What Is Trauma?

Trauma is an overwhelming experience with no power to fix it. It is unprocessed experience from the past that feels as if it were happening in the present. It is enhanced stress—or stress on steroids. It can come from events that are "too much, too soon, too fast" that hurt us or it can build up over time.

Trauma creates PTSD (post-traumatic stress disorder). PTSD happens when the amygdala in our brains, a region that plays a central role in processing memory and emotions, hijacks the brain's executive functions and causes a fight, flight, or freeze response. Trauma is our response to the event, not the event itself. And traumatic stress is stored in the brain in a way that is counterproductive for us.[37]

Individual trauma involves a traumatic event or events that happen to an individual, but trauma can also impact entire communities of people. Trauma experienced as a group is known as collective trauma, or ancestral trauma. Trauma can live in our genes and be transmitted epigenetically down through generations so that even family members who did not experience the event firsthand are affected by it. A large number of us have been collectively traumatized by patriarchal domination.[38] I suspect that many Western women, for example, carry fear and trauma in our bodies from either the witch-burning reign of terror in Europe or the Salem witch trials in the United States.

What Is Codependency?

In the era of #metoo, the actress Glenn Close gave an amazing performance in *The Wife*, a film based on the novel of the same name by Meg Wolitzer that tells the story of a young female college student named Joan who is awed and attracted to her handsome, married professor. With a force of personality and charm, he advises her that a "writer must write."

Ten years later, after he divorces, she marries him. But drip by drop over the years, Joan subsumes her dreams of being a writer and puts her tremendous talent into supporting her husband as his ghostwriter. Meanwhile, he goes on to have multiple affairs with younger women, which slowly erodes Joan's self-esteem. Years pass, and eventually he receives the Nobel Prize in Literature for the writing that she has done on his behalf over the years. Though Joan continues to participate in the deception, it becomes increasingly intolerable to her. Her breaking point comes on the night of the Nobel ceremony when he praises her as his "support, muse, and soulmate" and ignores the critical role she has played in his success. Finally, she puts her foot down and tells him she is divorcing him. Knowing he is nothing without her, he dies shortly thereafter.

The message of the film is driven home when the king of Sweden, who is seated next to Joan at the Nobel dinner, asks her, "And do you have a profession?"

"I do," she replies. "I am a kingmaker."[39]

I too was a kingmaker. Raised to be one from the cradle, I had deep neural pathways in my brain to be a "good wife," which have been hard to erase, though I have made great progress in differentiating my functional parts from the pathological.

It took me a long time to recognize my own trauma and specifically how codependent I was. I had been "doing my work," trying to grow and grow up, for as long as I can remember. I had the support of great therapists, workshops, and books, not to mention a first-class education. So, when my marriage came crashing down, I was shocked (and, I admit, a bit insulted) when two therapists whom I deeply respect said I was "very codependent and a love addict." Yikes!

Looking back, I see that I was raised to be a corporate, codependent wife. I learned it from my mom, who was more shackled than I was by traditional and predetermined gender roles. A product of her time and class, she turned down a great job and salary so she could be fully available for my dad. In her social circles, it was not a good look to encroach on her husband's role as provider.

The traditional family model, the bedrock of patriarchy and the world of work as we have known it, depends on women playing this role: supporting men, being homemakers so that men can go off and slay the dragons. To many outside observers, my marriage of twenty years to the "love of my life" and father of my children came to an end because of my ex-husband's anger and drinking, but I was faithfully behind the scenes enabling him into big dysfunction.

Codependency is probably the largest manifestation of trauma for women on the planet. As patriarchy is global, so too is codependency; wherever there is patriarchy, there is codependence. Codependence is, to a great extent, internalized patriarchy and pervasive among women worldwide. But since the first wave of feminism, we have been lifting the fog. Both patriarchy and codependence proclaim the myth of the superiority of the masculine over the feminine. Humans, of course, are interdependent, which is part of the beauty and joy of being alive.

Codependency is a learned pattern of chronic neglect of self in order to gain love, approval, or validation.[40] Codependents typically put their own needs to the side, a behavior that patriarchal domination reinforces.[41]

Codependency is a disease of attention. What we place our attention on grows. For too much of our history, women's attention has been on men, enabling their power and capacity with the expectation that they will then take care of us and protect our children in return. As the "second sex," we have been taught to serve.

Our attention is powerful. Energy follows attention and if we are placing it on others, we empower them and deplete ourselves. It's a wonderful fantasy that someone will take care of us. Sometimes, this exchange happens cleanly, but more often, if you ask others to take care of you, they will control you. The myth of Prince Charming is, in fact, a myth. He isn't coming. In the words of feminist writer Anaïs Nin, "How wrong it is for a woman to expect the man to build the world she wants, rather than to create it herself."[42]

Codependency is a big deal. Changing it, healing it, divesting ourselves of this crutch as women, will have monumental positive repercussions for our life on this planet. The reality is patriarchy persists because we, as women, enable it. If and when we pull the plug, it will crumble.

How Trauma and Codependency Impact Us in Negotiation

Over the last number of years, I have heard many women, either sarcastically or jokingly, refer to the "burned at the stake" gene that has stopped them from claiming more power in negotiation and leadership. They are referring to the body memory of the witch trials in Europe (and similar events in other parts of the world).[43]

Those witch trials, of course, were a long time ago and women, for the most part, are no longer getting burned at the stake for heresy. Nonetheless, it is surprising how often the "witch hunt" term is used in our present-day nomenclature and conversations. It lurks in the ethers as perhaps the ultimate hex that stops us in our tracks for going after what we want and insisting on our equal value as humans.

Have you ever disassociated? Gotten kind of foggy-brained and disconnected at a moment when you needed to be dialed in? According to a seasoned therapist Debbie Bern, MSW, a specialist in trauma and codependency, when we experience an emotional trigger, our mental capacities can go offline, which makes us more compliant or frightened rather than a present, engaged, and highly formidable adult. Hilary Heyl, MSW, a clinician specializing in trauma therapies, describes it like this: "What happens with unhealed, retriggered trauma is that you get small. Your higher executive functioning has been hijacked by the flaring up of the amygdala, the bellybutton of our primitive emotional responses towards threat to selfhood. You don't stand up for yourself. You lose your connection to your sovereign self which you need to be able to negotiate and collaborate well."[44] An emotional trigger activates the frightened part of the brain and stops us from deep engagement in the negotiation. And if the person we are negotiating with is famous or powerful, it ups the ante; our reactions (silence or meekness) might become even more magnified. As Bern says, "This is a pattern that has been going on for a long time." She consoles us: "Let's remember, it's not that long ago women were not even allowed to kiss the pope's feet!"[45]

Trauma and codependency kill our self-esteem and

self-confidence—just like the trauma of racism has killed the self-worth of so many Black and Brown people. But it can be healed. Clearing and healing trauma and codependency readies us for showing up cleanly, clearly, and powerfully for a New Negotiation. Doing the work results in an aliveness and presence that is worth every bit of the effort. It makes us unstoppable. Not doing so impacts everything: our ability to speak truth to power, claim value in negotiation, say no to the destruction of nature and military escalation; it causes us to submit, defer, or accommodate in the face of conflict. In other words, it contributes to our tendency to put up with bullshit and not say "enough."

It is probably not realistic to think that we can clear all our triggers and past pathologies. We can't always have perfect days, but the more we do, the more we can bring our powerful presence to every negotiation and conflict in which we engage. Here are some simple techniques we can use when we feel emotional triggers arise in a conflict negotiation. I have found all of them useful at one time or another.

- Breathe (always).
- Ground and center yourself—keep your butt in the chair, your feet firmly on the ground.
- Ask yourself: How am I feeling? Am I staying present? Am I disassociating? Am I afraid? Willing to concede too quickly, defer, or accommodate?
- Take a break. Breaks are always good.
- Notice when you are triggered. What or who is triggering you? Awareness can help you regain some of your power.
- Be kind to yourself on the journey.

Reflections on Trauma

- *Do you carry any trauma?*
- *Write out the events or experiences that you think may have had a traumatic impact on you.*
- *What has helped you heal?*
- *How have those traumas impacted your ability to negotiate or claim your power?*
- *Please be gentle with yourself as you engage in these reflections.*

Reflections on Codependency

- *In what ways are you codependent?*
- *What are the signs of codependency in your life?*
- *Has codependence impacted your personal power and ability to take care of yourself?*

Reflections on How Trauma and Codependency Impact You in Negotiation

- *Do you dissociate?*
- *Do you negotiate against yourself?*
- *In what ways do you give your power away due to trauma or codependency?*

CHAPTER 3

Get Comfortable with Conflict

> *What are little girls made of?*
> *What are little girls made of?*
> *Sugar and spice*
> *And everything nice*
> *That's what little girls are made of*
> —A popular nineteenth-century nursery rhyme, *Mother Goose*

It was 1989, and Mandela was about to be released from over twenty-seven years of unbroken incarceration in South Africa. He predicted a civil war would break out with his release and so he set up a system of local and national "preventative councils" to keep the peace. He chose trusted and popular members of the community, including midwives, teachers, magistrates, and housewives. More than half were women. As part of their work, these women were trained to intervene in violent conflict situations, calm things down, and keep the peace.

For example, if a conflict arose in one of the townships in Cape Town and someone was going to be "necklaced" (a horrific practice of filling a car tire with petrol, lighting it on fire, and putting it around someone's neck), the trained women rushed to the site, walked into the middle of the melee, often a shouting mob of violent lynchers, and with their hands raised, shouted, "Stop this! Go home! Your mother would be ashamed of you!"

And there would be complete silence. The crowd would disband. The women were able to get the men to stop.

Dr. Scilla Elworthy, founder of Peace Direct, told me this story. She said there are literally thousands of examples of interventions like this from trained, grounded, and powerful women. The women's trainings created "a quality of consciousness in them in how to take their stance," she said.

> This was not a group of worried women running in slightly hunched over into a terrifying situation. This was a group of women in their Zulu and other tribal grandeur, shoulders back, heads up, communicating "Make way!" in such a manner that the people thronging around the massacre were obliged to let them pass. There's a big difference between entering a negotiation and quietly saying, "Oh, please can I speak with so and so?" versus saying, "Stop. Now listen." I think there's a lot women can learn from that, about how to stand, how to carry ourselves with a kind of regal courage. We need regal courage because we've been stepped on as underdogs for so many generations. Now we need to be regal.[1]

Peace Direct funds, promotes, and learns from local peace builders in conflict areas who are working to prevent war in their regions. Dr. Elworthy says that the organizations that are woman-run are having the greatest impact.

What Comes to Mind When You Hear the Word "Conflict"?

As mentioned in chapter 1, it's the conflict in negotiation that people generally find the most difficult. If there were no conflict, and people could work out a fair solution, then they would simply go on with their day. But when there is conflict, most of us get stuck and find it more challenging—whether we are an individual or a nation. The best process to address conflict, the one where we have the most control over the outcome, the one that is most relational, least expensive, is negotiation.

Before you read ahead, reflect on this question:

What comes to mind when you hear the word "conflict"?

Take out a piece of paper and pencil, set a timer for a full minute, and jot down your thoughts. Don't think too hard. Allow yourself to free-associate and brainstorm whatever words and ideas naturally come to you.

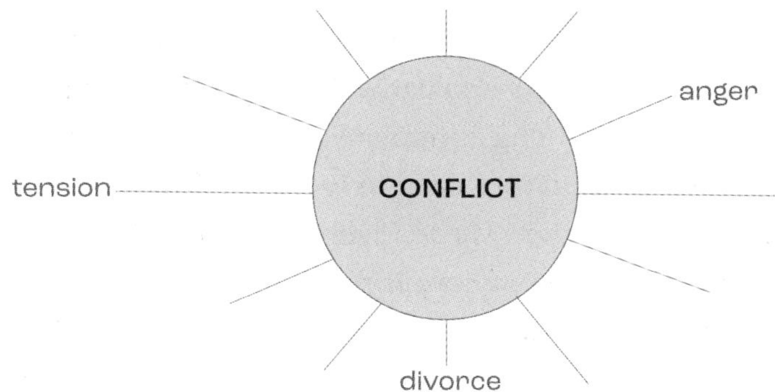

Now review your list. How would you characterize the words you have chosen? Are they negative? Positive? Neutral?

These are some of the typical words I have heard in my workshops (from mixed-gender groups and from all over the world):

anger	disagreement
tension	the world
violence	win-lose
fighting	war
divorce	misunderstanding

How would you characterize this list? Mostly negative, right? Generally, most people's associations with conflict are negative. But why is this so?

Conflict is everywhere. Life is full of conflict and can be overwhelming to so many of us these days. Just turn on the news. We see toxic fighting, polarization, and war. Space on the planet is shrinking. Resources are diminishing. Humans and nonhumans are colliding. Nature is straining under our weight. When I was at Harvard in the eighties, Roger Fisher, the coauthor of *Getting to Yes*, said, "Conflict is a growth industry." It still is.

But the truth is, conflict itself is neither good nor bad. It just is. Conflict is a necessary and natural part of life and a fact of human existence. As long as humans are on the planet, there will be differences that we need to work out. That's reality. What matters most is how we deal with the conflict. The reason we have negative connotations is not that conflict exists; it's because of how it is handled. We have negative associations with conflict, because we engage it in destructive ways so much of the time. "It sounds counterintuitive," writes negotiation specialist William Ury, "but we need more conflict—not less. By that I mean healthy conflict that enables us to grow, change, challenge injustices, and evolve as a democracy."[2]

How would you define "conflict"? I like this very simple definition: Conflict is things opposed. What's opposed can be something of enormous consequence, like a war between two countries, or it can be something really mundane and small, like whether we should have lentils or chicken for dinner.

And what causes conflict or sets it off? Lots of things. An "ambitious" colleague. Scarce resources or the perception of scarce resources. Inequality. Injustice. Value differences. Substance abuse. Greed. Disrespect. Sexual harassment. Low self-esteem. Cultural or identity-group differences. Change.

Bottom line, conflict is caused by unmet or frustrated human needs—inside of us, in our families, communities, workplaces, or in the world. Humans are need-satisfying creatures. If our tangible needs like food and shelter are frustrated, or our psychological needs for respect are in question, we will experience conflict.

Reflections on Our Associations with Conflict

- *Are your associations with conflict negative or positive? Why?*
- *Does your gender influence your associations with conflict? How so?*

Reflections on the Messages from Our Families of Origin About How to Resolve Conflict

- *What were the primary causes of conflict in your family of origin?*
- *As a kid, what were the messages you received from your adult role models about how conflict should be handled? What were the messages from your mother? Your father? Other key caretakers? Your community and culture?*
- *How do those messages show up in how you negotiate and resolve conflict today?*

The Lotus Flower Blooms Out of the Muck

When clients are able to see their negative associations with conflict, I might ask them to brainstorm their positive associations too. These are often more difficult for them to articulate, but once they have mulled it over for a moment, they get going. Here are some typical responses I have heard:

creativity
peace
opportunity
reality
transformation
excitement
win-win
relationships

What can be said to be good about conflict? Conflict can help us grow. When we are in the middle of a difficult conflict, looking for the lemonade in the lemons can make us seem like a Pollyanna, but it's worth the effort. While I have never lived in a war zone, my marriage after many good years became one. I experienced violent threats and fear, and it was hell. Nonetheless, the breakup of my marriage is the life experience that has grown me the most. I would not be the person I am today without having gone through it, and I am grateful for the maturity I gained. It was a conflict that helped me evolve and it increased my ability to be more useful to others.

Here are some conflict truisms I like:

- It takes a lot of pounding to make a good bar of steel
- The lotus flower blooms out of the muck
- Out of the shit come the vegetables . . .
- We grow through what we go through
- (From the Greek) Aspera ad Astra (i.e., "through adversity to the stars")

Conflict is fundamental to creativity. You can't create something new without there being some kind of limitation, tension, or opposition. The moon, which was created when an asteroid hit the earth and broke off a piece of the planet, is a great metaphor for how something amazing can come out of a rupture. Conflict has the potential to create something truly beautiful. If we use conflict as an opportunity to grow, it can shine light on needs that deserve our attention, either for you or others.

Albert Einstein is often quoted (perhaps inaccurately) for the idea that in the middle of difficulty lies opportunity. Though Einstein had a small role in the creation of the atomic bomb, he also was a Holocaust survivor and a strong advocate for cooperation and peace. The atrocities of the Holocaust and World War II deeply impacted people's views of conflict, war, and peace and birthed the fields of negotiation, peace, and conflict studies within social psychology. For instance, Kurt Lewin became one of the pioneers of the field of social and organizational psychology after he fled Nazi Germany. Lewin had a big impact on the conflict field and on me. I often quote him for the idea that "everyone understands authority, but democracy is a learned behavior."[3]

Reflections on Conflict and Growth

- *How has conflict helped you grow?*

Putting into Practice

This week, notice what is causing conflict in your life.
How is it affecting you?
How are you managing it? Resolving it?
Journal on your thoughts.

Two Paths: Collaboration and Competition

In the Chinese language, two characters (*wei* and *ji*) together mean "crisis." One character symbolizes danger and the other opportunity. That is the way it is when we are in conflict: It can feel dangerous and there is opportunity. The danger part is why so many people have negative associations with conflict and are often slow to see the opportunity in it.

Danger and opportunity also mirror the two main strategies of negotiation—competition and collaboration. Win-lose. Or win-win.

Approaches to Conflict and Negotiation

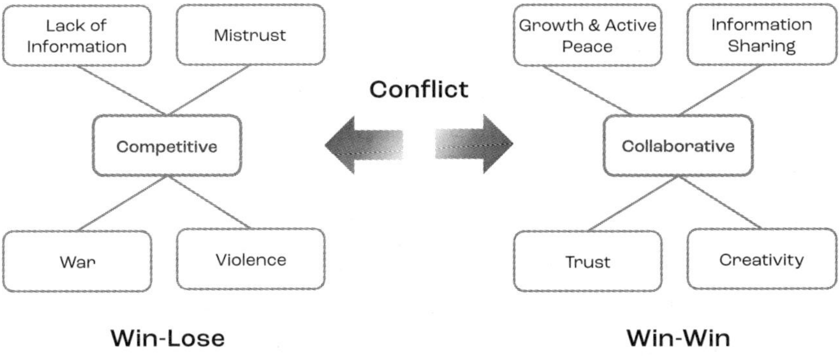

Lack of Information
Mistrust
Competitive
War
Violence

Conflict

Growth & Active Peace
Information Sharing
Collaborative
Trust
Creativity

Win-Lose **Win-Win**

The two main drivers of whether a conflict will move in the direction of competition (win-lose) or collaboration (win-win) are "trust" on the one hand and "lack of information" on the other. If we don't trust the person we are dealing with, how freely do we share information with them? Or to use a poker analogy, how much more likely are we to "keep our cards close to our chest"? There is a close correlation between lack of or unreliable information, mistrust between people in conflict, and a competitive climate. On the other hand, if there is trust and information is shared, things tend to move in the direction of a more harmonious vibe and collaboration. At the outer end of each pole on this spectrum, competition can lead to violence and war, and collaboration can lead to growth and an active peace.

These ideas are based on the seminal work of one of my significant mentors, Morton Deutsch, whom I worked with at the International Center for Cooperation and Conflict Resolution at Columbia University.[4] Mort was also deeply affected by the Holocaust and is sometimes referred to as the "grandfather" of conflict resolution (at least, in the West). One of the things he found in his research is what is sometimes referred to as "Deutsch's Crude Law," that collaboration leads to collaboration and competition leads to competition.

Think about competitive and collaborative situations you have been in and see if this further description of competition and collaboration resonates. In a competitive environment, trust is low, and communication is closed. There's often suspicion and even hostility between the parties. They might emphasize their differences as opposed to what they have in common and they might resort to threats, name calling, powerplays, and deception. One of the most predominant characteristics of competition is the presence of one-upmanship, or who is better than whom? Who is the master? Who dominates? Who serves? This is at the core of patriarchal relations.

Competitive negotiations often include what I call "group-o-centrism," where people from opposite sides of the conflict will predictably polarize around identity group differences. In today's world, identity group polarization runs rampant—whether it be male/female, Black/White, or old/young. The division occurs between whatever identity group is relevant in the particular situation and is often instigated by authoritarians that want to divide and conquer.

The characteristics of collaboration, in contrast, are the opposite. In a collaborative negotiation, people are likely to emphasize the importance of their relationship, listen for other's needs and interests, communicate in a nonaggressive style, highlight common ground, and respect worldview differences. They are looking for a win-win and when they change the climate to collaboration, identity group polarization, name-calling, all of it predictably will diminish.

With collaboration, people are looking for commitment rather than compliance and parties understand that if everyone engages in the decisions that affect them, they are much more likely to abide by them. If decisions are imposed on them, they will push back if they can. This is why mediated settlements are more stable than litigated settlements (the latter of which tend to get appealed) and why democracy in general is a good idea.

Awareness of "Deutch's Crude Law" and how collaboration leads to more harmony and peace applies to just about every arena of our lives. When I was in a negotiation with my children when they were young, I said "yes" to them wherever possible and picked my "nos" carefully (and of course a firm "no" whenever safety was concerned). I aimed for agreement with my children so that they would be committed to the decision and not feel like I was arbitrarily imposing an outcome on them. My kids did well with this approach; they've grown up to be strong adults with great conflict negotiation skills. A spirit of collaboration with our children lends toward raising empowered people who are less likely to be impressed with coercion and violence as a preferred method of influence.

Competition can be fun and useful. It can help us be our best in sports, innovation, work, and school. But destructive competition in a conflict or negotiation where you care about the long-term relationship usually does not make sense. And competition without guardrails can have very negative consequences. For instance, can you imagine a good sports game without rules? Competition and capitalism without guardrails have caused some of the most existential challenges on our planet today. Capitalism, when it turns predatory, concentrates power in the hands of a few and ironically undermines useful competition.

People can find out quickly how much of a competitive versus collaborative mindset they instinctively have in one of my favorite exercises, which I call "Across the Line." Picture two long lines of participants with each person having a partner facing them. I tell them to imagine a line running between them and that "everything on their side of the line is their territory and everything on the other side of the line is their counterpart's territory." Next, I give everyone one minute to get their counterpart into their territory, using whatever method they would like. What unfolds is very revealing and sometimes quite funny. People grab their counterpart and force them across the line, some hand over candy or money to see if they can persuade, and some just do not move. Very quickly, the exercise reveals the internalized refinements of competition and collaboration that all of us are playing out every day:

- Impasse—Neither side moves. Neither side gets what they want. Lose-lose.
- Persuasion—One side takes money out of their pocket to convince the other to come over to their side, or tells them that the view is much better from where they are at, or promises to take them out to dinner. All variations of persuasion. But if it works, the outcome is a win-lose because one side succeeds in getting their counterpart into their territory, but the other does not.
- Force—One side grabs the other and pulls them over. This is clearly a win-lose. When force happens, I always ask, "What will happen next time around if these two are engaging with each other? Will there be trust? Unlikely."

- Reciprocity—I'll come to your side, if you then come to mine. In other words, if you scratch my back, I'll scratch yours. With this option, people move delicately to build trust, but it could backfire if one of the parties chooses to renege.
- Integrative—There is nothing stopping the parties from simply switching sides except for their win-lose mental framework. If they switch sides, both get what they want. It is a pure win-win.

Very few people think to switch sides right away, at least in the cultures and climates that I have worked in. Creating a more collaborative world and environment will help all of us think more win-win in our individual negotiations and conflicts.

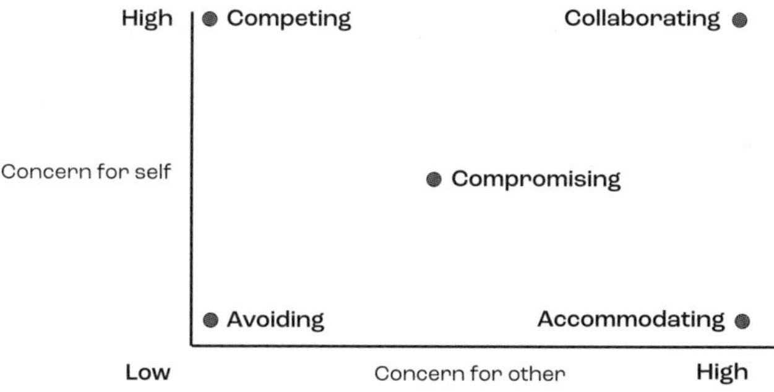

The "Dual Concerns" model shown in the chart above provides more insight into our choices when faced with conflict.[5] Imagine you and a friend are having a small argument. Your friend wants to watch TV and you want to play cards. This presents you with "Dual Concerns"—your concern for yourself, and your concern for your friend. If you have high concern for yourself, and low concern for your friend, you are said to be competing. If you have low concern for yourself and low concern for your friend, you are said to be avoiding. If you have high concern for your friend's interests and low concern for your own, you're accommodating. And if you have high concern for your own interest and high concern for the interests of your friend, you are collaborating. In other words, when you are collaborative, you pay strong attention to meeting both your own interests and those of the other side. Win-win. All of the five strategies presented in the Dual Concerns model can be useful depending on your circumstance, and it's always best, in terms of becoming more conflict intelligent, to be able to use them all. To everything there is a season. But most of us tend to "hang out" using one of these strategies too much of the time when it doesn't serve us. Is this true for you?

Reflections on Collaboration and Competition

- *Do you tend more toward collaboration, or toward competition?*
- *When you compare collaboration and competition, which of these strategies do you prefer? What's your hunch about women as a group planetwide?*
- *By "collaborative," is it possible you really mean accommodating and thus you lose, they win?*
- *Where do you tend to "hang out" on the Dual Concerns model? Does that work for you?*

Putting into Practice

Intentionally use all five of the Dual Concerns options. What do you notice? Write about this in your journal.

Women and Conflict

Are women more collaborative? Do we experience conflict differently?

There is plenty of evidence that, indeed, women are more collaborative, not always, but generally. It also appears, when looking at the big, long arc of time, that we have been cowed by the thousands of years of male violence and threats unleashed by patriarchy that have left us deferential, avoidant, scared, and disempowered in the face of conflict. The rise of patriarchy brought male violence and female silence. I suspect that that muzzling has dampened our conflict intelligence and what we might otherwise have considered sensible ways to manage difference, conflict, and good negotiation.

In my lifetime of experience in the world of negotiation and conflict resolution, it has become clear to me that women are more drawn to a collaborative approach to resolving conflict and difference. When alternative dispute resolution (i.e. other approaches to adversarial litigation like negotiation and mediation) became popular in the 1980s in the United States and other parts of the world, women stormed into the budding profession of mediation. In countless negotiation and mediation trainings, I witnessed thousands of women rejoice with the realization that collaboration is a real and respected approach to conflict. It's no accident that many women, including yours truly, wanted to learn about and utilize collaborative as opposed to competitive negotiation approaches.

In 2012, I published an article with my colleague Dorothy Weaver, "Women and Negotiation: Tips from the Field" in *Dispute Resolution Magazine*. As we wrote:

> Being introduced to collaborative negotiation was life-changing. We have seen a similar reaction for the thousands of women we have coached and trained over the years: relief at finding a way forward that is not about confrontation, fighting and aggression, but rather addressing both sides' needs and interests, integrating emotions, and respecting cultural differences. Learning collaborative negotiation enhances one's ability to be a good listener and helps build and improve relationships. We see that many women respond positively to this kind of negotiation; it feels safer and in keeping with their values. Armed with the collaborative negotiation skill-set, they become more willing to engage in difficult conversations and more confident in general about their ability to negotiate. They also advocate for their interests within this framework and do not simply accommodate (lose-win).[6]

In a 2018 paper, "The Suffragist Peace," Joslyn N. Barnhart, Allan Dafoe, Elizabeth N. Saunders, and Robert F. Trager wrote about their finding that "at each stage of the escalatory ladder of conflict, women prefer more peaceful options":

> More telling is to compare how men and women weigh the choice between backing down and conflict. Women are nearly indifferent between an unsuccessful use of force in which nothing is gained, and their country's leader backs down after threatening force. Men, by contrast, would much rather see force used unsuccessfully than see the country's reputation endangered through backing down. Approval among men is

> fully 36 percent higher for a use of force that achieves nothing and in which over 4,000 US soldiers die than when the US president backs down and the same objective outcome is achieved without loss of life.[7]

When I have offered the question "What comes to mind when you hear the word 'conflict'?" to groups of women, here's a sampling of the answers I have heard:

- I avoid conflict at all costs.
- I avoid, I avoid, and then I blow.
- I defer.
- I accommodate.
- I'm a shape shifter.
- I have been avoiding conflict my whole life.
- I don't deal with conflict; I just avoid it.
- I contort myself in my intimate relationships with men to keep them happy.
- My dad has always been king of the house, and my mom has catered to him completely. If he says it's green, it's green. If he says it is red, it's red. I'm now forty years old, and I am finally beginning to disagree with him.
- I grew up in the Middle East, and I was told by my parents that whenever there was a conflict, I should always apologize and specifically apologize to my father. Now as an adult, I avoid conflict.

Of course, some women thrive on adversarial conflict, but from what I've seen, it is not the norm. The majority of humans don't like conflict much, and I have observed that women like it even less. Or perhaps it's not so much that we don't like conflict, but rather we don't like the violence that comes with it. The PWC has not been safe for conflict; we have been threatened by "might-makes-right."

As part of our growth with negotiation, women need to truly understand what collaboration means. In my practice, I have seen that when many women hear the word "collaboration," they think of a lose-win. In other words, they see collaboration as a way to avoid conflict, accommodate, defer, or gloss over. But a lose-win and a win-win are not the same! In a lose-win, we sacrifice our own needs or overgive at the expense of serving the other.

In the years I spent at Columbia University, Mort Deutsch often got a laugh when he said, "Conflict is like sex. It should happen with a regular amount of frequency and both parties should be better after than before. And, like sex, you want to avoid premature conflict resolution . . . getting to a 'solution' before both parties are ready." The laughter from the audience was often nervous but, like with many jokes, there is great wisdom in his comment. Traditional sex (male-centric, missionary sex) has taught many women to fake orgasm in very much the way we can smooth over conflict or accommodate when we negotiate. We might accommodate missionary sex even though we do not feel the most pleasure in that position in order to keep the peace. It's just a glaring example of how we can accommodate all the way from the bedroom to the boardroom.

Many marriage counselors will ask struggling couples, "Would you rather be right, or would you rather be married?" I don't think this question always serves women. Many of us are too good at accommodating and avoiding and this question encourages us to keep doing it. Just like we need to insist on maximizing our pleasure during sex, we also need to sweat the small stuff in conflict—not all stuff, but the stuff that matters. The more we do this, the better we get at it. We build capacity, what we call in Gestalt the "small units of work." (From 2002-2009, I received extensive training in applying Gestalt theory to coaching individuals, groups and organizations.)

Patriarchy has been a big cultural wind that has influenced how all of us approach conflict and has baked in a sort of simplistic and binary win-lose and fight-flight. Many of us have learned the culture of violence and fighting even if it might not be our inclination. In 2016, when I was working with senior women from the Afghan government, I remember so poignantly doing the "across the line" exercise and how quickly the women went to the force option, how they struggled and pushed each other across the line. I got to know all of them, a very lovely group of people, and I could see their response wasn't anything inherent in them but the result of living in the middle of intense and prolonged violence.

And, many of us have been taught to silence ourselves and be sugar and spice. In my family of origin this led to another of the biggest conflict situations I have lived through. My sister Linda is one of the most beautiful human beings I know. She was the epitome of "sugar and spice and everything nice" . . . until she blew. And when she blew, she blew big time.

We didn't talk about conflict or feelings much in my family of origin. We were typically British American, "WASPy." Not quite as uptight as the British Royal Family, but kind of like that. Throughout my growing years, we were a closed system. But when I was in my twenties, I started therapy with a woman named Lee who was the polar opposite of my mother and my culture. She was a brilliant Jewish lesbian, and a "red-diaper baby" (i.e., raised by Communist parents). Lee basically reparented me. When I told my mom that I was in therapy, she said, "Susan, we don't talk about our private lives outside of the family." Somehow, I knew on a gut level that keeping the dysfunctional stuff inside a closed-loop system was a bad idea.

For both Linda and me, powerlessness was in the wallpaper at our birth, as it was for so many girls in my generation (and still is for many girls around the globe). We were given neither voice or authority. Linda was probably less of a fighter than I; she was milder, less competitive. I was more feisty. As the younger sister, I rode her around the house as if she were my horse and kicked her to make her go faster. Linda was always rewarded for her caretaking, loving kindness, goodness, and servitude. A "well-adjusted" female, as Gloria Steinem might wryly describe her.[8]

In the early '70s, revolution, transformation, and big social conflict were in the air, and Linda and I both chose to attend the newly formed Hampshire College in Amherst, Massachusetts, a bold experiment in education that, among other things, attempted to embody gender equality. We were thrilled to be in such a vibrant place filled with possibility and social change. I'll never forget my traditional New England grandmother almost fainting when she found a male student peeing in the gender-neutral bathroom during one of her visits. While at Hampshire, I asked Linda to join me in a class called "Poverty and American Capitalism," and she agreed. The professor, Charles Sackrey, asked us as a group to chart our access to wealth and privilege. As it turned out, there was a substantial amount of privilege in the class—from connections to the Bushes, Peter Stuyvesant, "Mayflower" families, and other elites.

Then the professor opened our eyes to the level of income inequality that existed in the country (sadly, it is far worse now than it was then.)[9] Shortly after the class ended and shocked by the reality of what she had learned, Linda dropped out of school, moved to Portland, Maine, and joined a radical leftist cell, an offshoot of the Weather Underground.[10]

Once Linda went underground, I had very little contact with her. This lasted for years. When I did hear from her, it was always in hushed tones over payphone lines to avoid being wiretapped. It was both exciting and painful. But, on occasion, I did get time with her. I remember meeting Ray, the French-Canadian charismatic leader of the cell and Linda's lover. Once, the three of us took a walk on a wintery Long Island beach. I can still feel Ray's power and stormy aura, which matched the turbulent surroundings of the breaking waves, gulls, and wind.

In Linda's memoir, *Radical Descent: The Cultivation of an American Revolutionary*, a gripping account of her experience, I learned that Linda brought Ray back to my family home, and they had sex in my parents' very formal living room.[11] The spot she chose for their lovemaking had unconscious perfection in my view—a blanket on the floor underneath the portrait of my young brother, who is posed on the arm of a couch with a posture that foretells all the power and privilege that was before him unlike his three sisters.

Linda is now a Buddhist nun and chaplain and has taken a vow against violence. She has supported many incarcerated women in writing their stories through a HerStory project, most of whom were domestic violence survivors. What my sister did, the violence she was navigating, was extreme. I almost lost her to jail, or death.

Reflecting on Linda's story now, I believe with near certainty that if there had been true gender equality in my home, a deep respect for women's voices, and a climate that prized collaboration over competition with the modeling of excellent conflict resolution skills, Linda would not have exploded as she did. She blew because both her voice and power were muffled in the gender hierarchy of my family, as was her ability to assert and claim value for herself. Instead, her role was to be sweet and subservient.

Let's firmly and fiercely build on our collaborative instincts, embrace conflict, and not shy away. Women have been shape-shifting for way too long. Let's be the conflict gurus on the planet, the conflict maestras, and say a resounding no to the violence of patriarchy. Let's lead the way with high-functioning responses to conflict and negotiation and stand up to the small stuff in our lives so that we can address the big stuff on the planet. Creating a more peaceful world is not soft; it is not lose-win. It is win-win. It's time to lead that way boldly.

Reflections on Collaboration and Women

- *Do you believe women are more collaborative? What's the evidence?*
- *Has patriarchal violence cowed us into a more deferential stance?*
- *Is conflict like sex? How so?*
- *Have you ever faked an orgasm so your partner would feel OK? How often? How many situations have you glossed over because you didn't want to make waves?*
- *How comfortable are you with conflict? What might help you expand your comfort level?*

Putting into Practice

If you find yourself in a conflict this week, practice managing your anxiety, staying present with the situation; breathe.

Reflect on the opportunity inherent in the situation.

Journal.

CHAPTER 4

Speak the Powerful Language of Needs

> *There are three ways of dealing with difference:*
> *domination, compromise, and integration.*
> *By domination only one side gets what it wants;*
> *by compromise neither side gets what it wants;*
> *by integration we find a way by which*
> *both sides may get what they wish.*
> —Mary Parker Follett, *The New State*, 1918

Legal systems were created by men. That's not necessarily a criticism. Just reality. The rule of law is certainly a great improvement over the divine right of kings. Some laws are great (like those that protect freedom of speech, assembly, worship, and reproductive rights), and some laws are terrible and just a reflection of the idea that "he who has the gold makes the rules."

The United States is a super litigious society. There are more lawyers per capita in the United States than in any other country; probably two-thirds of them are centered in New

York City. In the United States, our system of law is known as common law. You get to the truth by working each case and controversy. The idea that truth can be discovered by two people duking it out seems like a very male idea to me. Notably, our system is referred to as "the adversary system," which is contentious and binary, and it tends to escalate conflict. In the best of senses, this legal system is the bedrock of a rules-based order that is needed for democracy; in the worst of senses, it is the foundation of a PWC.[1]

As a kid, I had a front row seat to Wall Street and lawyers. My dad was a partner at the prestigious firm Davis, Polk, and Wardwell. I often visited him at the top of 1 Chase Manhattan Plaza in downtown Manhattan. It had a wraparound view of the city and a Dubuffet sculpture out front. I went to law school because it was what I knew. My mother was a homemaker. And my dad was the dutiful provider; he put on his gray suit, got on the train, and went to Wall Street every day to slay the dragons. In college, when I woke up to my gendered conditioning and realized I wanted more power and a way to make a living that didn't involve depending on a man, I followed his professional lead.

In 1983, I graduated from law school and practiced commercial litigation at Reboul, MacMurray in the heart of New York City at Rockefeller Center where I could look out our window during a break and see the Rockettes sunbathing on the rooftop below. For me, it was a weird job in many respects. You could tell that I didn't quite fit in by the ear cuff I wore in protest of the required man-mode suit. The job was a grind. It was assumed that I would get there by nine a.m. and leave no earlier than ten p.m., preferably later. At one point, when I requested to leave early for personal reasons, the rigid female senior associate enforcer in dour attire looked at me and said, "We don't have 'personal' here." It was super clear to me that there would be no "work-life balance" with this kind of a job.

I remember sitting around boardrooms with men smoking cigars, traveling to Boston with my male senior colleague while I wore the nicest of suits—only to be relegated to the basement of the John Hancock building for whom we were doing "discovery" around a litigation concerning windows that had blown off the building. A lot of litigation seemed kind of stupid to me, a never-ending series of one angry letter responding to the next. Attack, counter-attack, counter-counter-counter, Attack. We billed our clients by six-minute intervals as we went. My fellow associates and I would always laugh that we would never sue anyone. It seemed that any time we started one of these litigations we were simply building another wing on the senior partner's house. And, the entire vibe at Reboul was pretty alienating. I felt like I had been recruited into the firm to be part of the Anglo-Saxon WASP tribe, but I preferred to hang out with the Jews, who the WASP partners referred to as the "bagel boys." (There weren't any Black or Brown lawyers there at the time.)

After three years, I knew I had to get out. In 1986, I left Reboul to look for greener pastures. Luckily, I found them at the Program on Negotiation (PON) at Harvard, ground zero of the newly brewing interest-based revolution. At the time I reached PON, the book *Getting to Yes* and its corresponding movement had been around for about four years. The fundamentals of "principled negotiation," where negotiators and mediators focused on underlying interests as opposed to initial adversarial stances, was a welcome relief after witnessing as a litigator the crazy and often seemingly childish escalation of disputes.

After graduating from Harvard and my time with PON, I returned to New York City and rode the wave of the burgeoning alternative dispute resolution (ADR) movement. I felt lucky to be in the right place at the right time. "Alternative" meant alternative to power-based processes like litigation, which I hoped (and still hope) would take second place to a focus on needs and interests. I didn't use this language then, but might now say "alternative" to a patriarchal dispute resolution system and one with more of the feminine.

Around this same period, when I was first teaching negotiation, a groundbreaking book for women, *In a Different Voice* by Carol Gilligan (1982), was released. In that book, Gilligan references a study that showed that when little boys get into a fight, they apply the rules of the game to solve it, but when little girls fight, they abandon the rules of the game to preserve the relationship.[2] Suddenly, what I had witnessed with men and women was reflected in research data. It felt true to my experience and helped me come to terms with why I wasn't resonating with the legal world.

Before leaving Harvard, I had told my professors at PON and MIT (Massachusetts Institute of Technology, which also participated in PON) that I wanted to focus on "intercultural negotiation." I sensed that negotiation was heavily influenced by culture, and perhaps the culture of gender, and I wanted to learn more about that. They told me that there was no such thing. Nonetheless, about a year later, I met Ellen Raider, who would become my business partner. Ellen had been specializing in intercultural negotiation for about ten years conducting training workshops for global companies around the world. She had begun this specialization when she developed material for USSR/US trade negotiations—but when the

Soviets invaded Afghanistan in 1979, the project fell apart and she created her own business, Ellen Raider International. We subsequently joined forces as Coleman Raider International.

Over the next decades, Ellen and I worked and trained tens of thousands of people from different parts of the world in what we started to call "collaborative negotiation skills." We were known for integrating an intercultural focus into everything we did. I think of our work together as a Camelot of sorts; those were amazing years and the work rippled around the world. There was a hunger for it, especially among women. And women continue to be hungry for it today. Our popularity ruffled the feathers of the traditionalist war and peace folks at Columbia University; students from all parts of the university system came to our programs in droves.

Ellen's and my story is a story of the power of two women, speaking together in a different voice, breaking free of an adversarial PWC, building on our mutual excitement about the power of collaboration, intercultural communication, and supporting each other with confidence and chutzpah. It's a story of what we can do as women when we feel the rightness of our life-force energy and the power of our vision.

Are You Needs-Literate?

All human behavior is an attempt to get a need met.

Generally, you can't get needs met without being able to name them. Naming needs sets in motion their fulfillment. What we put our attention on grows.

The language of needs is the language of the feminine and a fundamental part of a New Negotiation. Speaking our needs and the needs of others with confidence is not weak or stupid; rather, it is part of the feminine reemerging.

In our society today, there is a common argument about whether it's good or bad to meet people's needs. Some call meeting the needs of another a "handout" or "socialism" (especially the advocates for zero regulation of industry). Some say it's impossible to meet needs more broadly. These beliefs come from win-lose and scarcity thinking. People think that there isn't enough to go around. But in reality, we can reward entrepreneurial creativity and have a kinder, more communal world order that meets people's needs. It's not that difficult to imagine and it has happened and continues to happen effectively in some places.

In every conflict, you can choose to place your focus on power, on rights/rules/laws, or on interests/needs. Legal systems focus on rights and rules. The language of rules is necessary, but it is not the language of needs. Rules provide helpful guardrails for competition and life. However, when people start using the language of rights and rules, the discourse can quickly escalate into coercion, threats, and attacks. Patriarchy privileges the language of rights, rules, and coercive power.

As a global sisterhood, women around the world differ by culture and worldview but every one of us has the same categories of need. Because our cultures have different sets of challenges, how we meet needs can differ, but our basic needs are the same. They are fundamental to being human.

There are many models of human need, but throughout my career working with conflict and negotiation, I have always preferred Abraham Maslow's. A humanistic psychologist practicing in the 1960s, Maslow is most famous for this hierarchy of needs model in which he identifies the categories of need that all humans have from the basic to the spiritual.[3]

Recently, I have become aware that Maslow's development of this model was inspired by his time on the Siksika Nation's Blackfoot reservation in Gleichen, Alberta, Canada.[4]

Maslow's Hierarchy of Needs

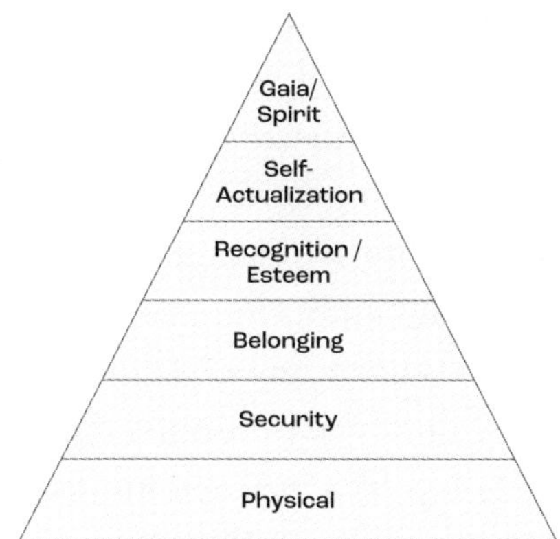

Physical—At the bottom of the hierarchy, we have physical needs: food, water, rest, and sex. These are our basic survival needs.

Security—Next comes our need for safety, which can be met by a good income or job, a secure home, a bank account, and the absence of war.

Belonging—All humans have a need to be part of a group. We need affiliation and community. Depending on our culture, some of us have a much greater need to be part of a group than others—but we all have a need to belong, whether it be to a family, organization, or community.

Self-esteem/recognition—Self-esteem is an inner feeling and recognition comes from outside of us. Recognition can come in the form of a promotion, a compliment, or a paycheck. Inner self esteem can be a hard nut to crack for many women, especially given the patriarchal messaging of our secondary status. Outer esteem comes from being seen by others for the value that we bring to whatever we're trying to do or contribute.

Self-actualization—Fulfilling our life's purpose helps us to self-actualize, and being our authentic self with purpose and meaning is considered a core need. In today's world, figuring out how to self-actualize has become an even bigger deal for people. And for women, finding purpose, as opposed to supporting the purpose of others, offers us a deep sense of inner power and meaning.

Gaia/spirit—Transcendence. "Transcendence" was Maslow's original word; I have changed this to Gaia because it's more holistic, less patriarchal, and more connected to the earth. The need for Gaia is our need to be connected to a spiritual dimension or power greater than ourselves. Gaia lives in the laws of the cosmos and nature.[5]

In summary, the idea of a need hierarchy is that if we are starving, we will find it hard to focus on the upper levels of need. If our house is burning down, we will, of course, focus on safety and security before thinking of much else. This is a reason so many people have a hard time focusing on the need for rapid climate action: because they are simply scrambling to survive and get food on the table.

When we get good at articulating needs we put their fulfillment into motion. When my family and I moved to a semirural community about fifty miles north of New York City, we landed, much to my surprise, in the middle of intense, almost come-to-blows conflict. Before our arrival, I had a somewhat quaint and even condescending projection about rural life. *It's going to be so bucolic and peaceful*, I thought. Far from the truth!

On its surface, the conflict we walked into was about money and taxes and the needs of the elementary school versus the needs of retirees living on a fixed income. Putting my organizational consulting skills to work, I helped all stakeholders—faculty, students, parents, staff, community—name their needs. Through a series of interviews and questionnaires, I supported everyone in articulating what was needed—a ball field, a new gym, and tax rebates—and reflected this back to the whole system without pointing fingers or blame. Lo and behold, over the next number of years, the needs that were identified as most important began to get met, one by one. Naming the needs had lessened the hostility and started the process of their fulfillment.

One powerful technique for helping someone articulate their needs is to focus on the positive thing they are trying to create, not the negative thing they are trying to avoid. You could also call this the positive fulfillment of the need as opposed to the frustration of it. So, for example, if I say, "Don't think about a pink elephant," I'm sure you just did. What we focus on grows.

At one point in my relationship with my daughter, I was experiencing a great deal of stress. If anyone could trigger me, it would be them. But I noticed that, rather than saying, "You're not doing this" or "You're being so cold," I instead focused on the positive thing I wanted to create with them—more time and connection. Things improved. It took some managing of myself to not get caught up in my own reactivity.

Getting in touch with our needs takes practice and self-attunement. I do a needs assessment in my journal as a daily practice and I highly recommend it. It's a powerful way to check in with myself and think about, for that day, how I am meeting each category of need. This helps me move beyond codependence (i.e., expecting somebody else to meet my needs) and empowers me to take action on my own behalf.

Conflict is created by frustrated needs. Pleasure is created by satisfied needs. Pleasure is the antidote to patriarchy.

When we start with what we need, we can then think about the best ways to achieve it whether it's through a negotiation with our counterpart or not. Notice that there are often ways to meet our needs (i.e., our BATNA) other than via the other party. Paying attention to this can increase our power and might give us ideas about alternatives that we hadn't thought of.

Reflections on the Powerful Language of Needs

- *Can I speak the language of needs and feel its power?*
- *Am I able to identify my own needs in a conflict situation?*
- *Can I name an example of where the articulation of needs has put into motion their fulfillment?*

Putting into Practice

Assess your level of needs satisfaction. Big picture, in this moment, which of your needs are most satisfied right now? Which needs are most frustrated?

In the following chart, identify one way that you are currently meeting each category of need.

Needs Assessment

Write down 1-2 ways you are meeting or working to meet each of these categories of need in your life today.

Gaia/ Spirit	______________________
Self-Actualization	______________________
Recognition / Esteem	______________________
Belonging	______________________
Security	______________________
Physical	______________________

Build Your Collaborative "Core"

I've taken a few Pilates classes, and I've come to understand how important it is to strengthen your "core," the muscles that provide deep stability to your body. This is a good metaphor for one of the first steps in collaborative negotiation: We need to practice and develop the core framework and skills that allow for a win-win to happen.

These include

- identifying the positional "clash;"
- discovering the needs and interests which underly the positions;
- reframing the conflict at the needs level into a joint problem to be solved; and
- creatively brainstorming alternative ways to satisfy the needs/interests of all concerned.

There are three other "elements" other than those four:

- climate (is the atmosphere competitive or collaborative?);
- emotions; and
- worldview (which includes culture).

These additional three are not exactly a structural core but exist more in the background and influence the vibe around the negotiation. While not part of the core, they are critical. If any is not handled well, it can easily derail any negotiation and often does. Because of that, emotions and worldview each have their own chapter . We have already addressed "climate" in talking about competition and collaboration but here is a bit more on that front.

Can you feel in your gut when situations are more adversarial/competitive versus collaborative? Can you feel in your gut which fundamental strategy is being pursued by you or the other side—competition, collaboration, or a mishmash of both? This is what I mean by "climate." Climate incorporates all the verbal and nonverbal communication that is creating the atmosphere surrounding a negotiation. How are you feeling in it? Are you tense? Are you angry? Fearful? Are you feeling like you shouldn't share information? Trust yourself! If the climate is hostile and the negotiation is competitive, people are very unlikely to be transparent and reveal their underlying needs. Instead, they stick to positions and provide justifications for why their positions are correct. Like in a lawsuit, they argue that the law is on their side (their position) and provide lots of justifications (legal and otherwise) to support their point of view. On the other hand, if the climate is collaborative, people are more likely to share their true needs and concerns and alternatives can more easily be discovered. They open up.

Whether the climate is collaborative and needs are revealed, or competitive with parties focusing on positions, justifications, and threats will impact the types of negotiated outcomes that are possible.

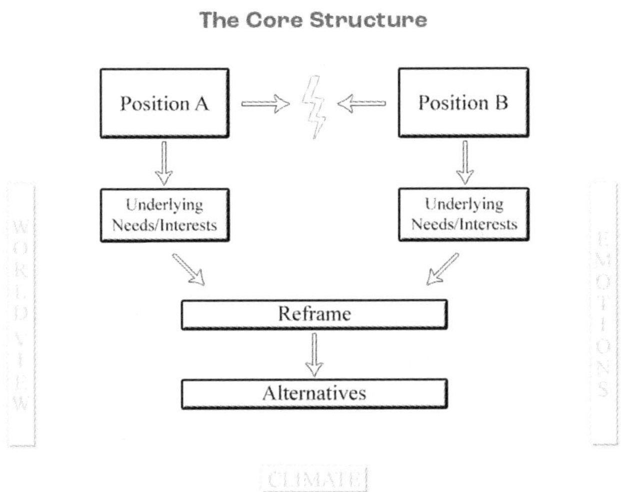

Separate Positions from Needs and Interests

> *Focus on interests, Not positions.*
>
> —Fisher and Ury, *Getting to Yes: Negotiating Agreement Without Giving In,* 1981

There is a classic negotiation story about an orange. It's been taught tens of thousands of times around the world, and it always resonates in important ways. It goes like this.

Let's assume your two kids are fighting over an orange. Their positions are: "Mommy, I want the orange." "No, I want the orange." You come in to help them resolve the conflict. How should you do this? Most people say, "Cut the orange in half." Tired parents say, "Take the orange away." But if you ask, "Why do you want the orange?" you will find out the underlying needs of each kid. It turns out that one wants the orange because she wants to eat it; the other wants the skin to make candy or marmalade. Their position is they want the orange—but their needs are different.

It's not surprising that it was a woman who first articulated the importance of separating positions from needs/ interests. Mary Parker Follett (1869–1933) was an American social worker, management consultant, and pioneer in the field of what is now organizational theory and behavior. Sometimes referred to as the "Mother of Modern Management" and called by some "an unsung hero," she brought in more of the feminine: Instead of emphasizing industrial and mechanical components, she advocated for people as the most valuable commodity present in any business.[6]

What does it mean to separate a position from a need or interest? Remember, conflict is simply "things opposed." In negotiation, what are opposed are basically negotiation positions. Positions are our preferred solution to the negotiation, our first best idea about how to get our needs met. Typically, they are stated as a demand, a preference, a request, a blame statement, or an accusation, like:

"Get out of my office."

"Take out the garbage!"

"You owe me $2,000!"

"I deserve a raise."

Positions can frame the conflict in the negotiation and help us understand what the "fight" is about. Notice that if people agreed on the positions, there would be no need to negotiate.

Positions come from asking, "What do I want?" "What does the other side want?" It's crucial to understand that a position—even though it's our preferred solution—is just one way to get our needs met.

If our position comes from asking, "What do I want?" our underlying need or interest comes from asking ourselves, "Why do I want it?" Beneath positions there are needs and interests. Your needs and interests are the reason you are negotiating. Needs and interests can be long or short-term but are specific to a particular negotiation.

The terms "needs" and "interests" are basically interchangeable though needs have a deeper connotation. PON generally used the term "interests," which was more acceptable in the male culture of the time; Ellen and I started using the softer, more feminine, and perhaps deeper term "needs" in addition to interests.

You and the other side might have both tangible needs and psychological needs. In general, you must satisfy both sides' priority needs and interests (in other words, the most important need that is driving your position) to have a stable negotiated outcome. Because needs are the reason we negotiate and because we are needs-satisfying creatures, if we are not getting our needs met in the process, we will either give up or try a different process (like a lawsuit or some kind of force) and the possibility for a negotiated agreement is likely to unravel.

Going back to the orange, if you, the parent, decide that the fairest way to resolve the kids' dispute is to cut the orange in half, each will get 50 percent of what they want. (Or you might divide it into two-thirds, one-third, or even 100 percent—zero.

In negotiation terminology, these are versions of "splitting the difference.")

Or perhaps you tell the kids you will do with the orange whatever they tell you to as long as they stop arguing. But imagine they don't and they continue to squabble. In negotiation terminology, they have reached an "impasse." Both splitting the difference and impasse are outcomes of "win-lose" or "lose-lose" negotiations. But if you ask, "Why do you want the orange?" you uncover the real underlying needs of each and can give them each 100 percent of what they want. One takes the skin and the other takes the fruit. This is known as an "integrative solution" or a "win-win" because it satisfies the fundamental need of each side.

A lot (and I do mean a lot) of conflict and negotiation gets stuck at the level of impasse. When that happens, value gets left on the table because people are not able to shift to a more cooperative climate and communicate their real underlying needs and interests. Problem-solving negotiations in which needs are revealed tend to result in integrative or win-win solutions—a direct contrast to more distributive, win-lose, zero-sum solutions. Distributive or zero-sum simply means that for every bit that I win, you lose the same amount and vice versa.

To discover the other side's needs and interests, we need to ask them why they are taking the position they are taking. This does not need to be confrontational. In every negotiation, we need to know our own needs, and we need to try to understand those of the other side. Many times, when people hear a position in a negotiation, they often assume, consciously or unconsciously, what the underlying need is. For instance, people often assume with the orange story that both kids want to eat the orange. It's very good practice in negotiation to not make assumptions because you just might offer the wrong "need satisfier" and, as a result, add unnecessary conflict to the negotiation or offer more than you need to. Or as we have often said in our workshops, "When you ass-u-me, you make an ass out of you and me."

Stable negotiated outcomes result from meeting or satisfying priority needs of both sides. People may have no idea of the distinction between a position and a need but, if their needs are met, they will give up the fight and forget about the issue. There will be peace.

Needs can exist at any level of system—your family, your community, your nation, the world—all have needs. Take, for example, an international organization like the UN. Just like individuals, the organization has physical needs—staff members, a physical plant; security needs like funding, security systems, diplomatic immunity; belonging needs like compacts and treaties with others; recognition needs like respect, dues paid by members, and the like. Nations too. For example: physical—water, energy; security—revenue from taxes, defense; belonging—allies; recognition—respect in the world from other nations. The organizational work I have done has almost always been about creating a more needs-based focus to increase collaboration in the whole system.

Reframe

When you reframe, you move your attention from positions to needs or interests. In the old frame, you're in a power struggle, a positional clash. When you're in the reframe, you're coming together and moving from opposite sides of the table to the same side (metaphorically or actually). You are now looking at the problem together to see what the solution might be. Reframing is an attempt to restate the problem so that both sides' priority needs are considered. Or, as the *Getting to Yes* authors described it, "However precarious your relationship may be, try to structure the negotiation as a side-by-side activity in which the two of you—with your different interests . . . jointly face a common task."[7]

Reframing is not rephrasing but rather refocusing the parties on needs instead of positions. People may say to each other, "You give up some of what you want, and I'll give up some of what I want. We'll meet in the middle." This is a classic compromise or split the difference tactic in which you can lose a lot of value. In reframing, the two sides say to each other, "Let's work together to discover how both sets of priority needs can be reasonably well satisfied." In most cases, reframing changes the atmosphere of the negotiation in positive ways.

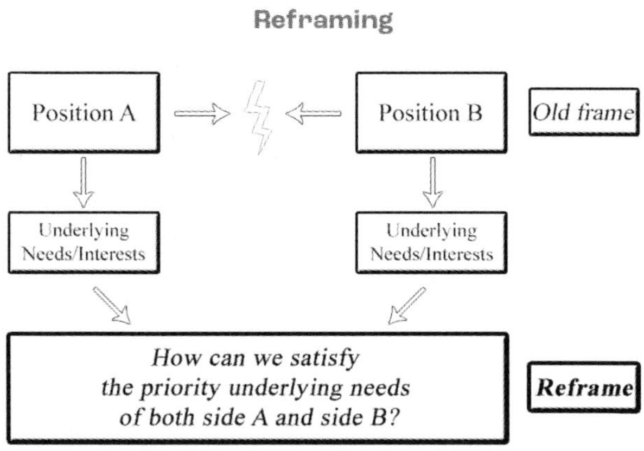

Reframing a negotiation to focus on needs instead of positions is a giant step toward bringing negotiations to a satisfactory conclusion. As someone who has mediated many conflicts, I can tell you that when you get to this point, you can feel the difference!

Brainstorm Alternatives to Meet Needs

Brainstorming invites us to think creatively which is always useful in negotiation and conflict. In any negotiation, we can brainstorm all the ways we could address needs—from what we can exchange with each other to how we might get those needs met from other sources. Take the following example from Mary Parker Follett, *Creative Experience* (1924): Two people (A and B) are sitting in a library. A wants the window open, and B wants it closed. These are their positions. The reason A wants it open is to get some fresh air. The reason B wants it closed is because they are cold. The reframe is, "Is there a way to create more fresh air and make sure that you're warm?" Some brainstormed solutions might be: One gets a shawl, one could open a window in the room next door to create more circulation, and so on. Simple, right?

Or a creative brainstorm could go like this:

You want to go on holiday to Italy. Your spouse wants to go to Greece. (These are positions.) You want mountains; they want the sea. (These are interests/needs.) Where can we go where we can have the mountains and the sea? Now you can together brainstorm places where both of your needs are met.

Here is a simple creativity exercise that perhaps you know. Can you connect these nine dots with four straight lines without lifting your pen or pencil? Give it a try before you look at the solution (solution on page 104).

•   •   •

•   •   •

•   •   •

This exercise captures the kind of mindset you need when you are brainstorming solutions after a reframe.

Possible alternatives can be further broken down into "Bargaining,"º or "chips" (like carrots), and "Bargaining Chops," or "chops" (like sticks). We try to get our needs met in negotiation either through getting our position met, or by getting something from the other side that will meet our needs. Thus, there are two kinds of need satisfiers in negotiations—positions and "bargaining chips." A position is a proposal by one side to get their own needs met, like "Give me the orange." A bargaining chip is an offer you make to your counterpart of something that might meet their needs, like "How about an apple?"

When people are adversarial, they also use "chops." "Chips" come from asking, "What are the things I could offer that would satisfy my counterpart's needs (and that don't undermine my own interests)?" "Chops" come from asking, "What are the things I have that would thwart my counterpart's needs?" You can think of chops like a karate chop.

Remember: There are three main things that give you power in a negotiation: your ability to meet needs (chips), to thwart the other's needs (chops), and your BATNA. Assuming you are staying in the negotiation and not walking away, the quantity and quality of your bargaining chips and chops determine your power. Using chops, however, may create an adversarial climate, which you may not want to do.

Many people assume that power just comes from hierarchy, status, or wealth, but that's not always the case. If you have a bunch of chips and chops, you have a lot of power to influence, either by meeting the other side's needs or by threatening to withdraw something valuable from them.

Bargaining chips are only worthwhile if they are perceived as valuable by the other side. Very often, negotiators think they have a wonderful bargaining chip that will close the deal or settle the conflict. They sense that it gives them power to influence, only to find out that the other side doesn't really want it.

Chips might not always be easy to identify, they're often creative, and you need to know the other side's needs to know if the chips will even work. Sometimes you offer a chip just to see if it reveals something about the other's needs, but you have to be careful not to undermine your own interest in the process.

Reflections on the Core Elements of Collaborative Negotiation

- *Am I able to distinguish a position from a need/interest?*
- *Can I reframe, and separate the person from the problem?*
- *Am I a good, creative problem solver? What strategies do I use to brainstorm and think creatively?*

Putting into Practice

Think of a current conflict situation you are in, or have recently been in. What is your preferred solution (i.e., your position)? What are your underlying needs or interests?

And what is the position of the person on the other side of the conflict? What do you think might be their underlying need or interest?

Nine Dots solution—The only way to do it is to "think out of the box," bring the lines outside of the imagined square around them. Like this:

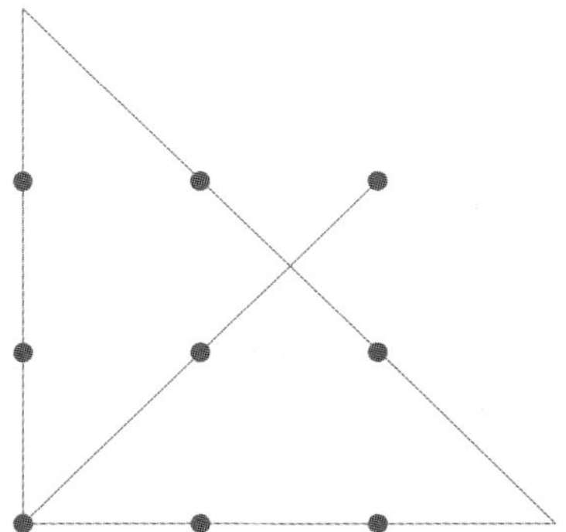

Don't Shy Away from Positions If You Need Them

> *It took me sixteen years to realize that "no" is a complete sentence. For a long time, I had no agency, no volition; if someone offered me a role, I took it. I wasn't very happy in my career because of that, you know.*
> —Jane Fonda, Film Society, 2017

If you are experiencing a conflict, you will feel far more heat if you focus on positions. Indeed, sometimes it's best to start by sharing your needs and interests, and sometimes you may never want to state a position. Having said this, being one of those women who learned the skills of accommodation, stating one's position and feeling the heat of it might be exactly what is most warranted.

Both our "no" and our "yes" can be important negotiation positions for women. They can help us unearth and stand up for important underlying needs that we want to satisfy and desires we want to meet. Too many women negotiate against themselves before negotiating with the other side. "Oh, I won't say that; he many not like it," we think. Or "I shouldn't ask for that. I doubt they will say yes."

Positions clarify the starting point and what we really would prefer. I have had to do a certain amount of hand holding with my avoidant female clients to help them state clearly what their preferred solution to the conflict is (i.e., their position) and to understand that it can simply be stated in a firm, clear way. Knowing what you want, and stating it, is powerful. And sometimes what you want to say is "no." "No" is a position. It's a complete sentence.

Too many of us are deeply acculturated to following the lead of a man or the PWC in general. We support what they want. At the deepest level, we have learned this somatically by not having the right to control the boundaries of our bodies. The culture of sexual assault and not having decision-making power over our bodies have had a profound impact on our ability to say no in negotiation.

When I was in high school, the male school doctor fondled me while he was doing my gyn exam. It was only when I was older that I thought, "Wow! That was not OK!" In the words of Gloria Steinem, "We have the right to vote, but we still don't have the right to our own bodies. We are still subject to bodily invasions at a rate far exceeding that of men."[8] Somatic learning runs deep and can sabotage us even when we are outwardly looking our professional best.

Getting comfortable with hearing "no" is also an important muscle to build. It won't kill us. After getting real with ourselves about what we want and asking for it, we can learn how to be more comfortable when we hear "no" as an answer. The world has gotten used to our services and we need to change the mindset. If we aren't hearing "no" enough, we're probably not asking for enough. But let's get comfortable with hearing "yes" too! Getting what we want can sometimes be a challenge. Having and receiving are critical skills to develop for those of us who have been trained to serve. I remember so well being struck by a comment from Mama Gena in her Mastery program that, in the end, what we were learning was ultimately about learning to receive. Negotiation is, after all, ultimately about both giving and receiving.

Reflections on No and Yes

- *Am I able to say "no" when I need to? How does it make me feel?*
- *Can I say "yes" to myself?*

Putting into Practice

Say "no" to something that you really would like to but might have otherwise avoided.

Say "yes" to something that you would really like to.

Pay Attention to Which Language You Are Speaking: Power, Rights, or Needs/Interests

As mentioned, in every conflict situation, we have a choice whether to focus on: needs and interests; rights and rules; or power-over, coercion, and force. They are each like TV channels that we can turn to.

The rules-based channel in the orange conflict might sound like this: "I saw it first." "Yes, but I picked it up first." Note that, in some societies, it's already established that the elder is absolutely going to get the orange, because that's the way disputes are resolved. Women are rarely "on top" of that arrangement.

And notice here that rules are often "reified" negotiation outcomes, something that started with a conflict and ended up as rule, either through negotiation or some sort of struggle. That's why so many rules and laws can favor the dominant group. "He that has the gold makes the rules."

A power-based channel might sound like this:

"If you don't give me that orange, I'm going to beat the hell out of you." Or "If you don't give me that orange, I'm not going to share my bicycle." Ever heard that channel being played or played it yourself?

And that's why, if your goal is to create a collaborative climate, you can be firm, you can even be fierce, but it's best to avoid rights-based or power-based language in a New Negotiation. This can be tricky. Rights and power-based language can emerge very quickly because so many people and cultures are primed to use fighting words. Triggering a more competitive, win-lose, adversarial debate goes right to the heart of a patriarchal way of doing things.

Focusing on interests, speaking more of the language of needs, is a sign that the Goddess is reemerging. This, of course, over the millennia, is two steps forward and one step back, but I choose to believe, like Mahatma Gandhi, that we are on a path in the right direction toward a more needs-focused, and therefore kinder world order: "When I despair, I remember that all through history the way of truth and love have always won. There have been tyrants and murderers, and for a time, they can seem invincible, but in the end, they always fall. Think of it—always."[9]

Reflections on Power, Rights, and Interests/Needs

- *Can I tell which channel I am on—power, rights, or needs/interests?*

Putting into Practice

Pay attention to which "channel" you are on—power, rights, or interests/needs. Play around with intentionally switching channels and see what happens. Journal about this.

CHAPTER 5

Use AEIOU to Guide Your Communication

A Fable of the North Wind and the Sun

Once upon a time, the north wind and the sun were arguing about who was the stronger. They saw a passing traveler and challenged each other as to who could remove the cloak of the traveler first. As the wind blew hard and cold, the man wrapped the cloak tightly around him. Then the sun shone and its warmth made the man take off his cloak.
—Aesop

How we communicate with each other has everything to do with the kind of world we want to live in. The PWC privileges a certain kind of tactical language—fighting words that sow disrespect, division, distrust, and hyper-masculinity. A New Negotiation and the more collaborative feminine uses and privileges the opposite.

Joseph McCarthy, Roy Cohn, Richard Nixon, Roger Stone, Paul Manafort, Steve Bannon, and Donald Trump are the sorts of American, scrappy, right-wing gladiator communicators and beneficiaries of the PWC. They are all connected to each other in a kind of lineage.

Joseph McCarthy was well known in the '50s for accusing everyone and anyone of being a Communist. Paul Manafort and Roger Stone began their notoriety with a lobbying firm in the '80s based in Washington, DC, where they worked on behalf of prominent Republicans, businesses, and foreign governments. Manafort catered to Russian oligarchs. Roger Stone, an advisor to Richard Nixon and later to Trump, is famous for the very large tattoo of Nixon he has on his back. Once he said to a reporter, "What I admire about Nixon was his resilience, it's attack, attack, attack."[1] Steve Bannon has been a political strategist for Donald Trump with eyes on long-term, right-wing global domination.

But none of the above was anything quite like Roy Cohn, who wrote the bible on twentieth-century PWC tactics. Cohn was a lawyer, prosecutor, and "fixer" in the 1970s and '80s, gay in spite of his homophobic vitriol, and one of Donald Trump's main teachers.

Cohn's playbook was as follows:

> Rule 1—Attack, attack, attack.
> Rule 2—Admit nothing; deny everything.
> Rule 3—Demand loyalty.
> Rule 4—No matter what happens, claim victory. Never admit defeat. You have to be willing to do anything to anyone to win.[2]

Sound familiar? Kind of like a Mob boss, right?

These rules and tactics are military in nature and ultimately lead to violence and war. They exemplify the toxic worldview of dominance that is the cornerstone of a PWC. For us women, these rules create a "permission structure" for male domination over us.[3] Immediately after winning the 2024 presidential election, adult male pro-Trump men screamed a disturbing refrain: "Your body, my choice."[4]

When I arrived at the Kennedy School at Harvard in 1986 and fortuitously found the Program on Negotiation (PON), I was fleeing the scrappy world of New York City litigation that embodied so many of these PWC tactics and rules. But as much as I appreciated PON at the time, and still do, it was a pretty male vibe of a place. The way they taught negotiation felt more like from the neck-up—two-dimensional and less emotional. While I enjoyed it and did well in the program (I won that year's negotiation prize), I didn't know what I was missing until I moved back to New York City to pursue a career in intercultural negotiation and met my soon-to-be partner, Ellen.

Ellen's voice, her style, her way of moving in the world, was much more a product of a woman's mind and sensibilities—much closer to the feminine.

What especially stood out was Ellen's communication model—"AEIOU"—that she and I then improved upon over the years.

AEIOU stands for Attack, Evade, Inform, Open, and Unite, the five types of communication tactics we can use in negotiation depending on our skill level and intention. AEIOU became our signature model—and over the years, it was translated into many languages and used around the world. Even though it is based on English language vowels, it still resonates with folks from just about every continent.

Fast-forward to 2021. I was attending the Women & Power Conference at the Omega Institute and was listening to its brilliant founder, Elizabeth Lesser, give the keynote.[5] Lesser was telling us about some research that she had just become aware of: In 1930, a clinical psychologist named Dr. Walter Cannon, who was the chairman of his department at Harvard Medical School, was interested in how humans reacted under stress and conflict and brought people into his laboratory to measure the chemicals and hormones released in the blood under simulated traumatic experiences. He discovered that stress triggers two primordial reactions, aggression or withdrawal. He called this "fight or flight." Since then, Elizabeth went on, "'fight or flight' has become doctrine. Under stress, humans fight or flee." But in 2002, seventy years after Cannon's experiment, Dr. Shelley Taylor, a clinical psychologist at UCLA, noticed something interesting. The people Dr. Cannon had brought into his labs were all men. "Now this wasn't unusual. Female subjects have historically been excluded from medical research. And this has had grave consequences for women who respond differently to all kinds of conditions like heart disease and Alzheimer's and lung cancer," Lesser said. Taylor and her team were inspired to see if men and women respond differently to stress.

In her book *The Tending Instinct*, Taylor wrote, "Early studies on the human stress response were done by men on male participants to explore arguably male scenarios from a male perspective. The dominant metaphor, fight or flight, represents the threatening social landscape as a solitary kill or be killed world." Dr. Taylor and her team brought women into the research labs and repeated the earlier studies and discovered that fight or flight was not the only response that humans have to stress and conflict. "Different chemicals, different hormones were released in women," she wrote. Their studies revealed that under stress, women may sometimes have a fight or flight response, but their primary reaction to stressful conflictual events was to "care, connect, and communicate." Dr. Taylor called this "tend and befriend" to describe how "women offer care, seek emotional connectivity, and create circles of belonging to deal with personal and collective trauma" and that "'befriending rather than fighting' is the primary gender difference in adult human behavioral responses to stress."[6]

At the end of Lesser's talk, I walked out into the cool, fall air with a brightness in my step. The research she had shared helped me understand why our AEIOU model has worked so well, why so many around the world have been drawn to it, and how it is such an elegant integration of the more masculine "fight, flight" (Attack, Evade, Inform) and the more feminine "tend and befriend" (Inform, Open, and Unite).

AEIOU

Great communication skills are probably the most essential part of negotiation, resolving conflict and, for that matter, building a more peaceful world. This includes what, when, and how we are communicating.

AEIOU supports us in setting our intention and following through. It helps us diagnose things if we hit a train wreck. It is the nitty gritty of the ways that women can be the collaborative leadership force that our planet needs right now.

Assuming we speak the same language, shouldn't communication be straightforward? If only it were so simple! Even between people who know each other intimately, never mind countries, there are probably hundreds of daily miscommunications.

Let's take a heteronormative husband and wife who are from the same culture. The wife "encodes" a communication to her husband based on her life experience. The husband hears what she is saying by decoding that communication according to his life experience. Sometimes, their life experiences align and there is synthesis between the intent of the speaker and the impact it has on the receiver. But often, the same words will conjure different images to them both. For example, the wife, speaking about another woman nearby, says, "She makes a lot of money." Well, how much is a lot? Is it $50,000, is it $200,000? It just depends.

Having the confidence to say what we need to say when we need to, to state clearly what we want, to assert, to listen to other's concerns when that's warranted, to contain ourselves from using fighting words that may ultimately undermine the way we want to proceed—these are the specific "devil in the details" that ultimately give us the road map to do what we want to do, and have the influence that we would like to have.

People of any gender can use all of these behaviors, but whether one chooses to be collaborative, competitive, or have a patriarchal, power-over worldview will likely influence their approach to communication. A New Negotiation and leadership requires mastering Informing, Opening, and Uniting behaviors to parry the Attack/Evade of the PWC.

Here is a description of each of the five behaviors. This will be followed by when and where you might or might not want to use each.

Attack

> *You cannot shake hands with a clenched fist.*
> —Mahatma Gandhi

"Attacking" involves any type of behavior that is perceived by the other side as hostile or unfriendly. It includes: threatening, criticizing, insulting, and blaming the person or group with whom we are negotiating. It also can include using hostile tones of voice, facial expressions, and gestures, as well as interrupting, discounting the other's ideas, patronizing, stereotyping, challenging, and defending.

Attacking behavior usually is directed at the person, not the problem under discussion, and it is frequently unfair or not accurate. A shorthand way to identify Attack communication is if it has an implied "you are an idiot" tone to it. There's a lot of Attacking behavior in a PWC.

Here are some Attack examples from clients I have worked with. (See the responses, not the prompts.)

Parent to teen daughter
Mom: Honey, can you please turn down the music?
Daughter: Mom, you are not the only one who lives in this house. Give me a break!

In an international NGO for kids
Government representative: Could you tell us about your plans for the zone?
Person A: Mr. Government Representative, we'll see what we can do about that zone. But we really have many other priorities for the moment. We really don't

understand how your government could allow such a situation to continue with so many children at risk!

A nurses' union (a nurse and her supervisor on the hospital floor)
Maria: I would like to go to lunch at eleven-thirty.
Claudia: Who do you think you are, coming in my face and asking me to go to early lunch? You always get what you want—you must be the teacher's pet. As fat as you are maybe you should miss a meal!

In a telecommunications company
Supervisor: I've been having trouble with two team members. Their arguments are polarizing the entire work unit.
Manager: Well, I see you still haven't figured out how to manage your people. Perhaps I promoted the wrong person for the job.

Evade

What you resist not only persists but will grow in size.
—Carl Jung

"Evade" behavior includes ignoring, changing the subject, withdrawing, postponing, "tabling" an issue (postponed for consideration at an indefinite later date), and "caucusing" (a private meeting of parties on one side of the negotiation).[7] For the recipient, Evade can feel like getting blown off or ignored and thus can have the same impact as an Attack, because we feel disrespected. On the other hand, if a party requests that an issue be tabled or asks for a caucus, while indicating their interest in subsequently continuing with the negotiations, the other party is not so likely to feel shunned.

But perhaps there are things that are worth ignoring. We cannot negotiate everything; we must pick our battles. There are times when we may need to step away to get the "charge" out of our body before we engage. Sometimes a negotiation between two parties may involve several issues that need to be resolved, one of which is a major disagreement. It may be best, in shaping the agenda, to table the major issue while trying to resolve the smaller ones. If the smaller ones can be dealt with successfully, the resulting spirit of cooperation might lead to a more productive negotiation when the two groups finally begin talking about the major issue. This is a positive form of Evading behavior.

Attack and Evade are essentially fight and flight behaviors coming from our old, reptilian brain.

Here are examples of what Evading behavior might look like in different contexts:

> ***In a company***
> Female staff member: We are establishing a subcommittee on sexual harassment, and we feel that your group's input is important. Can we count on you?
> Male manager: Hum, it's a possibility. We'll have to discuss it at next month's staff meeting.
>
> ***Between two fictitious countries***
> Sularia: I am sure that our military assistance will help you with the Bandor situation.
> Rodan: Yes, the military aspect is an important

consideration. Now, let me ask you about one of the priorities you mentioned earlier.

At the office

A: Thanks for coming, B. I wanted to talk to you about this report. It's clear that you put a lot of work into it, but . . .
B: Did you see the Champions League game on TV last night? Incredible second half.

In the kitchen

A: Could you wash the dishes before you go out?
B: (Doesn't look up from newspaper)

Inform

Speaking your truth is the most powerful tool we have.
—Oprah, *The Path Made Clear*, 2019

"Informing" behavior includes stating what you want (your position); backing up your position with data, opinions, justifications; communicating your underlying needs; and revealing your underlying emotions.

Perhaps you have heard about "I" messages and "you" messages in popular psychology. "I" messages are communications about you; "you" messages are about blaming the other. Informing in negotiation is a similar idea. Informing behavior refers to when we, directly or indirectly, explain our perspective to the other side and is consequently an essential ingredient of any negotiation. Both sides must provide information to each other if a genuine negotiation is to take place. We can Inform on many different levels, including our positions, needs, interests, worldview, feelings, facts, figures, and justifications.

Information given about our needs, feelings, or worldview is usually not negotiable. It is unwise to try to persuade someone to not feel what they feel, not need what they need, or not value what they value. What is negotiable are positions. And, if our underlying needs are satisfied, our original positions, justifications, and worldview arguments may fade away or become completely irrelevant.

Similar to the channels of power, rights, and interests/needs talked about in the last chapter, the "Levels of Information" diagram below shows a different view of "channels" going on in a negotiation. We can use Informing in both competitive and collaborative negotiations. If it's a collaborative process, the flow of information moves from the "channel" of positions to channels of interests/needs and then to the channel of feelings, if there is enough trust to share on that level. In a competitive process, the flow of information is opposite; it starts at positions and flows to justifications, facts, figures, opinions. This flow reminds me of my old litigation practice. If justifications didn't work, lawyers moved to threats, which are a form of Attack.

Levels of Information

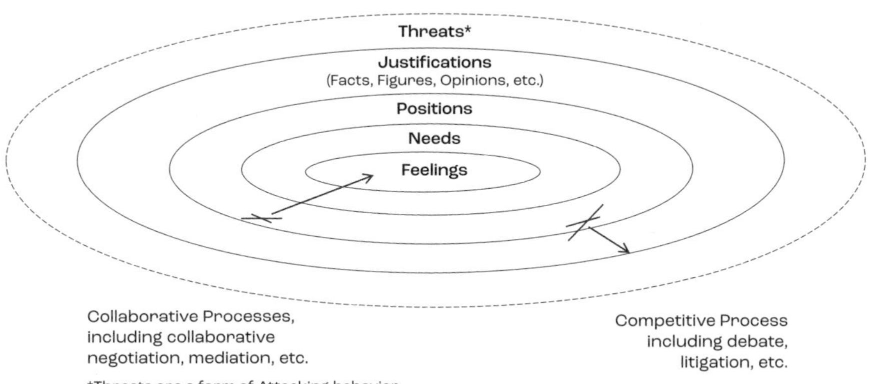

Here are examples of what Informing behavior looks like in different contexts.

At a credit card company
Sales manager: I want you to extend credit to the ABC company. They want to put in a large order that will push my commissions up by 20 percent for this month.
Credit manager: Sorry, I can't extend any more credit to them until they pay their past due bills. I've heard they're a big credit risk.

At home
Partner 1: Can you load the dishwasher?
Partner 2: I can't do it tonight. Have to get on a Zoom.

On a team
Ray: Could you revise this memo?
Fiona: I'm feeling like I'm doing too much of the work and sharing too much of the burden on this team.

One of the things that people sometimes have a hard time accepting is that even if you genuinely intend to Inform, it may land on the other side as an Attack, especially depending on body language, tone, and context. What matters most in negotiation communication is our impact on the other side, not our intent.

Open

> *We have two ears and one mouth so that we can listen twice as much as we speak.*
> —Epictetus, circa 100 CE

"Opening" behavior includes: listening quietly but intently; probing, asking questions nonjudgmentally; and listening actively by paraphrasing and summarizing understanding.

Opening behavior is essentially the reverse of Informing behavior. When Informing, we are telling the other side where we are coming from; when Opening, we are finding out where the other is coming from. Opening behavior includes any kind of communication behavior that "opens up the other side." A negotiator engages in Opening behavior primarily by:

- asking questions about the other's needs, positions, feelings, and values (in a nonjudgmental way);
- listening carefully to what the other side is saying; and
- testing one's understanding by summarizing what is being said without necessarily agreeing with it.

Opening Behavior

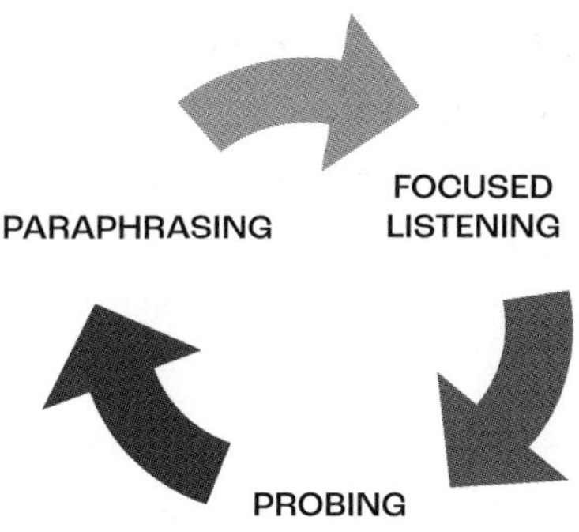

Opening behavior might sound like:

- Tell me more about the situation from your perspective.
- So, if I understand what you are saying . . .
- Can you tell me what you are most concerned about in this situation?
- How would my preferred solution (i.e. my position) impact you?

For years, I have said, and the research shows, that Opening behavior is the most powerful and the most difficult of all five behaviors. The best negotiators know how to listen. Collaborative negotiators are not just looking to win; they are looking for a mutually agreeable solution. We can only find out what that is if we pay attention and listen for the other's needs or interests as well as our own.

But while Opening behavior is the gold star, Informing behavior can be the most challenging behavior for many women who are not accustomed to speaking their wants and needs.

And, for those of us inclined to competition, Opening can be difficult. We might prefer to spend time talking about where we are coming from and why we are right. Many of us in this group may feel that if we allow the other side time to talk and give them our attention, we will be showing weakness or giving something up. If we are being Attacked by the other side, we may instinctively want to defend ourselves or Attack back. But Opening can be powerful for two main reasons:

> 1) Opening behavior reduces hostility. One of the best ways to counter Attacking behavior is to Open. People Attack as a strategy to meet their needs. When we use

> Opening, we are listening for their frustrated needs. 2) Opening behavior helps us identify the other's needs so we can link them with needs satisfiers, aka bargaining chips. We find out whether our chips are valuable by Opening, by asking questions, listening carefully, and summarizing what we hear. Offering a chip after the other side has stated the need to which it is linked maximizes the potency of that chip. Bingo!

Opening behavior is especially important when we are transcending identity group or cultural differences. To be effective we need to understand the other side's worldview, not attempt to negotiate it away. The only way to understand them is to get in the shoes of the other side, see the world through their eyes as best we can.

Using Opening behavior should not mean that we forget about our own position, needs, and worldview. It just means we need to include and respect the views of the other. Collaborative negotiation becomes possible to the extent that the people on both sides are open to the views of their counterparts and are willing to grow. We grow when we meet something different from ourselves. When both sides use Opening behavior, the negotiation can transform itself from a confrontation into a shared effort to reach a resolution.

When you are "Opening," keep your questions simple. It is so easy for all of us to make things too complicated. For example, if you have been trained as a lawyer, you know to ask yes/no questions. This keeps things simple, but it is the opposite of what you want to do when "Opening." We want to simply get the person to tell us more specifically about their perspective.

Here are some examples from different contexts:

Corporate

Director: I have been getting reports from customers that your department is poorly managed. Are you are giving any attention to this?

Manager: Could you tell me specifically what kinds of concerns customers have expressed?

School

Teacher: I am still having trouble with the class I was talking about, and I am wondering if you are going to help me.

Principal: It sounds like this is a frustrating situation. Tell me what you think might be causing the difficulty?

School

Parent: My child has not been doing well with his classwork in spite of the support he is getting from my husband and me. There must be something going on in your class that is giving him trouble.

Teacher: I can see that you and your husband are very worried about your son's progress. Tell me what exactly you think might be going on in class that is creating the trouble?

Unite

> *Let us put our minds together to see what*
> *we can build for our children.*
> —Sitting Bull, Lakota Sioux Leader, 1876

Uniting behavior creates the relational glue in a negotiation. It brings you together when conflict or difference is pushing you apart. It includes: building rapport, highlighting common ground, reframing, and proposing solutions that address the other's interests.

Building Rapport, Creating the Climate, Ritual Sharing

Creating a good climate for a negotiation or difficult conversation, picking the right time and place, can make all the difference. This is the stuff you can control. In one of my favorite books on facilitation, *Don't Just Do Something, Stand There!*, my brilliant colleague Sandra Janoff recommends, "Control the hell out of what you can control (which is not much) and let go of the rest."[8] It is a good motto for negotiators.

Ritual sharing might include the typical "Hello, how are you?" or it may get more involved with a longer conversation about family, hobbies, or even arranging a series of social events before the real negotiation.

This kind of relational behavior is most typically used at the beginning of a negotiation, but can and should be used throughout when there is need for some "relationship glue" to help the negotiation along.

In collaborative negotiations, it's important to be aware of what we need to do to make the other side comfortable. Building trust in the relationship is our goal. How we do this will depend on the reasons for the negotiation, the individual with whom we are negotiating, and their cultural perspective.

For instance, asking some people questions about their personal lives may be culturally inappropriate and will feel to them like an invasion of privacy. Not asking others about their personal lives, however, will strike them as cold and unfeeling and will distance them from you at the outset of the negotiation. Know who you are talking to.

Highlighting Common Ground

Throughout the negotiation, use the opportunity to highlight common ground whenever possible. During a negotiation, expressing common values, needs and interests, and shared perspectives can be a useful way to diffuse the tensions that often arise. If the folks on both sides are tired or discouraged, a restatement of the common ground you share or the specific agreements you already have reached can give everyone the extra energy you need to resolve remaining issues.

One finds the common ground in a negotiation by discovering both sides' underlying needs through effective Informing and Opening behavior. At the level of positions, there will typically appear to be no common ground, but rather a clash of preferred solutions to the problem or issue.

Reframing the Issue

This is the same reframing described in chapter 4. It appears here again because when we reframe, we Unite. Reframing when done well changes a tense climate to "How can we satisfy both sets of needs?" which invites creative problem solving.

Proposing Solutions to Meet Needs and Interests

Negotiation, ultimately, is about solving problems, making offers, and reaching agreements. Here, you and the other communicate proposed offers and link them to the needs expressed by you both to determine whether, in fact, they satisfy those needs. If they do, you will have reached an agreement.

Here are some examples of what Unite might look like in different contexts.

School

Parent: My husband and I are very concerned about our son's poor math scores. We have been working with him and we still are not seeing any improvement.

Teacher: I am so glad to have the chance to speak with you. I want you to know that I have been very concerned about his progress too. Perhaps we can put our heads together and develop the support that he needs to do better.

Married couple

Arial: I'm feeling like we need more downtime together, just time to hang out.

Taranah: I'm feeling exactly the same way.

At the office

Secretarial supervisor: I am glad to hear of your concern, but I still feel that my staff's low morale during this downsizing is becoming a serious issue. I just don't know what else to do.

Manager: Well, let's toss out some ideas. Maybe together we can come up with something that will work.

Reflections on AEIOU

- *When is Attacking behavior useful, if at all?*
- *Do you Evade in situations where you need to negotiate for your interests?*
- *Which is easiest for you—Informing or Opening?*
- *Look back at the definition and behaviors included with Uniting. Can you do each of these—create a positive climate, highlight common ground, offer chips to link with the other's needs, and reframe?*

Putting into Practice

Identify a conflict or negotiation situation that you have had or currently have. What might be an Attack phrase you could use, an Evade phrase, Inform, et cetera.

My Scenario:

Attack	
Evade	
Inform	
Open	
Unite	

Speaking Up with IOU—
Your Perspective, Your Voice

Our voices as women are essential to a post-patriarchal world order. When Oprah says our truth is our most powerful tool, she is right.[9] But knowing our truth and knowing what we truly want are essential first steps. Figuring out how to communicate those truths effectively is a growth edge for many of us. But our honest, vocal expression is key to creating both gender balance and the balance of the masculine and feminine in the resolution of disputes and differences. As one of my course participants said, "I'm learning to speak. I'm less passive aggressive. I'm transparent. I can't believe how silent I have been. There has been a culture of silence" (Laura, spring 2021, on finding her voice).

It's possible, and indeed desirable, to Inform and not Attack. We can be firm. Firm and fair. Fair—even if we are called "a bitch." It is OK to set boundaries. Women in many parts of the world have a lot of moral authority. We must use it.

Getting good at speaking our truth, especially when there is less at stake, helps us gain strength for all situations on our planet.

Putting into Practice

Pick a conflict situation in your life right now and write out:

- *I want* _______ *(your preferred solution)*
- *I need* _______ *(your underlying need or interest—why you are taking the position that you are taking)*
- *I feel* _______

While Listening (Opening) Is Key, "Over-Listening" Can Be a Problem

Being a good listener is super important, but as women, we need to be careful. With the backdrop of patriarchy's long arc of silencing us, we need to take care to not also silence ourselves or each other. A woman I was working with comes to mind. She described a scene in a restaurant where her male business counterpart was talking. And kept talking. She listened well. She nodded and listened. He kept talking. And she kept listening. Have you ever been in a situation like this?

Or at a recent college reunion, many of us went for a hike. I found myself coming down the mountain with a guy about my age whom I had never met from my very progressive college.

We walked. He talked, I listened. Occasionally, I said a thing or two about myself—intentionally something that would have been easy for him to follow up on. He didn't. He kept talking. I decided to let it happen and simply watch the experiment.

We say in Gestalt that there are things that we do well, but we can overdo. For many of us, this can be over-listening.

If we over-listen in the context of a conflict negotiation, we can miss an important opportunity to let the other side hear and understand our own needs and interests. Then we find ourselves calling the dude names under our breath as we walk away. Many women have been conditioned to stroke the male ego with over-listening (and we have probably facilitated the development of a lot of narcissists that way). So, when you are in a negotiation, try to balance Opening with Informing. They work together.

Putting into Practice

Using the same conflict that you used for the previous practice exercise, fill in these blanks.

- *They want* _____
- *They need* _____
- *They feel* _____

Reflections on IOU Communication

- *How effectively can you Inform about your needs?*
- *Reflect on the training (or lack thereof) you have received throughout your life in listening.*
- *Are you able to use IOU communication? What works best for you?*
- *Do you over-listen?*

Essential IOU for a New Negotiation

As I've indicated, there's a lot of Attacking in a PWC. Once when I was working with an audience of astrophysicists from different countries, a woman asked me for more clarification on what Attack sounded like. I told her to think of Donald Trump's tactics, and she smiled because she immediately understood.

In addition to A, there's also a lot of E and I in the PWC because the culture is largely competitive and adversarial– better to avoid than to have a genuine conversation.

In essence, IOU are all collaborative behaviors. A, E, and I are competitive. As my business partner Ellen Raider often said, "A shortened way of thinking about this is: I owe you the courtesy of telling you where I'm coming from (I), finding out where you're coming from (O), and together, we can come up with a solution that works for both of us (U)."

It can be that simple. And what a contrast to, "I'm going to tell you where I'm coming from (I), I might even scream it in your face because you're an idiot (A), and if that doesn't work, I'm going to ignore you if at all possible (E)."

Scilla Elworthy, Nobel nominee in the peace and conflict field, told me that she has witnessed several situations over the last four or five years where negotiations were going completely wrong because the "old modes" of A and E were being used until a woman stepped in. Men were saying what had to happen and interrupting each other—and then a woman came in and said, "Hold on a minute; you're just interrupting each other. May I just repeat back to you what I think I heard you say?" And that just changed the atmosphere completely. The simple act of asking, "Would you be so good as to repeat back to me what you heard me say, just to make sure we've got it right?" changes the pace of the negotiation and can alter the outcome.[10]

At the end of Elizabeth Lesser's keynote that day in October of 2021, she said,

> Can you imagine if throughout history, tend and befriend had been valued, respected, funded, taught, memorialized, and if vengeance, detachment, and violence had been discouraged? More and more, we are seeing women emboldened to strike their tend and befriend, everywhere from the personal to the political and relationships and family systems, in business, in leadership, in entertainment and education. And I contend it's not only women and girls who have a tend and befriend instinct; boys and men do too, if

> allowed to put down the shame of not always living up to the warrior code, and encouraged to develop their full selves. It may seem that fight or flight is too deeply entrenched in men and in our culture. But I am an evolutionary optimist.[11]

IOU works because what goes around comes around. We live in an interdependent world.

Attacking behavior almost always elicits an Attack or defend (counterattack) response from the other side unless that person is skilled in containing the impulse and understands the usefulness of changing the climate to one of collaboration. If your strategy is collaborative, Attacking behavior needs to be used very cautiously, if at all, because the Attack/defend spiral that it creates can be very difficult to break. When people are Attacking and defending, there is very little trust, and trust is essential if people are to reveal underlying needs.

A human rights and peace activist from South Sudan, Riya Yuyada, told me how IOU helped guide her response when she was being harassed and arrested by men pointing guns in her face. They claimed she was "spoiling women" with her work. She asked them, calmly, with a nonaccusatory tone, in other words, not Attacking, but Opening, "How do you come in such large numbers with guns to arrest me, only one woman with not even a stick? Am I that powerful? Or scary?" She attributed her ability to change the dynamic by using IOU. The tone and conversation changed. "They became softer," she said. "We actually talked and it turned out well."[12]

As the saying goes, "It's better to use the high road. There is less traffic up there."

So, for a New Negotiation, think IOU. Avoid Attacks and Evades. Listen for needs and interests. Communicate what you want (your position) flexibly so they understand your desire to negotiate. Communicate your needs and interests and feelings if useful. Build common ground and relationships.

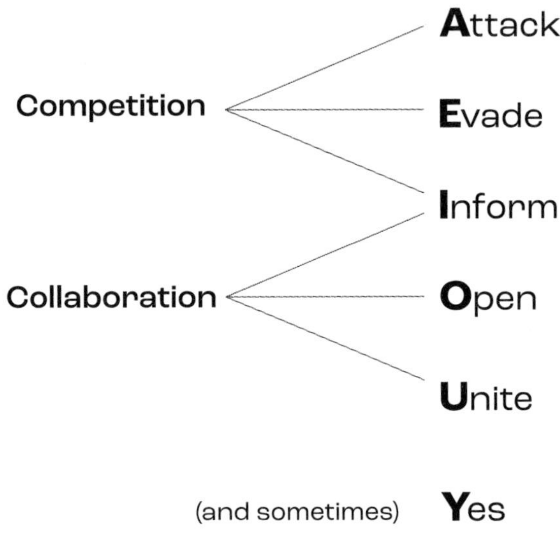

Putting into Practice

Try to express AEIOU nonverbally. Just act it out yourself. Then, try to observe the nonverbal ways that others communicate AEIOU.

If you are preparing, or are in the middle of a negotiation or conflict, try writing out examples of what some of your "Informs," "Opens," and "Unites" could sound like. Do the same for your counterpart. What could theirs sound like (even though, of course, you can't put words in their mouth)?

My I. O. U.	My Counterpart's I. O. U.
I	I
O	O
U	U

CHAPTER 6

Own and Honor Your Emotional Intelligence

> *Anger is like gas. You can light a match to it and watch it explode. Or, you can put it in your car and ride, baby, ride.*
> —A truism shared among many of us conflict resolution professionals

After high school, I stayed east and my friend Carey, science genius that she is, went west to study geology at Stanford. For years we did not see each other. When we met much later in life, she said, "Susan, you look different. You seem much more upright, shoulders back." It was true. I was standing up straighter. As it turned out, I had grown 1.5 inches (3.81 cm) in my sixties! I attribute my change in posture to my work with emotions.

The topic of Emotions is one of my favorites. That's probably because it's the area where I've grown the most over the years, from my early uptight Anglo Saxon, "WASPy" upbringing to learning how to truly feel my full range of feelings in my adulthood. "All eighty-eight keys on the piano" as Mama Gena referred to it.[1] Emotional intelligence is powerful because it helps us align with who we are and what our needs are—so we can then speak those needs with far more confidence.

Anger was never modeled for me in my family of origin. The culture was British American, erudite. You just didn't erupt. We kind of took our cues from the British royal family. When my dad was dying of cancer, I came across the Chinese medicine diagnosis of cancer as "prolonged resentments" and it resonated. My dad had no idea how to get angry, until it erupted in him and killed him. As the Chinese saying goes, "Many diseases, long life—one disease, short life."

Perhaps because of that, I was drawn to my now ex-husband who had no problem expressing his anger and rage. For a good decade, my kids and I lived in a cauldron of his explosions, with little or no room for the rest of us to express our anger or other emotions. This, I came to understand, was parallel to the way anger often plays out in our world: Those who have power or claim it are more entitled to display it.

Thank the Goddess for the School of Womanly Arts. Probably the single greatest full-bodied learning I took from that experience was something we called "swamping." Picture a room full of one thousand women emoting everything at full volume. We would be given garbage bags, shown scenes of all the rape culture crap that women are exposed to globally on a daily basis, and then we would have to fight our way out of the bag while surrounded by big, loud, angry music. It was cathartic: A lot of buried emotions got released, with a lot of screaming and pounding on pillows. I remember being shown one particular video of a woman tied down during labor. I know restraints were used on my mom during her labor with me. In her upscale hospital, they used velvet straps, but they tied her down nonetheless. I found myself triggered—and there is no doubt in my mind that I connected that day to some very early traumatic emotion around my entry into the world. But moving my body and voice allowed me to release years of built-up emotion. I became healthier than I had been in a long time. My digestion worked better. I was happier. Low-grade depression lifted. I had had a trauma release, a trauma healing. It took two physicians to tell me that I was no longer 5′7″ and now 5′8.5″ to believe it.

My journey around anger has been important for me both professionally and personally. Ironically, in spite of how popular Ellen's and my negotiation programs were in the early days at Columbia, we hadn't included emotions in our first models. Our bad. My hunch upon reflection was that we unconsciously sensed that emotions were too "feminine" and we were two women teaching the "masculine" topic of negotiation at an Ivy League school. To gain legitimacy, we instinctively thought it was safer to stick closer to the emotionally buttoned-up man mode.

Emotional Literacy: The Language of the Feminine

In any negotiation, nothing helps you know more quickly what is going on than when participants reveal how they are feeling. Feelings are a window into the soul—of an individual, a group, or a nation. And a window into what is needed.

Authenticity and transparency are deep values at the heart of a new collaborative order and a New Negotiation. For myself, and all the people I most admire, these are bellwethers of the world we want to create. Imagine two people in a relationship with a clear glass boundary between them that represents the natural boundary that exists between all individuals. Each time either one is dishonest, it's like putting a little bit of mud on the glass. The more lies, the murkier and more opaque things get.[2] That's not to say that we always want to reveal all, but just that truthfulness and showing our humanity is what ultimately creates the emotions of trust and connectedness—which are needed for collaboration.

Emotions and vulnerability are often disparaged in the PWC because they are considered the realm of the feminine. As such, they are revered in theory, but disparaged in fact. When we create space for emotions, especially those of fear, sadness, and shame, everything becomes more human. Emotions support our ability to take the perspective of the other party, which then can lead us toward wanting to give more and collaborate more. Emotions soften us. We are more alive to the extent that we feel and can articulate what we feel. As the adage goes, "If you can feel it, you can heal it." The world is crying out for more emotional healing. And as women, we need to stand up for and expand our emotional intelligence and our often-greater comfort with emotional content. In other words, we need to embrace our tendency to tend and befriend.

I remember a light bulb going off in my head one day early in my UN career when I was working with a group of young professionals all from very different countries (some of which I had never even heard of!), when I realized that every human on the planet has the same categories of needs, and the same categories of emotion. Needs and emotions just show up differently based on culture and gender.

When the idea of emotional intelligence (EQ) hit

management circles in the West (a feminine idea popularized by a man, Daniel Goleman), it was a kind of a eureka moment for many.[3] EQ became known as even more important than IQ in many respects, and you began to hear in organizational circles "the future is feminine." The key components of EQ are self-awareness, knowing what you're feeling and what the feeling is, managing those emotions, and having empathy for others' emotions. In contrast to an earlier era, Goleman brought in the idea that what sets people apart professionally is strong EQ. IQ might get you in the door, he suggested, but EQ would be a much better predictor of organizational success.[4]

Emotional literacy is as key to conflict negotiation excellence as is needs literacy. Neither has been seen as such in the PWC. As women we have the capacity to change this. When it comes to feelings, women and men are acculturated differently. Many men have been taught the warrior code, which doesn't give them permission to feel and cuts them off from an essential part of being alive. Generally, women are more allowed to feel. Though we can be criticized for it, it's a strength that we need to own, grow, and not apologize for.

Emotional literacy means being able to name what you feel. Thanks to my colleague, Bill Woodson, with whom I did diversity work for many years for this model of feelings—MAD-SAD-GLAD-SCARED-LOVING.[5] And, of course, there is theme and variation in each of these larger categories of emotion.

Emotions – Theme and Variation

Mad	Sad	Glad	Scared	Loving
Angry	Hurt	Happy	Apprehensive	Affectionate
Furious	Left out	Satisfied	Threatened	Compassionate
Resentful	Depressed	Enthusiastic	Overwhelmed	Respectful
Irritated	Regretful	Proud	Frightened	Understanding
Frustrated	Disappointed	Hopeful	Exposed	Considerate

Emotions Reveal Needs

But what are emotions exactly?

E-motion.

Emotions are energy released when needs are either met or frustrated. When our needs are threatened, or conversely when our needs are met, strong emotions arise. Undeniably, it is the more "difficult" emotions, like anger and fear, that can make negotiation and conflict challenging. If it weren't for emotional charge that often clouds people's thinking and causes things to escalate, most conflict negotiation would simply be a creative problem-solving exercise, with some problems easier than others.

But emotions are critical to the pathway through.

Emotions reveal needs.

Emotions are the energy that shows you whether needs have been met or frustrated. Needs drive why we are negotiating, so emotions are important to track. When we are aware of what the emotional content is, whether it's our own or our counterpart's, we get a window into what the needs and interests are that are either being frustrated or met. This is true whether the context is intimate, business, or global.

Let's return to the Maslow Hierarchy of Needs Pyramid and allow me to show you how I have connected the dots between categories of need and categories of emotion. For instance, if our physical needs are met, we generally feel wonderful.

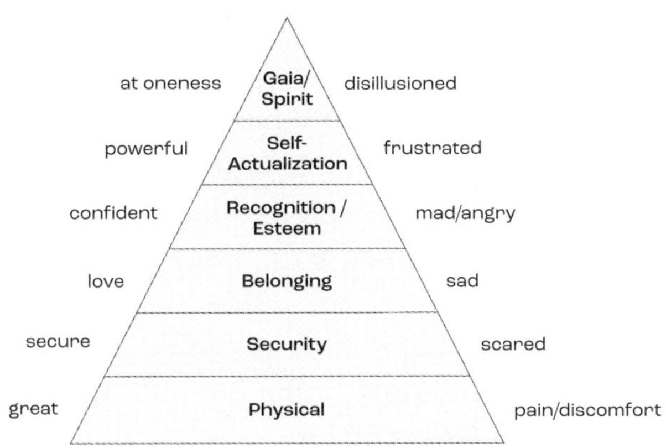

In contrast, if our physical needs are not met, we typically feel pain or discomfort. If our security needs are met, we feel secure, safe. If our security needs are not met, we feel fear. If our belonging needs are met, we feel love. If they are not met, we feel sadness and loneliness. If our need for recognition and esteem are met, we feel confident and proud, and, if they are not met, we might feel angry. If our self-actualization needs are met, we might feel powerful. If the opposite, we might feel frustrated. And finally, if our spiritual needs are met, we might feel oneness. If they're not, we might feel disillusioned.

I remember watching the facial expression of one of the

parties to a mediation. We had gone through some intense discussions. There was hurt. There was anger. But then there was a genuine apology. I looked over at her face. I could see that she was feeling resolved. Her need for acknowledgment and recognition had been met by the other side.

Whether we feel like our needs are being met or thwarted can change in a minute or over a lifetime. I wanted a true apology from my ex about the pain his behavior caused our children and of course me. The divorce mediator asked him to give me one: He complied but it didn't land. It was inauthentic and I don't think he really meant it. About a decade later, when we went out for dinner, he gave me an apology that was heartfelt. It was a "*chip*" that linked with my need for respect and recognition. It took him a minute to say, and a decade to be ready to say it.

Reflections on Emotional Literacy and Negotiation

- *Am I able to recognize the connection between emotions and needs?*
- *Am I comfortable with my complete emotional range, "all eighty-eight keys on the piano"?*
- *Do I allow myself to feel certain feelings more than others? Are some feelings more out of bounds, less acceptable?*

Putting into Practice

Assess your emotional literacy—your ability to feel the full range of your emotions and know what you are feeling.

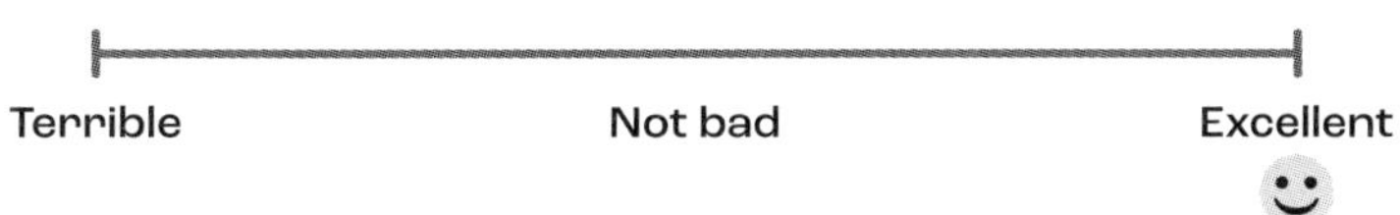

Anger Is Invaluable Life-Force Energy

Anger, like conflict, just is. It is a feeling that every human experiences regardless of how we might express it or suppress it. Like conflict, what's important is what we do with anger.

It is important to human health and well-being to feel the anger that we feel and it's empowering to be able to articulate it well. It is also important to not become addicted to feeling angry in lieu of expressing a range of emotions. Because many of us (all genders) are not good at these things anger can become a problem. Humans, in general, carry a lot of unexpressed anger. There's a lot to appreciate and love on our planet, but there is also a lot to get angry about! For instance, I feel huge anger at Big Oil and the devastation these executives have caused the planet that our children are inheriting. This is mostly so because oil companies have known about the problem for decades and have chosen to lie, prioritize greed over planetary health, and continue to support leaders like Donald Trump all over the planet who want to "drill, baby, drill."

When working with groups in a negotiation workshop, the energy that is released when the topic is anger is very noticeable. I invented an exercise long ago that has had great staying power. In part, its focus is hearing the needs behind emotions. Participants are in a long line, facing one partner with whom they will engage. I often start the exercise with "a time that you felt sadness," then "fear." Then, when I get to the simple question "a time that you felt angry," the energy that is unleashed is palpable. Life force. It starts flowing.

Why do we get angry? Why do people in general get angry? We get angry because we have needs that are being frustrated. That's also why we Attack as a communication style—it's a strategy we use to get our needs met. In Maslow's hierarchy, the category of need that is frustrated, and around which anger erupts, is respect, recognition, justice.

Of course, figuring out what is triggering us, what is making us angry, can sometimes be difficult. We are complex beings with moments in the present inextricably linked to events in the past which are often lost to our consciousness. The person we are fighting is often not the person we are really angry with. But the conflict we are having with them can be a useful catalyst to resolving unhappy or destructive feelings about an earlier relationship with another.

Some people when in conflict use anger like a drug like it seemed my ex-husband did. Righteous indignation can cover up much deeper, uncomfortable feelings of shame or lack of esteem that is at the heart of what's needed. When we get angry, adrenaline pulses through our veins and, like any other drug, can numb other more uncomfortable feelings. It's important, however, to recognize that becoming conscious of those feelings and feeling them are important pathways to growth, freedom, and healing.

When we deal with anger destructively, we can get stuck in what's known as the "fundamental attribution error."[6] We blame the other side for creating the situation that has made us angry. We avoid self-responsibility. This approach inevitably leads us to Attack the other side, creating a destructive Attack/defend escalating spiral of conflict. This approach also reinforces our powerlessness. It can take work, growth, and courage to own anger and other emotions and respond in ways that will bring us closer to meeting our needs and those of the other side.

Psychologists often refer to anger as a "secondary" emotion because underneath anger is often fear and sadness. What that means is, if we are honest with ourselves, we typically feel emotions like hurt or fear before we feel angry, even if only for an instant. The anger comes up as a means of protecting ourselves from those more vulnerable feelings. Underneath anger are those deeper feelings of sadness or fear, which connect to frustrated needs like belonging or a need for respect.

How we express anger matters a lot. Just like with conflict, the pathology we can have with anger is that we either stuff it, when it shouldn't be stuffed, or we become violent with it. Fight/flight. Attack/Evade. In an ideal world, we all could identify and express our anger, identify the frustrated need that we would like to satisfy, and express the primary emotions like hurt or fear that we might have about the situation. In a not-so-ideal world, a destructive emotional cycle of conflict might look like conflict—anger—rage—violence. This includes the human who "flies into a rage" and picks up a gun, or a human who buries their anger, accommodates objectionable behavior, slight by slight—sometimes for years turning it on themselves, often to illness and sometimes death.

In short, we need more *IOU*. And we need to "fight fair" through negotiation. We need a world that is safe for conflict, and safe for people to get angry without killing each other.

How to Negotiate When You Are Angry in a Negotiation or Conflict

The famous existential philosopher Jean-Paul Sartre once said, "Hell is other people."[7] Well, maybe. But life on the planet would be pretty terrible if there was no other human around, even if they are making us angry. Here is an approach (in recommended order) you can employ when another person or situation has prompted your anger.

1. What did they do or are they doing that is making you angry? What need of yours does it frustrate? What could you do about it? What could they do about it? Is there a way that you could satisfy your need independent of them?

2. Do you want to address it? Sometimes, the answer is no. We all must pick our battles; we cannot negotiate or engage with everything. But, if it's important to you, don't talk yourself out of it with "sugar and spice" or conflict avoidance conditioning. And, rest assured, if you miss one opportunity to address what's making you angry and it is important to you, it will inevitably come around again.

3. If You Do Want to Express Your Anger
   Pick your time and place. My Gestalt mentor, John Carter, always used to say, "There is no bad intervention, just terrible timing." That is sage advice. I don't want to stuff my anger, but I do want to be speaking from my prefrontal cortex (the part of the brain responsible for higher level cognitive functioning) as opposed

> to my old (reptilian) brain. If you can—think of yourself like a dog and wait for your hackles to go down before proceeding. Sometimes you might have had a blow-up, and need to calm down before picking the right time and place. But, if you are capable of a clear, firm response, setting a boundary in the moment—go for it!

Here's an example. While on the road in a foreign country, I was with my partner, driving a rental car in the middle of a very chaotic and anxiety provoking log jam of traffic. Neither of us knew where we were going. My partner, sitting shotgun, said, "I can't deal with this" and threw up his hands. I was furious and yelled at him, "I need you now!" Later, calmer but still angry, I picked a moment to have a more functional conversation about the situation and got his agreement. "Can we talk about that moment in the car?" Here were my *Informs:*

I want: "I don't want you to throw up your hands and leave me to deal with the situation like that on my own" (my position).

I need: "I need your help in those situations."

I feel: "I felt abandoned by you." Not coincidentally I suppose, my partner has many qualities that remind me of my dad, most of them positive. Nonetheless, I had some big abandonment stuff with my dad that was getting reactivated in this moment. I find it very useful to use this kind of language: "What I made up was that you were abandoning me." In other words, it's helpful to acknowledge that you are making an assumption and don't actually know what is going on with the other person.

At this point, you can move into listening to their side of things here.

Open: "Do you have thoughts about what I have said?"

Listen for needs on their side, summarize to see if you've got it right, and then move into a reframe—their need, your need—how to address both moving forward.

Expressing your Anger with IOU

I want (**Inform** at the positional level)

I need (**Inform** about your underlying need or interest)

I feel . . . (**Inform** about feelings that have come up—
anger and perhaps the deeper emotions underneath anger)

(Great to use language here like "What I made up about that was. . . ")

Open when ready

Putting into Practice—Expressing Your Anger

Pick something that makes (or has made) you angry. Write out:

- *I want* _____
- *I need* ____
- *I feel* ___
- *What I made up about (what you did was)* _________

How to Handle Another When They Attack You or Confront You in an Angry Way in a Negotiation or Conflict

When someone gets angry at us or is Attacking us, it's very easy to want to defend ourselves and try to establish that we are right and they are wrong. It is always best to contain this urge. Listening to someone who is angry at you is difficult but necessary for handling the conflict. Instead, if you can seek to understand, you may succeed in deescalating their anger as well as create an opening for them to listen to your concerns.

Assuming you want to engage and negotiate, here are some ideas on how to proceed.

First, acknowledge that there is a conflict between you, and that you want to understand how they see the situation as well as help them understand your point of view. You might need to take a deep breath before you can do this. Or you might need to postpone the discussion to a time when you are both more able to listen to each other.

Use Opening behavior to understand the perspective of the other, test your understanding of what has been said, and make space for the other to correct you or provide additional information. Be mindful and avoid flipping things around so that you are talking about your perspective; instead, try to capture the other's point of view in your own words, especially their needs, not necessarily their position. This can be hard, but with practice, it gets easier.

If you have summarized and it seems you have named their need correctly, you can switch to yourself. Express your needs and feelings using Informing (not Attacking behavior). In other words, it's fine to tell the other side that you are angry but avoid putting them down in retaliation.

Putting into Practice—Responding with Skill to Another's Attacking or Anger

Pick a time when someone has Attacked you or expressed their anger with you. Can you write out:

- *They want* _____
- *They need* ____
- *They feel* ___

What, if anything, does this reveal to you?

Clearing "Charge," Preparing for "Hot" Conversations

When emotions run high, it is helpful to take some time to first calm our nervous systems and "clear the charge." "Charge" is emotional energy (often anger or frustration) that builds up when we are not able to meet our needs either psychological or tangible. Often charge can be triggered by past trauma.

Charge doesn't have to be "rational." When we feel it, it is real for us. I spent too many years trying to talk myself out of my anger: "Oh, you shouldn't feel that" or "I just need to understand him better. It is my fault I am getting so upset." Charge is neither good nor bad; it just is. Once we accept it, we can get good at calming ourselves and then harnessing the energy and turning it into positive action.

Here are four tools I use for managing charge: (1) breathing, (2) spring cleaning, (3) taking a walk, and (4) talking things over with a trusted friend or advisor. All of them are a means to managing ourselves first because, of course, we only have control over ourselves.

Breathing

Assuming the situation doesn't call for you to run away, probably the single best thing you can do when faced with a conflict or a challenging situation is to breathe. The breath brings you into the present moment because the present moment is the only place you can find it. Breathing influences the involuntary nervous system. Some say breath is the doorway to the involuntary nervous system.

According to Dr. Andrew Weil, a doctor who specializes in holistic medicine, the involuntary nervous system has two components—the sympathetic and parasympathetic nervous systems. The sympathetic nervous system prepares the body for fight or flight responses—for emergencies. It speeds up heart rate, increases blood pressure, slows down digestion, and takes blood circulation away from the surface of the body to the interior. This is a logical response. If faced with an emergency, the thing that is most important is to maintain blood flow to the brain. Quite simply, if you fail to do that, you die. The heart speeds up, blood pressure increases, and blood is shunted away from the surface of the body to ensure that there will be no interruption of blood flow to the brain.

The parasympathetic nervous system does the opposite; it slows our heartbeat and returns blood to the surface of the body. The sympathetic and parasympathetic work hand in hand, presumably in balance.

In many languages, the word for breath and spirit are the same. In Sanskrit, the word "prana" means both breath and universal energy. In Hebrew, the word "ruach" means the same. In Greek, it's *numa,* and in Latin, *spiritus*. When you think about the link between breath and spirit, taking a breath can be a way of invoking spirit or universal energy into the difficult situation you are in. You can even "con-spire" or "breathe with your adversary." And breathing is contagious. When you take a breath in a difficult moment, so will the people around you. So, if you breathe, the other side may likely breathe—and it will help you both.

When you are angry, afraid, or upset, your breath becomes more rapid, shallow, irregular, and noisy. And conversely, when you are grounded and relaxed, your breath will grow deeper, quieter, slower, and more regular. If you are upset in a negotiation, you might not be able to get the anger or upset to go away, but you can always settle down the charge by changing your breathing.

Here are two exercises Dr. Weil recommends that I find very helpful.

> ***Exercise 1***
> Scan your body to make sure all parts are relaxed.
> Take a deep breath.
> Start observing your breath; follow it out and in.
> Now focus on making it deeper, slower, quieter, and more regular. Do this for a few breath cycles.
> Notice how you feel.
>
> ***Exercise 2***
> Exhale through your mouth completely.
> Inhale quietly through your nose for a count of four.
> Hold your breath for a count of seven.
> Exhale through your mouth for count of eight.
> Do this a few times.
> Notice how you feel.[8]

Spring Cleaning

I have been "spring cleaning" to clear charge for at least a decade. I learned the practice from the School of Womanly Arts (SWA) and I can't recommend it highly enough. Here's my version which is very similar to what I learned from Mama Gena.[9]

First, you need a spring-cleaning partner—someone who knows the practice. I have a group of about two to three women whom I call on regularly. The practice is generally reciprocal—person A spring cleans and person B holds space and then you switch.

> A – I would like to spring clean—do you have some time?
> B – Sure. How long would you like?
> A – Seven minutes is good. (Typically, I do from five to seven minutes, but sometimes it's three minutes and sometimes it's twenty. You and your partner need to agree on the amount of time.)
> B – What's your topic? (A topic can be anything you want to process for yourself and generally that you have some charge about.)
> A – My topic is "right now." (That's often a topic I pick, but it can be anything.)
> B – OK, I'm going to set my timer for seven minutes. "Sister goddess" A, I am here to hold sacred and confidential space for you while you spring clean for seven minutes on the topic of "right now." Are you ready to begin? (Sister goddess is a SWA term—as Mama Gena always describes it, "sister because all women are sisters to each other and goddess because every

woman has a touch of the divine.")
A – Yes, ready.
B – What do you have on right now?
A – I have xxxxxx. (Person B's job is to listen and when A is complete say, "Thank you." That's it! It's also their job to not let A go on and on. Just a few thoughts and then "thank you.")
B – (And then B repeats the "pull"—"What do you have on right now?")
A – I have xxxxxxxxxxx.
B – Thank you. What do you have on right now?
A – I have xxxxxxxxxxx.

This continues for seven minutes. When the timer goes off, B says, "You have three more pulls. What do you have on right now?" (And this happens three times.) Sometimes, B might offer another pull at the end if A doesn't seem complete and requests it, or sometimes two more pulls is enough. When the three pulls are complete:

B — Thank you. This ends your spring cleaning right now. It's been a pleasure and honor to hold space for you. How would you like to conclude?
A – I would like a few "frames" and a Trinity. (A frame is simply something that most stands out to B—not an interpretation or judgment, just something they most notice. Mama Gena does not do this or recommend it. I like it a lot.) A "Trinity" is a "brag," a "gratitude," and a "desire" (see below).
B – What stands out to me is xxxxxxxx.
A – Thank you. Well framed. Here's my Trinity.

I brag ______.
I'm grateful _____.
I desire_______.

A "brag" is something that you feel proud about. Do not brag about your children (women do this a lot); brag about something about yourself, that you did, that you accomplished, that you surmounted, shifted, a way you evolved, et cetera. You don't need to inflate—just own up to what is true.

You can also add at the beginning, "I swamp." This would be a "Quad," not a Trinity." I often do a Quad because there is so much out there these days to be upset about. A "swamp" is something that is generally something you are angry, sad, fearful about—anything from the intimate to the global.

SWA orthodoxy has it that after you have both spring cleaned you shouldn't talk about it. While I think this is generally a good idea, sometimes we cheat a little and process for just a few more moments.

This practice is amazingly efficient and effective. Give it a try.

Walking

If I have a tough problem, I go for my favorite walk up "to the chimney" where I get an amazing view of the Hudson Valley. Before I start, I name the issue in my head and then release it for the walk. Almost miraculously, on the way down, I notice how I have new insight and usually a way forward. Every time! What I'm doing is backed up by research. Indeed, the widely acclaimed effectiveness of EMDR is based on bilateral stimulation to the brain, which is what happens when you are taking a walk.

As my colleague, Peter Coleman, has observed, moving your body can get your mind unstuck. Of course, taking a walk with the person (or party) with whom you are having the difficult conversation (i.e., the celebrated walk in the woods) is also an excellent tool and often lauded by experts in negotiation. As Coleman writes, "moving forward together—literally" can be the secret sauce to resolution. "Moving together—side-by-side and ideally outside—has shown great promise for connecting disputants and helping to synchronize them in ways that promote more empathy, rapport, and flexibility."[10]

Talking with a Trusted Guide, Coach, or Friend

I have an amazing guide/therapist who is in her eighties. We have known each other for years now, and I give her a call to talk things over and gain insight when I have a difficult conversation coming up. She almost always adds another layer that I hadn't accessed. All of us need to have these kinds of people in our lives: therapists, coaches, spiritual guides, great friends, whatever their training might be. Ideally, they will be someone who (a) is a great listener, (b) can support you and validate your feelings and experience without necessarily agreeing with your version of the facts, and (c) can provide just the right amount of challenge for your growth. This takes skill, so finding these kinds of people is invaluable.

Reflections on How to Handle Emotional Charge

- *What helps you most to prepare for emotionally challenging conflicts?*

Putting into Practice

Give each of these practices a try: the breath exercises, spring cleaning, taking a walk either on your own or alongside the person you are in conflict with, and talking to a trusted guide. See what you think. Write about your experience in your journal.

If you don't already have one, see if you can find a trusted coach or guide.

Sisters, Let's Own the Power of Our Anger and Turn It into Positive Action

Big picture, is anger for men and fear, sadness, shame for women?

I wondered this when I was working with a group of male military officers in Cyprus.

My cotrainer James Williams and I decided to do the listening exercise on anger I described above. At first, I was hesitant. I thought, *Oh my god, these guys are all in uniform; they're going to think this is so touchy-feely*. But to our surprise, the opposite was true. They loved the exercise! It was like we had broken open a dam. In debriefing, James and I commented to each other about how folks like men in the military, and men in general, are not given the permission to feel fear, sadness, the more vulnerable emotions, but anger, well, that's OK. It made me realize how gendered emotional expression can be. In the same way that patriarchy has divided the human being in half—into masculine and feminine—the PWC has ascribed anger to men and fear and sadness and shame to women. All humans need to be able to feel their full range. Moving beyond patriarchy will make this more possible for everyone.

If women are supposed to be more sugar and spice and not generally free to express anger, we are definitely allowed to connect with our fear. Fear is such a predominant feeling for so many women around the world. Our codependency is in every nook and cranny on this globe and its core feeling state is fear, including fear of negotiation itself. For so many women, negotiation is scary. This is simply because when we negotiate, we are asking for something, we are challenging the order of things, we are deciding that we have needs that must be addressed and met, we are seeking to change the balance of power. We are asking to be paid what we are worth, for help with childcare or housework, and for a seat at the table. Fear, while useful information that sometimes can protect us, can also keep us small and not asking for enough.

Connecting to Our Anger Is Vital for Women

In a PWC, women have a lot to be angry about. In the language of Maslow, the PWC has frustrated us at every level of need—physical, security, and so on. It's no wonder we are pissed. Our voices have been stifled for millennia which means that our basic human need for recognition and esteem has been dampened, muffled, drowned out. If we are true to ourselves, this is infuriating. As half of humanity, we carry generations of suppressed, atavistic anger built up from living in a PWC. It's time to release it as one of the most powerful moves of self-care we can make. It's time to use our anger powerfully, forcefully, and with clarity so it serves us and future generations. Anger used well is our friend. No more "tyranny of the kind and nice."[11]

We need to allow ourselves to not get cowed by the violence that a PWC celebrates, for the most part enacted by male violence and anger. Both men and women can be violent, but the evidence is clear that the majority of violence on the planet is male-generated and men have used that violence to control women with fear. Women need to recognize that for what it is, call on our courage, and set limits with it. It is no longer acceptable and we have the capacity to stop it and to say enough! One of the best ways to deal with bullies, violence, and anger is to be firm with them, and sometimes ignore them. Obviously, sometimes there can be real harm. But part of what we, as women, need to do is not be afraid. Patriarchy has taught us to feel afraid.

If you are a woman who previously suppressed your anger, you may find that as you start releasing it, you may overdo it. Getting comfortable with expressing what makes us angry is great but spewing unconscious charge is not. We need to come to the table in our functional, adult selves, grounded, direct, with the fullness of our integrity and power.

Responding as opposed to reacting is powerful. We need to consider how best to express our anger, but express our anger we must. It is time to give life to this essential life-force energy! We also need to own and stand up for our generally skilled emotionally intelligent selves.

If you are part of a subservient group (as to greater and lesser degrees we can be as women), expressing anger can be dangerous, in our homes and in the world. People who have a stake in keeping others subservient can decide to do harm to "underlings" who speak out. We see this everywhere and throughout history. Expressing anger can be dangerous for any group that is below another group in our human hierarchy.

When we start connecting to anger and expressing it in constructive ways in negotiation or activism, it can unleash aliveness and force.

In the words of Nobel Laureate Leymah Gbowee (who you will meet again in chapter 9):

> Anger is very effective fuel. The way I describe anger is that it's fluid, like water. It's neither good nor bad. It's the thing that propels you into action. But the action you take determines whether you're a hero or a villain. All the heroes and villains of our history shared the common trait that they were angry—whether it's Hitler, Dr. King, Rosa Parks, Mandela—they used anger to fuel them. But what distinguished them is how they used their anger: in the service of violence or nonviolence . . . I feel like especially in the West, there are a lot of polite conversations around coffee tables about issues that affect women's lives, such as reproductive health and reproductive rights. When I see media coverage of panels of all men sitting in suits and talking about abortion when they can't even have their period, the question I ask myself is: Where are the women? . . . We need to make sure our voices are heard. We need to storm in and say we want to be part of the conversation. The kind of polite anger that women display does not disrupt the system and it does not get our needs met. It is time to be enraged, not be violent, but to take action.[12]

Reflections on Anger, Fear, and Sadness

- *What makes you most angry?*
- *How comfortable are you with expressing anger?*

- *Do you use the power of your anger well?*
- *Is it easier for you to feel fear or sadness than anger?*
- *How much was expressing anger allowed in your family of origin?*
- *How has your culture or tribe impacted the messaging you have received about anger and whether and how you can express it?*

CHAPTER 7

Celebrate Worldview Differences and Build Sisterhood Across Cultures

> *We emerged from "the great effulgence" commonly known as the Big Bang. One of the first principles of our beginnings was differentiation, that everything differentiated, nothing was the same. It wasn't a pile of gas that evolved, it was differentiated beings, differentiated things. Differentiation is one of the main principles in us and when we try to establish monocultures or mono races, we are working against the fundamental principles of Earth, and ourselves.*
> —Rabia Roberts, "Herstory"

Early in my conflict negotiation career, a colleague of mine and I were asked to deliver a program for a group of eighty participants from the New York City public schools. Racial tensions were running high, which was the motivation for the program. Participants came from a mix of school positions—principals, guidance counselors, teachers, and administrators.

Demographically, the group was very diverse in terms of race, gender, and age.

We divided the group into two groups of forty, but we kept an identical demographic mix in each. My colleague, a wonderful and skilled trainer, took one group and I took the other. He decided to start his program with a "prisoner's dilemma" game often played in negotiation programs that tends to simulate reality quite closely. In the game, participants are divided into teams and instructed to "win as much as you can." Without getting too deep into the weeds of the how the game works, the general upshot (that parallels research) is that if everyone competes, they get the worst global score, and if everyone cooperates, they get the best. The activity is fun but tense and moves quickly, and players are often quick to anger. Distrust builds if someone "defects" (i.e., refuses to cooperate). By the end of this exercise in my colleague's room, folks were seething and trust was in the pits.

In contrast, I started my group with a very different opener, a game called "In Common." A fast-paced exercise also, In Common begins with participants in dyads brainstorming everything they have in common. Then they move into fours, then eights, and the game ends with a group list of everything that everyone in the room has in common. It's fun, and people laugh and learn a lot about each other quickly. By the end of the game in my room, everyone felt a strong community spirit with high trust.

Lo and behold, after the games, when my colleague progressed into the negotiation content, the people in his group erupted and polarized quickly based on race. In my group, nothing like that occurred. There was a good vibe. And we were both teaching the same curriculum.

I left this experience with an important insight that has been reenforced for me over and over again in my years of working with groups around the world: Building awareness and sensitivity around difference of any kind is important, but if you create an adversarial climate, it will probably be to no avail. The group will very likely polarize around whatever identity group—Black/White, male/female, tall/short, whatever variable is relevant to that group and that conflict negotiation at that time.

At this point in my career, I feel fairly confident that, if you give me a diverse group in conflict, I can make them go to war with each other pretty quickly and, to the contrary, I can support their process of building peace. Creating a collaborative climate is everything and central to a New Negotiation.

Worldview, Culture, and Conflict

What is culture? What is worldview? And what is an identity group? And how do these factors show up when we are attempting to resolve conflict through negotiation?

First, culture. You cannot talk about negotiation without talking about culture because negotiation itself is a "culture-bound" concept. What does that mean? People around the world have different words for the process of negotiation and different ideas about what it involves. In many places, there isn't even a word for negotiation and in some, negotiation is something that women just do not do.

There are also key variables that affect how different cultural groups negotiate that are useful to understand, be aware of, and respect to enhance our effectiveness with negotiation.

On top of that, and most importantly, there is a predictable recurring phenomenon with the conflict inherent in negotiation. When we create an adversarial climate, people will polarize around identity group differences, groups that we identify as being a part of like Asian or European, young or old, Black or White, and so on. But, if we are able to create a more collaborative climate, this polarization will dissipate.

Finally, we need to understand that gender is a "culture," as is patriarchy. Patriarchy is probably the single largest cultural force on the planet today which, of course, impacts us in negotiation.

So, what is culture?

Some things are universal—the things that are shared with all humans, for example, the need for food and shelter.

Some things are individual. For example, no one has exactly my same smile.

And some things are cultural. These things are learned or taught. They are not genetic and are shared with one group as distinguished from other groups. An example might be eating utensils or social norms for behavior. A good working definition of culture that I have often used is from Geert Hofstede: "the collective programming of the mind, that distinguishes one group from another."[1]

I like to say that personality is to an individual what culture is to a group. Culture is a group's personality. A group's culture, in general, comes from the challenges and opportunities of living in that group's particular place on our planet and segment of society. For example, in small towns in Greece, people observe a "quiet time" between three and five o'clock in the afternoon, a siesta, and stores close. The climate is very hot, so people use this time to rest from the heat—a cultural adaptation to living on a very warm part of the planet.

When some people talk about "culture" they are often referring to "high culture"—the arts, music, theater, literature, and more. But in terms of negotiation, "deep culture" is much more relevant. For example, imagine an approaching iceberg. In such a scenario it would be smart to pay attention to not only what is on the surface, but more importantly what is below the water line. The same is true with negotiation: We want to pay to attention to what is obvious on the surface, but we also want to hold an awareness of "deep culture," important values that might be less visible.

Over the years, Ellen Raider, my other colleagues, and I began to use the term "worldview" in addition to "culture" because it encompassed a broader understanding of the phenomenon. Worldview comes from our ethnic or national culture and it also comprises our deeply held beliefs, attitudes, and values that come from both our personality and life experience. Worldview is the collection of one's personal philosophies, beliefs, and perspectives that inform how we see the world. It may come from, for example, our education, our gender, race, culture, socio-economic status, thinking preferences, or life experience. In the words of Anaïs Nin, "We don't see things as they are, we see things as we are."[2] This is important to understand when we are negotiating conflict.

Positions are negotiable. I want this; you want that. But worldview is not negotiable. Instead, it needs to be understood and respected or it will become the source of an impasse in negotiation.

Here is a simple example for how worldview and negotiation intersect: Assume you are negotiating with a man who has a hungry child. His position is he wants an apple, which you don't have, though you do have some beans, tomatoes, and pork you can offer him as bargaining chips to meet his need for food for his child. But suppose this man is a religious Muslim, a Jew, or vegan and your offer of pork violates a norm against eating pork, or meat generally. Your offer will likely be received more as a bargaining chop, something that thwarts his needs rather than a chip that would meet them. The offer will not meet the needs of your counterpart and it will not build rapport either.

When worldviews clash, conflicts can be difficult to solve through negotiation because people hold tightly, consciously or unconsciously, to previously acquired core values, attitudes, or beliefs. Each thinks their way is the only way. The more deeply we hold parts of our worldview, the more we will experience those parts as nonnegotiable. For instance, it's hard to convince a Catholic to become half a Jew in a negotiation, or vice versa.

Important Worldview Differences That Can Impact Us When We Negotiate

A lot can be said about culture, cultural differences, and worldview—and it's beyond the scope of this book to cover that vast terrain here. We do, though, need to be aware of how these differences can impact us when we negotiate and, in any given situation where they may be playing a role, do our homework and grow our knowledge of which aspect of culture or worldview might be most relevant to the situation.

When I was first getting started in this field, my professional library was filled with texts on intercultural communication. For example, I had Encountering the Chinese—A Guide for Americans" From Nyet to Da, Understanding the Russians" Understanding Arabs—A Guide for Westerners—and so on. I loved creating a file for just about every country on earth and what I might need to know about them from an intercultural perspective. We used "*Going International*—a video that had great vignettes about how, as an American, to do business with Mexico, Japan, Saudi Arabia, and England.[3] In reviewing those files for this book, I saw in my earliest files the recognition that gender was a culture and a desire to articulate what that might mean. I appreciated the work of Deborah Tannen, a linguist who wrote best-selling books around that time titled *That's Not What I Meant!* and *You Just Don't Understand*. In the early '90s, I did one of my first offerings for women around gender and negotiation and began to contrast cultural variables in the same way I was doing for national cultures. All of that research and reading helped expand my lens, which is what we all must do to navigate culture and worldview well.

As with the iceberg, we aren't always aware that cultural differences are affecting us because they are "beneath the surface." As we have said for years in our programs, "The fish is the last one to know that it's swimming in water." There are so many ways that we are different from one another—and we have different ideas around how we talk about things. Once when I was leading a negotiation seminar for a large group of scientists, I pointed out that the term "to table" in American English means "to postpone," but in the UK, it means "to discuss," just the opposite. Exasperated, a participant from the UK said, "Wow, I have been doing business internationally for forty years with people from the United States and have never been aware of this difference. It makes me wonder how many other differences like this we just may not know trip us up in our understanding of each other." As Oscar Wilde said about the UK and the United States, "Two worlds separated by a common language."[4]

Here are the key cultural variables I've identified over the years that show up in negotiation:

Time—We all have twenty-four hours in a day but humans around the world have different attitudes and norms around time. Some are much more relaxed with time, others much more precise. Some cultures are "monochronic," and some are more "polychronic." In a monochronic society, time is a priority. Time is money. Someone with a polychronic worldview is more people-oriented; relationships take priority. At an intercultural program I delivered for ATT International Services, a Latin American participant who was more polychronic in their worldview was running down the hall, late for a meeting, when they ran into a very important person. Instead of sprinting to the meeting, they stopped and connected with the person. A monochronic person would likely wave, point to their watch, and arrive at their meeting punctually. In a polychronic culture, you get things done through relationships, not through systems. The clock is a useful tool, but it does not dictate. I heard a participant in Benin say, "You in the United States may have a watch, but we here have time."

Belonging—While every human has a need to belong, some groups are much more "I" oriented and privilege individualism, and others are more "we" oriented and privilege the group. For example, in the United States, White, Anglo-Saxon men (the men of my family of origin) are some of the most individualistic groups on the planet. This can show up in conflicts about whether people should have to pay taxes or follow regulations for the collective good versus doing whatever they want.

Authority—Some groups pay much more deference to authority (whether it comes from status or wealth) and others are much more egalitarian and might challenge authority. Related to this, some groups are much more "high context" and others "low." In other words, a high context group will pay much more attention to all the nonverbal communication including who is delivering the message, and the low will rely on the specific words that are spoken. Much of Chinese culture, for instance, is very high context and, in a negotiation, it might be most relevant who shows up at the table versus what is said.[5]

Risk—Some groups are much more comfortable with the risks inherent in the future and others not so much. For example, the culture of the tech world is notoriously comfortable with risk and likes to, as they say, "fail early and fail often" and "don't be scared to break things."

Gender roles—Some groups have stricter and more traditional norms and attitudes about roles based on gender. Other groups are far more relaxed about gender norms. In some cultures, women can lead the negotiation team; in others they should be in the background, taking the notes, or not in the room at all.

If not handled well, all of these variables create can discomfort and misunderstanding in negotiation.

Many of us also tend to flock toward what feels familiar and are made uneasy by what feels strange or looks different. In my trainings, I have offered a simple but revealing exercise in which each member of the group gets a piece of construction paper of different shapes and colors and is asked to pin it to their shirt. Participants are then asked to circulate and form groups without saying anything more. Inevitably, people group up based on the most similar pieces of construction paper in color and shape. Birds of a feather flock together. I remember long ago arguing a motion before a judge. I prevailed, but the judge (a man) said to the lawyer on the other side (a man), "Sorry, Joe, but I have to give it to her."

Also, all of us, to greater or lesser degrees, are ethnocentric. To the best of my knowledge, if you go around the world and look at maps in school classrooms, you will find that most countries put themselves in the center of the world (unless the maps are coming from colonial countries). All of us put ourselves in the center to greater and lesser degrees and that's understandable. But whether we do this will also depend on how much work we've done on ourselves to dispel tendencies to believe that we and our group are somehow the best and the center of the universe or instead can see ourselves as part of one human family, and humanity a subset of nature. As Hillell says, "If I am not for myself, who will be for me? But if I am only for myself, who am I?"[6]

It's the PWC That Creates Toxic Polarization

Conventional wisdom probably would say that a lot of conflict and impasse in negotiation has to do with insurmountable cultural and worldview differences. Politicians and social and traditional media often contribute to this and, certainly in my country, like fanning the flames of the culture wars to gain political control, sell more newspapers, or get more clicks. But it's what I call "group-o-centrism" that causes the most problems and that we need to be on the lookout for in negotiation. Here's what I mean.

Mix an adversarial climate with worldview and identity-group differences and you get group-o-centrism. By definition, worldview and culture are a "collective mental programming of a group of humans." When we are talking about them in the context of a negotiation or conflict, humans can polarize around any identity group that is present in a group that has turned adversarial. This could include: nationality, ethnicity, gender, race, age, language, family status, physical condition, religion, class, sexual orientation, or profession. Perspective-taking is key to collaborative conflict negotiation and key to a New Negotiation. When worldview differences are at play, this becomes even more critical. In those circumstances, if we don't attempt to understand and respect worldview differences but remain in an ego- or ethnocentric mode, we will not only forego the richness of understanding multiple perspectives in our diverse world—we will inevitably escalate the conflict rather than resolve it.

Here's an example that may sound familiar to you using the cultural variable of time. If the atmosphere of the negotiation is competitive and adversarial and things aren't going well, monochronic people will likely call polychronic people things like "lazy" or "not serious" and the polychronic people will call the monochronic ones "cold and unfeeling." Do you know what I am talking about? Have you experienced this? In contrast, when rapport and respect are strong, these kinds of differences are often good naturedly joked about or simply appreciated.

Sometimes, when we negotiate at the level of needs and interests, apparent worldview differences will even disappear. Here's a scenario we created to demonstrate this: Imagine the mayor of a town, "Centerville," has called a meeting to address citizen complaints about a factory in town that is emitting powerful toxins that can cause respiratory illness. The owner of the chemical plant, the town's main employer, is present, as are three members of the Concerned Citizens of Centerville (plant workers and community members). The mayor cautions that the cause of the illness is as of yet undetermined but announces that the results of a preliminary environmental report require the factory to close for one week to see if it is the source of the problem.

The climate at the meeting is very hostile and competitive. The disputants interrupt, yell, contradict, and accuse one another as well as make it clear that each side sees the other as unreasonable. The position of the community group is to close the factory immediately. The chemical plant owner's counterposition is to keep the factory open. He says the factory is not the source of the illnesses. Then the community members use chops: They threaten to take the environmental report to the local newspapers. Similarly, the factory owner threatens to take his jobs and factory to another town. Then the community members name-call, using words that insinuate that the factory owner is just a greedy capitalist. In turn, the owner tells the community members and factory workers that they are a bunch of "liberal environmental crazies."

The hostile climate shifts when the mayor (serving as an impromptu mediator) presents a great reframing question that focuses on everyone's priority needs and interests instead of the positional clash: "How can we clear up the source of the symptoms and keep the factory and the economy of this town in good shape?" With a shift in climate into calmer discussion, it becomes clear that even though there is a clash at the positional level there is common ground at the level of needs and interests. The community's main concerns are for health, their jobs, and a good town economy, and the owner needs to protect the economic viability of his factory as well as the health of the workers in order to run it. In addition, they all have a need for accurate information about the source of the illnesses (and everyone wants their perspective acknowledged and understood). As more trust is built, the factory owner also admits his concern for his own health: "I live here too, you know." Finally, with common ground established, they reach a first step agreement that includes the factory owner's willingness to close the factory for a week and suffer the short-term losses, the workers agree to take their paid vacation (it is July), and the community agrees to support a tax break if the factory ends up not being the source of the symptoms. As they get their respective underlying needs and interests met, the apparent clash of worldview becomes irrelevant.

Negotiating across cultures or worldview is really about creating and managing a positive collaborative conflict climate. When there is a competitive, adversarial climate, the dominant culture will impose its norms on the subordinate culture—whether we are talking about a national culture, or the culture of gender and the large "negotiation" that is happening around this on the planet.

From working all over the globe, one of the things that I've learned about us humans is that we are much more alike than we are different. That's true of nations, tribes, genders, all of us. We have the same categories of needs: physical security, belonging, etc. We have the same categories of feelings: mad, sad, glad, etc. But how needs and feelings manifest is impacted by culture.

It may seem simple to say, but ever more important to emphasize in our shrinking and contentious world, that when you create a climate that is collaborative across difference, that allows people to meet their basic needs, you don't need coercive and violent police, and you don't need a hyper-militarized planet. When you build a collaborative climate in a family, a team, a group, or world, you do not get huge identity group polarization. You do not need to dominate one cultural group with another. You don't need to put trillions into weapons to impose your way, especially when that money is so sorely needed to heal our declining ecosystems.

A few years ago, I delivered a negotiation workshop in war-torn South Sudan, the birthplace of humanity. A young man named William, a native South Sudanese with very dark skin, and I were talking about culture, conflict, and negotiation. Somewhere in the discourse, I said, "William, you and I may be more similar in our genetic makeup than me and my White neighbor at home." He looked at me like I was crazy but I knew what I was saying was correct. We have made a whole hill of beans about skin color (just like gender) for the purposes of creating hierarchies that justify domination and exploitation. For instance, during the first Trump administration in the United States, the MAGA movement created an adversarial climate that stoked culture wars—from blaming covid on the "Chinese virus" to calling Mexican immigrants "rapists" and peaceful Black Lives Matter protesters "terrorists." The intention (which continues on in the second Trump administration) was to wreak havoc by pitting groups against each other. It was an example of the old trick of "divide and conquer," to create an adversarial climate of distrust to dominate and control. This is what authoritarians do best.

Transcend the PWC and Embrace a Global Sisterhood

As Rabia Roberts says, "Differentiation is one of the main principles in us and when we try to establish monocultures or mono races, we are working against the fundamental principles of Earth, and ourselves." Nonetheless, celebrating and respecting differences doesn't always come easy, especially in an adversarial PWC.

How do we proceed? Here are some ideas.

First, it helps to recognize that we are all cultural beings, even if we are the demographic majority in our country. We can stay in a familiar bubble or we can break down walls and celebrate the diversity of humanity and other people. Can you imagine if all birds were the same color and type? How boring!

Second, do your best to clear out bias. Prejudice is "prejudgment." When you see behavior that feels foreign to you, try to move beyond your own cultural lens that might lead to an inappropriate response or negative reaction. For example, when I worked in Afghanistan, I had to wear a head scarf. My initial response to this was negative. I assumed it signaled that the environment around me considered me secondary (which, to some degree, was likely true). Nonetheless, as I got to know the Afghan women I worked with, I realized they saw it quite differently. Indeed, many of them told me how much they preferred wearing their head scarves, for a variety of reasons including modesty prescribed by Islam, honoring their own cultural norms, and resistance to Westernization. My thinking shifted and I too began to appreciate covering, especially because it made my blond hair and "American-ness" less obvious. And when I got back to the States, I noticed how I kind of missed the head scarf for a time and felt a bit naked.

Third, notice when you feel stress. Sometimes when we see a foreign behavior and prejudge it based on our own cultural lens, we feel stress. That stress or discomfort can be our signal that we need to check our "filter." We can then seek out clarification or learn more about the difference. We can ask people around us who might be able to provide insight, or we can read books, watch videos, and then come up with a more flexible, relaxed, and enlightened response.

Fourth, be on the lookout for the combination of competitive escalation mixed with apparent worldview or identity-group differences. If the atmosphere is competitive, you are likely to see movement from negotiation positions to justifications to threats. This predictably leads to negative stereotyping and assumptions about the other based on identity group differences. For example, a woman might get called a disparaging word or name when she is not doing what someone wants her to do. In contrast, when you choose a collaborative strategy, the movement goes from positions to needs/interests, to a reframe, and toward alternative solutions. Behaviorally, you are listening to understand, respect, and manage differences between you and the other. You are moving from a single dominant perspective that might be based on an egocentric or ethnocentric worldview to an understanding that there are multiple perspectives each with a part of "the truth." This heightened ability to step into the shoes of another can be challenging, of course, but it explains why people who negotiate well across cultural difference create better long-term relationships and outcomes. We grow when we meet something or someone different from ourselves.

Finally, recognize the global nature of patriarchy and how it influences the dominant worldview norms on the planet. The

Harry Potter actress and gender activist Emma Watson said, "Patriarchy is the largest superpower on the planet."[7] This is another way of saying that it is the largest culture on the planet; it transcends all others. A few years ago, I delivered negotiation skills workshops to the global tool company Stanley Black & Decker. It was a cool gig. I started in Baltimore, then flew to Seoul, then traveled to Milan and back to New York to work with their people—my first round-the-world tour. One of the participants in Seoul was a woman from China. She said, "I love this material, but I can't negotiate at home. I just do what I am told. And, all of this money I make from my job? It goes to my brother." I heard something similar from a Dinka woman from South Sudan who had a good job but was required to give her salary to her husband to support his multiple wives who did not work. These are cultural norms, sure, but they also are the norms of a PWC and something we need to link arms with women around the world to change.

It is a relatively new thing that women are everywhere out in the world and increasingly having a voice and influence. The impact of our presence is still at a fledgling state yet to be realized. What kind of a cultural imprint do we want to make and how can we do it? In the last century, and globally, if you were Anglo-Saxon or at least white-skinned, tall and male, and spoke English, you would have had a strong edge. We have moved the needle on this somewhat but it's still a reality and something we must consider when we talk about culture, worldview, and negotiation. When I think about what stands out to me as the dominant characteristics of the PWC today, they are:

- Hyper-individualism over the common good
- Jockeying for status

- Competition over collaboration
- Domination over partnership and working together

According to the Program on Negotiation at Harvard Law School, "When it comes to different characteristics in negotiations, a growing body of research suggests that status consciousness varies depending on the gender of interested parties . . . men tend to care more about status than women do."[8] Patriarchy is all about status, one-up, one-down, hierarchy, dominion. Men have been much more schooled in that philosophy.

So, what is the gender-equal world culture we want to create now as women, and how do we do it? The African proverb comes to mind: "If you want to go fast, go alone. If you want to go far, go together."

When Barack Obama first took office back in 2008, two thirds of his top aides were men. A lot of female staffers reportedly complained about having to force their way into important meetings to be active in those meetings and feel like they were heard when they weren't. Rather than giving up or becoming aggravated, these women developed a strategy that would force the male staffers to listen to them. If one woman made a point or suggestion during a meeting, others would repeat it or highlight it to ensure it was recognized and given the proper weight. This practice, often referred to as "amplification," was especially prevalent during discussions in which men were more dominant or more likely to have their ideas heard and credited.

Melinda French Gates, in partnering with Michelle Obama and Amal Clooney to end child marriage, has said, "Women, I think, naturally work in collectives. I've talked to a number of women who are older than me who made it as CEO, or CFO, in their company. And there's some regret that they didn't do it in concert with other women. They didn't pull other women up and along with them. The generation that we've been part of—Michelle and I are essentially the same age—we've wanted to pull everybody up with us."[9]

A PWC divides and conquers. A global sisterhood unites.

Dismantling patriarchy is the key to dismantling identity-group conflict.

Reflections on Negotiation, Conflict, Worldview/Culture, and Gender

- *Have you negotiated across cultures?*
- *How much of "culture" and "identity-group polarization" is really the PWC?*
- *Do you believe in a global sisterhood? What is its promise?*

Putting into Practice

Make contact with a woman who is not necessarily in your tribe. Write about the experience in your journal.

In your next conflict or negotiation, notice worldview. What are the assumptions that each party may be making that are impacting the process?

CHAPTER 8
Pause, Integrate, Apply

This chapter is a little different.

Negotiation and conflict resolution can be challenging. That's why there is so much destructive conflict in the world; people aren't very good at it. We need to have patience with ourselves and each other. In this chapter, I give you an opportunity to digest, walk before you run, and integrate some of the ideas we have been talked about so far.

We progress with practice; the better we get with the small stuff, the better we are able to take on the big stuff on the planet that needs our attention.

In this chapter, I provide you with two tools. The first is what we have colloquially called a "Chip/Chop" analysis, which you can use to either prepare for a negotiation or analyze the process while it's in progress. The second is a negotiation "Bare Bones," which basically maps out an entire negotiation from beginning to end in its skeletal framework with all the steps and stages of what goes into the mix.

Before undertaking any negotiation, always check in and ask yourself at the outset: Do you want to pursue it collaboratively and use the principles of a New Negotiation? Wait for your "yes" before you proceed. If you want to make a different process choice, that's OK. Perhaps you want to ignore the conflict, perhaps you want to hire a lawyer, go to the press, and so on. It's worth reflecting on what you think is the best process choice because it's easy in today's world to get unwittingly pulled into an adversarial, patriarchal, man-mode way of doing things even if that wasn't really your intention. We have deep, baked-in, neural pathways both in ourselves and in our culture that have been carved over thousands of years that we need to redirect and reshape. So, taking a moment to pause and reflect is always wise before you dive in. Does taking this on make sense? Does a collaborative approach make sense? Do you and the other party have an ongoing relationship? Is there interdependence between you? Do you care? If the answer is yes, a collaborative strategy and the thinking and tools of a New Negotiation are probably the way to go.

The "Chip/Chop" Tool to Prepare for or Analyze a Negotiation

When I am faced with a challenging conflict there are basically two types of preparation that I do: the head work (the analysis), and the heart/emotional stuff. For the latter, please refer to "Clearing the Charge" in chapter 6. For the former, read on.

The academic research is clear: People who prepare get better outcomes and more of what they want in negotiation. "Seventy percent of good negotiation is good preparation," says my experienced negotiation colleague, Pablo Restrepo.[1] "Preparation is everything. If you prepare well, you are far more likely to reach a positive outcome."

Good preparation puts us into our prefrontal cortex—our

grown up, more functional adult selves. It takes us away from the "positional clash," where lies the heat of the conflict, and gives us a broader, richer, more creative perspective and response. When we react without pause, we tend to do so from our reptilian brain. As family therapist Terry Real loves to say, "Which part of you is talking?"[2] There is so much righteous indignation out there in the world. Preparation gets you out of it and helps you manage reactivity.

To prepare well or analyze an ongoing situation you must be asking these questions.

What are the positions?

Just about always, it makes sense to start with "the positional clash." Positions reveal the things that are in opposition to each other. They help you understand what the conflict is about and what you need to negotiate. For this reason, you will see on the Chip/Chop tool (pg. 191) that both side's positions are given the number one.

What are your underlying needs?

In other words, why are you taking the position you are taking? Why is this your preferred solution to the conflict? Try to do a thorough assessment of your needs and interests before the conflict begins and continue to refine as things unfold. Look at Maslow. Think it through.

What are the other side's underlying needs and interests?

What do you know for sure? What do you assume? Again, be as thorough as possible before you engage and then continue to refine as the process progresses. Remember, the more adversarial the climate, the less likely people are to reveal what's really going on, i.e. their true underlying needs and interests and feelings about the situation.

What might be a good reframe?

The hardest thing to get to in any conflict negotiation whether you are one of the parties to the negotiation or you are a mediator facilitating the process is to articulate a good reframe. When you succeed, you will feel it and know it. When people's needs and interests are named, rather than being caught up in the power struggle, things calm down. Also, it accentuates your reframe to add a statement that highlights the common ground between you (i.e., the needs and interests that both sides share) before you reframe.

What are your bargaining chips?

Look at what you understand to be the needs and interests of your counterpart. What can you offer them that might meet those needs and interests? Note that you can always agree with their position in exchange for chips from them that meet your needs. Or, they can always agree with your position in exchange for chips you offer them that meet their needs.

What are your bargaining chops?

Again, looking at the needs and interests of your counterpart, what might you be able to do to thwart the other side's needs and interests (ideally legally). But why think about chops if you want to pursue a collaborative process? For two reasons. The first is to make note of them so you don't unwittingly use them if you want to maintain a positive climate. The second is to assess your power. Chips and chops both give you power to influence the negotiation and get what you want.

What are their bargaining chips?

What could the other side offer you that could meet your needs and interests? Note that they could always agree with your position in exchange for chips you receive from them, or you can always agree with their position in exchange for chips they offer you that meet your needs.

What are their bargaining chops?

Again, looking at your needs and interests, what might your counterpart be able to do (ideally legally) to thwart your needs and interests? Why think about their chops if you want to pursue a collaborative process? Again, to make note of them so you can avoid your reactivity if they use them, and second, to assess your power as both chips and chops both give you power to influence the negotiation.

Your BATNA

What are your best options if this negotiation doesn't work out with your counterpart?

Their BATNA

What are their best options if this negotiation doesn't work out with you? You often won't know their BATNA but should always try to assess it.

Worldview

Ask yourself here:

- Are there relevant worldview differences between you that might be impacting the situation?
- What are the assumptions that each of you might be making about life or negotiation that might be different?
- Are there deep values you each may hold that will not be experienced as negotiable?
- What will it take for you to stand fully in your sovereignty, connected to your life-force energy? What will it take for you to know that you are not secondary in any way, feel confident, worthy of respect, equal treatment, and able to claim value?

Any conflict negotiation, no matter how big or small, intimate or international, can be analyzed in this way. It doesn't really matter the order you think through these questions, though, again I always think it makes sense to start with positions.

Note that if there are multiple parties you will need to do this analysis for each.

What follows is a "Chip/Chop" form and an example of this kind of analysis.

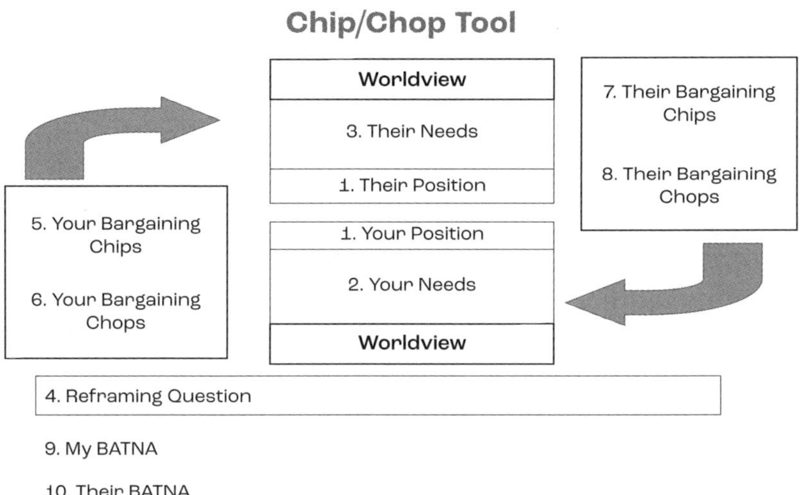

"Las Comunas"[3]

This conflict took place in in Medellín, Colombia, in the early 1990s and was mediated by a female mediator who was very familiar with "Las Comunas," a hilly area above Medellín that had experienced a lot of gang violence. A gang, made up of mostly teenagers in Las Comunas, demanded *una vacuna,* a "vaccine" (aka a bribe), from anyone who did business in what the gang considered its territory. The term "vacuna" had originated from revolutionary fighters in Colombia and then caught on with gangs. An owner of a bus company, "Don Pedro," refused to pay the bribe. As a result, the gang captured one of the drivers of the bus company, killed him, and burned the bus.

What were the positions?

The gang—Pay "the vaccine."
Don Pedro—I refuse.

What were Don Pedro's underlying needs and interests (in order of priority for him)? (These became clear as the mediation unfolded.)

- to provide a needed service for the community
- safety for his drivers and his equipment
- to operate within the law
- to not set a precedent of paying for "vaccines"
- for his enterprise to be financially viable

What were the gang's underlying needs and interests (in order of priority for them)?

- control of the territory
- respect
- to not have to lug their mothers' groceries up the steep hills in Las Comunas (The mothers of the gang members relied heavily on the bus service. If the buses weren't available to them, the kids would have to walk up the very steep paths with the groceries.)
- income, for themselves and their mothers
- their own personal safety
- to stay connected to/belong to the gang

What would have been a good reframe?

Ask yourself, what do you think a good reframe to this conflict could have been? After many attempts the mediator came up with the following:

"Since we are all concerned with the community, how can we provide the gang with a legitimate source of income while permitting Mr. Pedro to provide a safe transportation service in the gang's territory?"

With this reframe, the mediator opened up the way for a brainstorm of possible solutions. Ideas began to flow.

What were Don Pedro's possible bargaining chips?

- make them bus drivers
- allow the kids to name the bus
- name the service after the community
- make the kids bus assistants
- have the kids run a car/bus wash
- put a Virgin Mary on the buses
- start a school for kids
- provide home delivery
- make them mechanics
- provide a memorial to Escobar

What were Don Pedro's bargaining chops?

- cancel the service
- seek support from the paramilitaries (In that time in Colombia, the most common response to this kind of violence for someone like Don Pedro would have been to go to the paramilitary for protection. But Don Pedro

didn't want to do this because he believed it would put him and his company in the middle of a war between the paramilitary and the gangs.)
- go to authorities (Authorities like the police didn't want to go into Las Comunas because it was too dangerous.)
- refuse to talk to the gang members because he is "legitimate" and they are not

What were the gang's bargaining chips?

- agree to no more violence
- agree to a bus washing service

What were the gang's bargaining chops?

- continued violence

Don Pedro's BATNA

- potentially more murdered bus drivers
- more damage to his property

The gang's BATNA

- possibly the end of the bus service which their mothers relied on

Worldview

For Don Pedro it seemed to include: a strong work ethic, social responsibility toward the community, and operating within the law.

For the gang it seemed to include: a sense of community within the gang (often the name of the gang was synonymous with the name of the territory), resignation that violence was just a part of life (most of these kids had a very short life span),[4] and social justice.

The solution the parties agreed to was to have the gang members, i.e., the kids, wash the buses for income. This solution held for a long time.

Putting into Practice

Pick a conflict or negotiation in which you are or were one of the parties. Can you analyze it in this way? Use the "Chip/Chop" form and fill in the blanks.

"Bare Bones" Negotiation— Putting the Steps and Stages Together

Negotiation is a process, not an event. One negotiation can happen in a minute, another over years, or over a lifetime. For example, some of the conflicts between men and women about gender are "negotiations" that have been going on for millennia.

People generally don't think about process unless they are a "process person" like me and my colleagues. But when we see negotiation as a process rather than a static momentary thing and apply all the skill set and ideas, we improve our chances of a successful resolution.

"Bare Bones" is a map of the whole process. Negotiation is often messy and nonlinear, the way life is. Because emotion, drama, dysfunction, and mistrust are often part of a conflict negotiation, having a mental map of the whole process, from beginning to end, can be super helpful.

Bare Bones brings together core elements like positions, needs, reframing, and alternatives alongside AEIOU, with a prescription for an ideal stage flow to all of it. Because it's just a map (not a complete picture), it can help you diagnose where you are in the process, where you need to go next, and also why things might not be going well if they aren't and which steps might have been missed that you need to return to.

The stage flow of the whole process is: (1) Connecting, (2) Communicating the Issues: The Positions and Underlying Needs and Interests, (3) Highlighting Common Ground and Reframing, (4) Brainstorming Alternatives and Reaching Agreement. The steps of Bare Bones happen inside of these four stages.

"Bare Bones" Negotiation

Stage		
Stage I	1. Both A and B create good climate for negotiation (Unite)	
	2. A states position flexibly (Inform)	4. B states position flexibly (Inform)
Stage II	3. B probes for and paraphrases A's underlying interests/needs (Open)	5. A probes for and paraphrases B's underlying interests/needs (Open)
Stage III	6. Either highlights common ground 7. Either reframes (Unite)	
Stage IV	8. A and B brainstorm a number of possible alternative ways to satisfy their needs (Unite)	
	9. A and B evaluate the alternatives, pick the best combination for both sides, and summarize their agreement	

1. Both A and B Create a Good Climate for Negotiation (Unite)

A rule with few exceptions is "connect before content." You will have set yourself up well for success if you create a good climate for negotiation. Sometimes this looks like breaking bread with the other side, "ritual sharing," building a relationship through preliminary conversation in which we build rapport whether across countries, tribes, or teenagers. Sometimes it's as simple as naming the topic of the conversation you want to have, and a time and place you want to have it, and making sure the other person is in agreement. In AEIOU terms, you are "Uniting."

With intimate partners, friends, or family, we might say "could we talk about (our conflict—name it neutrally) that we had the other day. When would be a good time?"

With more formal situations or with people we don't know as well, it's good practice to not rush this step if at all possible. In casual conversation, we can glean critical information about the other person's values and interests which will prove useful when we get into the substance. It is also a time when we can build the rapport, trust, and common ground that might be needed to take us through a difficult dynamic.

Who we and the other are can matter a lot in terms of what kind of climate setting will work. Think about what might be best. People from different "tribes" will be inclined to talk about different subjects, will have different expectations about the length of time they should take connecting. For example, and stereotypically, two men might discuss the latest ball game in their "connecting"—while two women might admire each other's clothing and discuss where they shop. Another example might be that certain cultural groups might expect to take more time to get to know each other and build their relationship, whereas others might want to get right to the point.

In my early years of educating myself about international negotiations, I was impressed by a story of a Japanese company who wanted to do business in Mexico but before they got down to business they went to the effort and expense of sending their "company man" to live in Mexico for a year where he learned Spanish and how to play the Mexican guitar—both excellent ways to build a relationship.

In protracted conflicts, where trust is low or nonexistent, you may need to come back to climate repeatedly to build rapport, trust, and connection.

2. A States Their Position Flexibly (Inform)

At some point, one of you crosses the line, "gets down to business," and states your position.

Positioning is simple on its face, but emotionally can be more difficult especially for many women. There is tension in the "positional clash." Conflict avoiders may prefer to avoid the tension and Evade. We might be afraid that our request is not legitimate. We may want to "be nice." But here's the thing. Avoiding stating what we want, your position, will only give us less time to talk about it and work out a good solution. Way too many people do this. They wait until the eleventh hour, and then when urgency takes over for a resolution, they are more likely to polarize, reach an impasse, cave, or just split the difference.

Assuming your intent is collaborative, you will want to be clear about what you want and convey your desire to find a workable solution for all involved, in other words, communicate some flexibility with your position and a desire to negotiate versus the hard lines that competitive negotiators generally use.

When numbers are involved in your negotiation, should you put your number on the table first or should they? Many people wait to hear what the other person says. This is not always a good idea as stating your number anchors the bargaining part of the negotiation around it.[5]

3. B Probes for and Paraphrases A's Underlying Needs/Interests (Open)

Once you and your counterpart understand what the issue is (i.e. the positional clash), you can move to discovering the needs and interests that underlie. This can be difficult and may take time for you to be clear about your needs and interests—or the other. The person we are negotiating with may not be as skilled as we are and may not even be aware of their underlying needs/interests. We may need to help them by asking good questions and summarize what we understand at the needs level.

Sometimes starting with our interests and needs and then stating our preferred solution (our position) is softer because there can be so much tension at the positional level. This can certainly work well as long as you don't avoid what you really want.

4. B States Their Position Flexibly (Inform)

5. A Probes for and Paraphrases B's Underlying Needs/Interests (Open)

Steps 2 through 4 are the hardest in any negotiation. Take your time. If you can get past them, lots of times you will be home free and well on our way to reaching agreement.

6. Either A or B or Both Highlights Common Ground (Unite)

Again, naming the needs and interests that both sides have in common that are revealed from the steps earlier.

7. Either A or B Reframes (Unite)

Asking a refocusing question as to how we and our counterpart can satisfy both of our priority needs working together instead of struggling over positions.

8. A and B Brainstorm a Number of Possible Alternative Ways to Satisfy Their Needs (Unite)

9. Packaging and Reaching Agreement

A and B evaluate the alternatives and pick the best combination for both sides and summarize their agreement.

10. Both A and B Renegotiate Over Time as Needed

Bare Bones Example

Lee and Shiv During Dinner

Stage I

Ritual Sharing - Step 1
Shiv: This is wonderful chicken.
Lee: Thanks. It's a new recipe I found.

Position - Step 2
Shiv: I need to talk now about our proposed spending plan for the year.

Position - Step 4
Lee: Well, I would really rather not talk about this now. (He feels some anger around this because his wife oftens brings up difficult issues at inappropriate times.)

Stage II

Underlying Needs - Step 3
Lee: Why do you feel so much urgency to talk about this now?
Shiv: I need to know that we are going to deal with this and other difficult issues and not just avoid them.
Lee: So you need some reassurance from me that I want to engage with you about these issues and not just duck them?
Shiv: Yes, that's right. Can we talk?

Underlying Needs - Step 5
Shiv: Can you tell me why?
Lee: Heavy discussions at dinner give me indigestion.
Shiv: So, it's not that you don't want to talk about it, it's just my timing that is a problem. Is that right?
Lee: Yes, that's right.

Stage III

Reframe - Step 7
Lee: Let's figure out a good time for both of us to talk about our money plan and other difficult issues like that.

Problem Solving - Step 8
Together they generate the following options:
1) Fix a regular time after dinner to deal with these topics if we have any;
2) Rule out dinner as a time to deal with conflict; and
3) Talk about these issues on Saturdays when we are both relaxed.

Stage IV

Reaching Agreement - Step 9
Shiv: Let's regularly talk after dinner if we have anything that needs discussing and decide that dinner time will not be a time to deal with issues that cause conflict.
Lee: Sounds good to me.

Putting into Practice

Using your own example, write out a Bare Bones using the form below.

Bones Practice

Stage		
Stage I	**Ritual Sharing - Both A and B create good climate for negotiation (Unite)** 1.	
	Position - A states position flexibly (Inform) 2.	**Position - B states position flexibly (Inform)** 4.
Stage II	**Underlying Needs - B probes for and paraphrases A's underlying interests/needs (Open)** 3a. (probe for needs) 3b. (response from other party) 3c. (paraphrase) 3d. (if paraphrasing is incorrect, start again with 3a.)	**Underlying Needs - A probes for and paraphrases B's underlying interests/needs (Open)** 5a. (probe for needs) 5b. (response from other party) 5c. (paraphrase) 5d. (if paraphrasing is incorrect, start again with 5a.)
Stage III	**Reframe - (6) Either highlights common ground, then (7) either reframes (Unite)** 6. 7.	
Stage IV	**Problem Solving - A and B brainstorm a number of possible alternative ways to satisfy their needs (Unite)** 8.	
	Reaching Agreement - A and B evaluate the alternatives, pick the best combination for both sides, and summarize their agreement 9.	

CHAPTER 9

Stand Up to the Domination System

> *You have to dominate. If you don't dominate, you're wasting your time. They're going to run over you, you're going to look like a bunch of jerks, and you'll be the laughingstock of the world.*
> —Donald Trump, forty-fifth president, United States (to US governors and mayors in response to George Floyd protests), 2020

In 2003, Leymah Gbowee inspired the world when she and other women came together to end the horrendous civil war that had raged for over a decade in Liberia.

This story, elegantly portrayed in *Pray the Devil Back to Hell,* directed by Gini Reticker and produced by Abigail Disney, is a blueprint of what women can do planet-wide as we connect to our power and voice and say no more to violence, sexual violence, and war, all consequences of the PWC.

Liberia is a West African country of three million people and was founded in 1847 by freed American slaves. The civil war erupted in 1989, and as a result, Liberia suffered prolonged periods of violence. By 2002, over two hundred thousand people had died, and one out of three people had been displaced. There seemed to be no end in sight until an "ordinary woman did the unimaginable."

"I am five months pregnant, my son is three, and my daughter is two," Leyma said. "So under rains of bullets we leave the house, and we walk for like seven hours to my parents' house. And it was hell on earth. My three-year-old is sitting down, sweat pouring off his body, and he says to me, 'Mama, I wish just for a piece of doughnut this morning. I am so hungry.' I'm sitting there and thinking, 'Where am I going to get a piece of doughnut for this three-year-old?' The anger built up again, the pain was there, and I said to him, 'Nuku, I don't have a piece of doughnut to give you.' He said, 'I know. But I just wish for a piece of doughnut.'"[1]

Leymah and other women ignited a nonviolent movement. Together they unified three thousand Muslim and Christian women across tribal lines and they wore white as a symbol of their demand for "peace now." They called themselves "Women of Liberia Mass Action for Peace." They kept their message simple: "We are tired of the violence and we want peace now." Their white robes also signified that they would refuse sex with their husbands until the hostilities stopped.

In a critical moment, when thousands of women were seated and blocking the entrance to where peace negotiations were taking place, one of the henchmen of the corrupt Liberian President Charles Taylor demanded, "Who's in charge here? You're obstructing justice, and I'm going to arrest you." Leymah stood up indignantly: "Fine, come and arrest me."

As he approached, she began to strip. In her culture, seeing a mother naked would send a person to hell forever. Immediately, the soldier backed off, and the negotiations went forward. The civil war was ultimately brought to an end. The women did not back down. They said, "Enough!"[2]

Leymah was honored with the Nobel Peace Prize in 2011. Her leadership and example deeply inspired me to think about the power of women working together to build a world beyond armed conflict and I hope it inspires you. "I had a dream . . . And it was like a crazy dream," Leymah said.

> We decided to protest, we wore white signifying that we were out for peace . . . Muslim and Christian were coming together from different walks of life. These women had seen the worst but they still had that vibrance for life. So, we said well, if I should get killed, just remember me that I was fighting for peace . . . We stepped out . . . and did the unimaginable to send out a signal that we, the Liberian women, we are tired of the killing of our people.[3]

Can you negotiate with warlords? When you look at this example from Leymah and the Liberian women, the answer is clear. Yes, you can.

Leymah's use of withholding sex until there was peace, while not her main strategy as she tells it, brings to mind stories of women throughout time who have withheld sex as a means to influence toxic male power. Lysistrata, in ancient Greece, brought an end to the Peloponnesian War when she led women to deny men sex until there was a negotiated peace.[4] In 2019 a movement emerged in South Korea called "4B."

"B" is a shorthand for the word "no" in Korean—and the "4" stands for the four things women had agreed to say "no" to to protest the conservative political environment and the loss of their reproductive rights: No sex. No dating. No marrying men. No children.[5]

In 2024, after the election of Donald Trump, whose leadership has consistently subordinated women as equal citizens, a right-wing podcaster named Nick Fuentes coined a taunt that went viral: "Your body, my choice." On my blog, I wrote:

> Please sisters, don't get freaked out by men like Trump, but do stay away from them. I know many of us can get drawn to dominator types. I did and I paid a high price. It can feel like a fantasy, like they will protect you. But they won't. Hold on to your power instead, and build it. Take responsibility for your own life and your best way forward. Don't give them your support, your attention, or your body (but do protect our younger sisters from their toxicity). Men like Fuentes are going to lose women; they will lose our beauty, love, divinity, not to mention our power to bring their children into the world.[6]

How do you negotiate when you are dealing with aggression or a threatening or dominating force?

A fellow congressman calls you a "fucking bitch."

After you reject your boss's sexual advances, he isolates you at the firm and you no longer get any choice assignments.

Your husband, who you are trying to separate from, is threatening to kill you or bankrupt you.

Your country is under fascist or authoritarian rule by

a leader like Putin, Bolsonaro, Teodoro Obiang Nguema Mbasogo, Donald Trump, or Erdoğan.

What are tools of the domination system? Domestic violence, sexual harassment, coercive psychological forms of violence like gaslighting, rape, and rape culture, White supremacy, colonialism, imperialism, militarism.

Let's get real, sisters. In a PWC, there are a lot of opportunities out there to "Negotiate with the Domination System," both inside our homes and in the world around us.

Assuming your counterpart has much more power than you, whether that is physical, economic, or more, how do you proceed? How do you disarm a bully with composure, moral authority, style, and firmness? How do you bring a party to the table if they believe you are so beneath them that you are not worthy of their attention? How do you respond when you are overwhelmed with the threat of violence? What do you do when the other side can just dismiss you, dominate you, crush you, or kill you?

Patriarchy, White supremacy, colonialism, imperialism, and human supremacy all share a dominator worldview. Negotiating with people or parties that have this worldview often must move beyond negotiation to various forms of "corrective action," by which I mean all the nonviolent and violent methods of influence other than negotiation that build up your power to a level where the powerholders agree to talk to you (i.e., negotiate.)

Perhaps by this point, you have been able to use the collaborative model of a New Negotiation successfully in a number of situations—but you have yet to bring it to a truly challenging situation. You might be thinking, "Well, collaboration is great, but what do I do when I am dealing with someone who is adversarial and aggressive? What if the other party has a win-lose mentality? What if they have way more power? What if I can't even get them to the table?" These are great questions and best thought of in levels of intensity.

Negotiating with an Adversarial Negotiator

It can be difficult to stay in a collaborative frame of mind and get an adversary to play a more collaborative game, especially if they have more perceived or real power over us. While certainly sometimes negotiation is just not going to work, the reality is, too many of us move up the "process ladders" (remember from chapter 1, negotiation, mediation, litigation, force/power) way too quickly. We need to remind ourselves that resolving conflicts informally, at the level of need and interest, and at the level closest to those involved, usually creates better, more stable outcomes. It's also more relational and satisfying.

There are also, of course, many people who take an adversarial, competitive, Attacking style with negotiation whether it would behoove them to do so or not. Often, this is just simply out of ignorance. Remember, Attacking is just one behavioral way to meet needs. The adversarial, more patriarchal approach is knee jerk to many and "baked in" to a lot of our social systems. Attacking can feel good. To some, it helps them feel more dominant, more entitled. To others, it just comes from laziness, lack of skill or self-mastery. Our job is to recognize the Attack, see it for what it is, and not get triggered by it or take the bait.

So how does one respond to Attacking behavior? We covered some of this in chapter 6, but let's review and go deeper.

First, recognize the Attack.

Breathe.

Use Opening behavior in response (i.e., silent listening, probing, active listening). When you use O behavior and use it well, you are not countering force with force (i.e., A with A) but rather leading with O and taking the wind out of the other's A. Most of the time, they will calm down if you are able to articulate and reflect back their need or interest.

This takes functional adult containment and nonreactivity. Nine times out of ten, if we do it well, it will put the other on track to be less difficult, more cooperative, less Attacking. You get more with honey than with vinegar as the saying goes.

You may not deescalate the other side in one move. There might be multiple A's from the other side and you may need to use multiple O's. But the likelihood is, the Attacks will lessen.

Reducing Defensiveness and Hostility

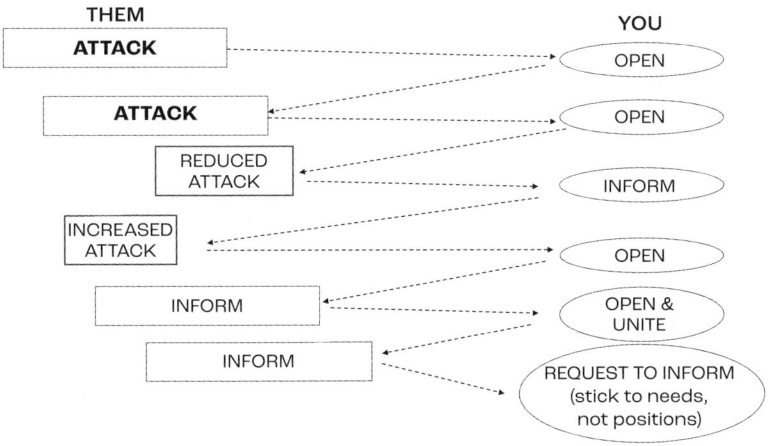

THEM

YOU

ATTACK

OPEN

ATTACK

OPEN

REDUCED ATTACK

INFORM

INCREASED ATTACK

OPEN

INFORM

OPEN & UNITE

INFORM

REQUEST TO INFORM (stick to needs, not positions)

In negotiation training, my colleagues and I have demonstrated this using an adaptation from martial arts. You stand opposite a volunteer participant—your palm is pressing on theirs as a representation of A behavior. If both sides are Attacking, the palms pressing against each other will rise (i.e., escalate). If you are equally strong, there will be a stalemate, or one side will overpower the other.

In contrast, using O in response to an A, I ask the volunteer to continue to press against my palm no matter what, and then instead of countering force with force, I begin to step back and lead them where I want them to go as they continue to press. This is exactly what happens with effective use of O behavior.

Basically, we are countering A behavior with O behavior. Sometimes we are using U. We only are using I when things have calmed down enough to do so. If we use I too quickly (in other words, communicate about our side of things, our needs and interests), the A from the other may escalate.

To do this well, you need to stay regulated, keep your cool, and focus on the positive thing you are trying to create, not the negative thing you trying to avoid. Don't react. This requires being true to yourself. Do you have charge inside you? If you do, you must clear it as much as possible beforehand or take a break.

When you get good at O behavior, you get good at taking the wind out of Attacks and inviting more constructive problem-solving responses from the other side.

Take your time, take a breath, get grounded. Don't react! If possible, stay calm, or let some time pass for everyone to calm down (E, for the short-term).

Be firm, fair, boundaried, and future-focused.

For example, my neighbor, Sarah, who was escaping a toxic and abusive marriage to an ex-cop with whom she has two young children, came to me frightened. She nervously told me, "He wrote to me, he wants his money back, he is threatening me and making accusations that just aren't true!"

"Don't bite," I said. "Don't respond tit for tat. Ignore his threat, stay relational, don't put up with his BS, and don't get intimidated. Hold your ground and focus on the positive thing you are trying to create."

She did and he backed off. From what she told me later, it seemed he could sense her newfound strength.

In summary, use OUI, generally in that order. Avoid A! Set boundaries ("No, that isn't possible," etc.) with clear "I" statements as needed. Keep Uniting and focus on the positive thing you are trying to create. Reframe if and when you can.

Reflections on Dealing with an Adversarial Negotiator

- *Are you comfortable with a competitive, adversarial negotiator? Can you stay composed when confronted with one?*
- *Are you able to listen for another's needs under the pressure of their Attacking?*

Disarming Bullies

> *No one can make you feel inferior without your consent.*
> —Eleanor Roosevelt, *This Is My Story*, 1937

A bully seeks to harm, intimidate, or coerce someone perceived as vulnerable. A bully wants you to believe that he (or she) has more power than you do (sometimes they do, sometimes they don't).

Disarming bullies requires a firm connection to our sovereignty, power, moral authority, and yes, a deep knowing that we are not secondary in any way. It also requires an effective use of boundaries. However dangerous they might seem, bullies are often fundamentally childish, immature, egocentric, and unevolved humans. I want what I want, and I want it now!

Being "nice" to a bully, or trying to appease them doesn't work. It can even inflate their power and cause them to go for more. Counter-Attacking, or playing at their level, will only escalate the problem. Instead, be firm! Even if the bully is scary and dangerous, which they often are, try not to be cowed or intimidated. Get support.

A bully wants you to believe that you are vulnerable, you are a victim. You are not! Unenlightened men (and some women) have been acculturated to use threatening behavior to get what they want and control women. Don't bite.

Ask yourself these questions. Does the bully have a monopoly of power? (Probably not, though they certainly want you to think so.) Ask yourself—what do you want? Are there ways to get it without locking horns with the bully? What is your BATNA? Are there ways to simply work around the bully? Ignore him? Detach?

Pay attention to your leverage. For example, Terry Real sees a lot of bullies in his marriage counseling work with high-net-worth individuals. He refers to these men as "masters of the universe" who are used to getting everything they want. He helps these grandiose and powerful male clients think through the consequences of their behavior, for example, losing their marriage or access to their children, both things they don't want. The problem, says Real, is that grandiosity and false empowerment can feel so good, so it can be hard to bring these men down from their (lonely) pedestal even though they are about to lose their marriage.[7]

As Timothy Snyder, author of *On Tyranny*, advises, "Do not obey in advance."[8] Do not give your power away. Any ground you give to a bully he will take, so resist the temptation, even if you are scared.

I appreciated this great modeling of dealing with bullies by a US congresswoman, Alexandria Ocasio-Cortez, when she spoke openly on the floor of the US House of Representatives in response to another member of Congress calling her "a fucking bitch:"

> Representative Yoho put his finger in my face. He called me disgusting. He called me crazy. He called me out of my mind and he called me dangerous.
>
> In front of reporters, Representative Yoho called me and I quote, "a fucking bitch."
>
> These are the words that representative Yoho levied against a congresswoman. The congresswoman that not only represents New York's fourteenth congressional district, but every congresswoman and every woman in this country. Because all of us have had to deal with this, in some form, some way, some shape at some point in our lives. And I want to be clear that Representative Yoho's comments were not deeply hurtful, or piercing to me. I have encountered words uttered by Mr. Yoho and men uttering the same words as Mr. Yoho, while I was being harassed in restaurants. I have tossed men out of bars that have used language like Mr. Yoho's, and I have encountered this type of

harassment riding the subway in New York City. This is not new. And that is the problem. Mr. Yoho was not alone. He was walking shoulder to shoulder with Representative Roger Williams. And that's when we start to see that this issue is not about one incident. It is cultural. It is a culture of lack of impunity, of accepting of violence and violent language against women in an entire structure of power that supports that. I want to thank him for showing the world that you can be a powerful man and accost women. You can have daughters and accost women, without remorse; you can be married, and accost women; you can take photos, and project an image to the world of being a family man, and accost women, without remorse, and with a sense of impunity.[9]

Reflections on Responding to a Bully

- *What do you think works best with bullies?*
- *How well can you hold your ground and not get intimidated by bullying behavior?*
- *Are you able to ask for help or support if you need it?*

Engaging with Heavy or Scary Negotiations

The threat of violence (i.e., rape culture) has been a primary method that men have used to control women, both at home and out in the world. Did you know that home is the most dangerous place for women?[10] Domestic violence is a huge and global pressure on women; across the world, so many of us experience danger in our own households. This has been movingly captured in art installations like one created by a Turkish artist who hung 440 high heels on a building in memory of women killed by their domestic partners, or *The Wall of Dolls* in Milan that condemns femicide and violence against women.[11]

A number of years ago, I watched a documentary on the life of Tina Turner that showcased the violence she endured at the hands of her husband Ike.[12] I related with the feelings anyway even if not the facts. While I've never been a famous musician like Tina, like her I have lived a life with plenty of privilege and opportunity. And like Tina, though the details of my situation were not even closely as extreme or prolonged, I lived with a violent partner. It took me a long time to get out of my denial about this. My ex, once his addiction was in full swing, was scary and often physically and verbally violent. There was no room in our home for anyone's anger but his. He regularly slammed his fists on our kitchen table when he didn't get what he wanted. He was like a two-year-old having a tantrum, but with a big, muscular, scary, adult form. I have many memories of my terrified young children running out into the woods or up into their bedrooms where they could bar their doors with furniture. For years, there was a big hole in our bedroom door where my ex had slammed his fist through it in displeasure because of something that I had said or done.

Years later (as alluded to in the introduction), when I was in Kabul conducting a negotiation program for high-level women in the Afghan government, we did an exercise that involved kicking out the lovely male translators and sequestering ourselves (about forty of us) to a private space where we sat in a large circle and shared our intimate and private stories. I was the first to share. The Afghan women couldn't believe that an affluent American Caucasian woman from a "fine family" might be subjected to domestic violence. But the truth is that domestic violence touches women in homes of all income levels and nationalities.

Violence, war, and the trauma that gets created affects us individually and for generations. We are learning so much about epigenetics and how most of us are born into a traumatic field. That was certainly true for my ex. In the years I lived with him, I worked in both Germany and then the southern United States, where there are still scars and signs of those two huge wars, WWII and the US Civil War. It got me thinking about the connection of these conflicts to the violence I was experiencing in my home.

My ex's story with World War II is long and complicated. His mother was British and a driver in the motor pool in London. He grew up with her stories of lying in an empty swimming pool while watching the bombers fly overhead during the Blitz. His mother's family, once very affluent, lost everything in the war; her brothers became horrendous drunks; and she married a captain in the US Army (my children's grandfather). Eventually they moved to a house with a dirt floor in rural Georgia, with no money for her to buy more than a paper dress. Her father, my ex's grandfather, came to live with them. Once on the pinnacle of London society, a freemason of the city of London, he now had an advanced drinking problem, and while he seemed to have a soul and a laugh, his dysfunctional part regularly caught the yard on fire.

My ex also grew up in rural Georgia and knew a kind of violence left over from Jim Crow and slavery in his childhood that I had not been exposed to in the industrial north of the United States. There were times when he was raging at me that I wondered where he had learned that behavior. What had he been exposed to?

He would jokingly say that he was always "getting the shit off his shoes"—clearing the shame that he carried personally and as a product of the rural South that had been so ravaged and dominated by the North in the American Civil War. When he was angry at me, which he was far too often, he called me a "Long Island bitch" which kind of captured it all—me from the more affluent and industrial North and him from the agricultural south.

These traumas, individual, collective, and ancestral, play themselves out until they are healed.

I used every negotiation tool in the book to save my marriage and get on a better footing. People said, "No one worked harder than you, Susan, to save your marriage." But truth be told, I was a hooked participant, and terrified of what was on the other side. I didn't want the shame I felt would come from being a divorced woman. I didn't want the difficulties divorce would bring for my children or having to manage life on my own. I didn't want to face myself, and the part of me that had brought me to this place.

It can take a long time to accept that you have lived in agreement with an oppression. But this is what you must do. You must figure out how to get out of there and create a new reality. You need to build your BATNA. You need to seek out great support. I thought about Mandela a lot during this time. If he could live through years of solitary confinement on Robben Island and yet stay strong with his integrity intact, I could weather what I was going through.

The day Putin invaded Ukraine (2022), my ex sent me an aggressive email reopening an old issue from our divorce about money. Somehow, it all felt like the same stuff—the domination system.

How do we do we move beyond it to a better place?

First, we need to start with ourselves which is, whether we like it or not, the only thing we really have the power to control. So often we want to blame others for our predicament. In many cases, it is warranted, but blame leaves us powerless because as much as we might keep banging our head against the wall and trying, it's very difficult to make others do what we want them to. A lot of life is an inside job.

We cannot negotiate unless we are willing or able to walk away. The more we build our capacity, our power, our finances, our BATNA, our "fuck you" number, the more we can stay in the conversation, start a conversation, or dictate the terms to get what we want, if that's what we choose to do. Building ourselves up involves building up our physical, security, belonging, esteem, self-actualization needs, our BATNA, our voice, finding our "no," being able to say it and mean it even if the circumstances are dire, getting clear about the present/future of what we want. Self-care will be required here including internal growth, healing trauma, finding a community of support.

This might take the strength and prowess of Athena . . . and is asking a lot of many women around the planet. The story of a woman from sub-Saharan Africa comes to mind. She couldn't muster the courage to refuse to have sex with her husband even though she knew he was sleeping around and HIV was rampant. Perhaps it was the smarter choice. Perhaps her refusal would have ended in her death or the death of her children.

Sisterhood is key because, while there are many enlightened men out there, women need to create support for each other. An enlightened sisterhood is our "union," as the #metoo movement demonstrated. Women standing with women is powerful.

Unfortunately, some women are often our worst enemies. Under patriarchy oppressed men oppress women, and codependent women can operate like "union scabs"—willing to take our place if we object to substandard treatment. When my ex didn't want to accept my request that he stop raging and coming home drunk, he found a woman who didn't mind. When my sisters and I were young women trying to insist on our equality, my brother found a traditional wife who demonstrated to us how a "good" wife was supposed to behave. This kind of societal undermining happens in all oppressed groups—like Uncle Tom for African Americans.

If we fail to embrace the feminine, ignore nurturing our sovereignty, our worthiness, fail to support each other as women, continue to "collude with the enemy," we will never win this game and achieve true gender equality, mission critical I believe for our planet and our children's future.

Reflections on Heavy, Scary Negotiations

- *How can you strengthen your capacity? Grow yourself? Make yourself stronger, more formidable?*
- *If you are living in a less than ideal domestic situation, do you have a BATNA?*
- *How can you strengthen your community of women? Your support system?*

What to Do When Those in Power Refuse to Negotiate

Negotiation is only useful if someone is willing to negotiate.

If you have a poor BATNA and poor chips or chops, you don't have power (at least in a negotiation sense). Accept this, see it clearly, and take action if you want to change things.

When our counterparts won't meet us at the negotiation table, we have many options to shift the balance of power. Typically, in Western countries, when negotiation doesn't resolve things, people first seek redress through the courts. But, when that doesn't work, and those in power have overwhelming power and are genuinely not willing to negotiate, we must consider what I call "Corrective Action," the strategies that change the balance of power to make negotiation possible.

Corrective actions can be nonviolent or violent. I personally don't believe in violence and don't believe it works better than nonviolent methods in any case. I'm with Thoreau, Gandhi, Martin Luther King, Gloria Steinem, Mother Teresa, Malala, John Lewis, Scilla Elworthy, Rabia Roberts, and the tens of thousands of pacifists and peace activists who have advocated for nonviolent options. When you spank a child, you are communicating use of force. Violence begets violence. War creates more war. Hurt people hurt people.[13] When I imagine someone hurting one of my children, I feel a tremendous fierceness in me and can understand the desire for retribution. But there is too much "offending from the victim position" in our world, and the more we learn about generational trauma, the more we learn how long it takes to unravel cycles of violence. Holding out the possibility of a collaborative outcome is important.

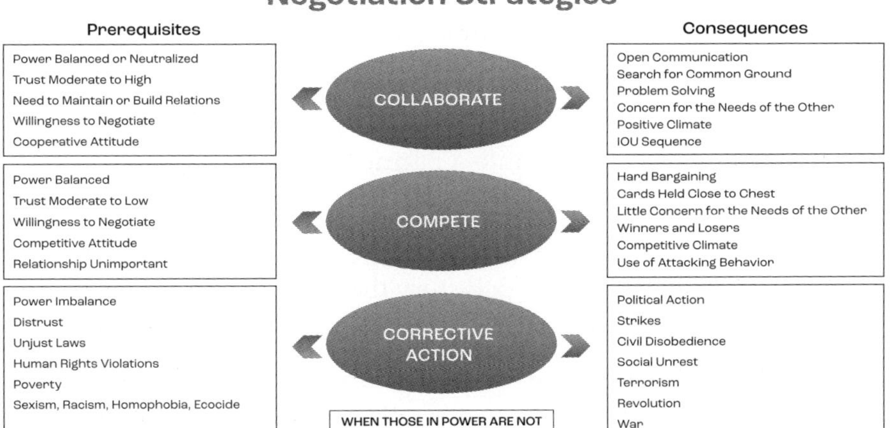

The stories of corrective action that are working to dismantle the domination system and create a more enlightened world are many, including

- scientists and explorers helping us understand our cosmos and dispel religious fundamentalism,[14]
- enlightened educators,
- legal activists that have changed laws around the world to create a more gender-equal world,
- therapists and trauma healers,
- activists and organizers for gender, climate, and racial justice,
- those building democratic institutions to ensure ballots over bullets, and
- conflict resolution professionals and peacebuilders who are creating group processes (both small and large) to resolve conflict and build common ground.

To summarize, when power is unequal or negotiation isn't working, we need to find our wisdom, and our courage, find each other, and say no to what is unacceptable. Dealing with bullies and oppressors is hard and requires us to transform the domination system into a partnership one—at home, at work, and in the world.

In the words of Mahatma Gandhi, "When I despair, I remember that all through history the way of truth and love have always won. There have been tyrants and murderers, and for a time, they can seem invincible, but in the end, they always fall. Always."[15] Let's remember that a man in a simple loincloth brought down the British empire.

Reflections on Dismantling the Domination System

- *Do you believe there is a place for violence?*
- *Are you politically active?*
- *What kinds of actions do you take to dismantle the domination system?*

CHAPTER 10
Fire Up Your Money Power

God bless the child that has "her" own.
—paraphrasing Billie Holiday

It was about 2010. I was in midtown Manhattan on my way to the Charles Schwab office. It was one of the first of my many visits to get myself ready to do what I knew I had to do.

My estranged ex had repeatedly threatened, "If you touch that money in Schwab, you will trigger litigation." He was referring to a joint account we had that had virtually all of our liquid assets. I had been cowed by that threat in the past but was increasingly letting go of its hold on me.

A few weeks later, while my husband was on a stoned-out dalliance in the Caribbean with my son's best friend's mother, I made my move. I called Schwab, and with my heart racing and my hands trembling almost uncontrollably, I instructed the male Schwab representative on the other end of the phone to divide our account exactly in half, giving my ex the benefit of the doubt if there were securities that couldn't be evenly divided.

It felt like I was violating some deep rule that lived inside of me—breaking a code that was not to be broken.

But when I looked online and saw that the transfer was 100 percent complete, I drew a big sigh of relief, and a smile of satisfaction crossed my face. I texted my ex to let him know.

I mark the true beginning of my financial freedom from this moment.

My ex was livid, gushing expletives, threatening, and demanded that I put it back. But it was my money every bit as much as it was his, in spite of his claims to the contrary. I told him I would do no such thing. I knew he was returning from the Caribbean and felt I would need protection for a while, so I called the cops and described my ex's blue Porsche. He was good with guns and good with anger. Neither of those were my forte.

This is my story, but I know how many versions, regardless of economic class, there are all over the globe having to do with women, money, power, and threats of violence. I know how frequent it is in all corners of the globe for men to feel they have a proprietary interest in women's resources, as they do our bodies, and how often we let them get away with this. I know also how much, especially when money is involved, the "burned at the stake gene" can light up for many women.

My money story is a complicated, topsy-turvy story. First, I was choosing to be "downwardly mobile" and leave behind the shackles of my economic class in order to contribute to a more just and equal world. But then, I was also trying to be "upwardly mobile" when it came to not giving my power away to men—my brother, my ex-husband—around money. I wanted to be strong and capable in my own right with the ability to use money well, have what I need, and be able to give from overflow.

I now do my best to have enough money so that I have what I need for me and my family, including some extra, enough so no one can control me, get paid what I am worth, and be of service. I'm also doing my best to tread lightly and with humility on our fragile planet with the food that I eat, the clothes and things I buy, the travel that I do. I'm not a purist, but moderation, generosity, and contribution are the values I strive for.

The Money Hex

> *Sooner or later women are going to realize*
> *that they are the slaves of the earth.*
> —Warren Buffet, as paraphrased by
> his first wife, Susan Buffett

If we really want to understand what's going on, in a family, an organization, a country, the world, follow the money. Women's relationship with money is really about power—our ambivalence about it and men's ambivalence about giving up the control it provides them with women and the world. Indeed, in general, how we as women are about money is parallel to how we are about negotiation and about power.

It would be a big oversight to write a book about negotiation for women without exploring the topic of money. Many negotiations are about money and many are not. But follow the money and you will see pretty clearly what's going on in the world in terms of gender equality, how it is impacting women's lives everywhere, and what we might do to change it. We face many external obstacles as women, but the codependent money hex inside most of us, along with class warnings to stay in our lane, we luckily have the power to change. As Marley sings, nobody but us can free our minds.[1]

What I like about money is that it's a very clear metric. When I feel a need for more control over the chaos and complexity of life, I sometimes find just balancing my checking account, whatever the balance is, to be calming. It is specific. It is tangible.

But what is money? And what does it represent for people? Money can mean so many different things: love, time, freedom, status, power.

But money is money. In the end, it is simply a means of exchange, a tool, to get our needs met.

Money doesn't have any intrinsic value in and of itself. It's only valuable because we make it so. I remember having a conversation with a multinational group at the UN about what people valued the most. An Irish man said that in Ireland people value "a person who can tell a good story." The Americans in the group agreed that, in the United States, it is "money."

Many societies throughout time have lived well without money. Maybe we will live well without it again in the future. Money is based on made-up systems. And when it comes to gender, it is a made up (and false) fact that men should have and control the money and resources on the planet and women should not. In the realm of negotiation and money, articles or blog post titles like "Asking for More" and "Negotiating Salary" resonate with many women, but, at the end of the day, our attitudes about money and early messaging can run deep and affect us in identifying what we truly want and asking and negotiating for it.

Strangely, the strongest message I got about money from my family of origin came from food. My mother, like many women of her era that were dependent on the male gaze, was always in "fighting trim" (staying thin) as she put it. When food was put on the table, the largest plates would always go to my father and brother, and the smaller portions would go to my two sisters and me. Indeed, my mom would glower at me if I added more food on my plate. It's no coincidence that this later translated to my brother being super rich and lavish with money and my two sisters and I suffering from both physical anorexia and serious underearning given our education. The message was, accept less money and resources, make yourself attractive for men, and take care of them so that they will take care of you.

I know I am not alone in this. There are powerful messages in the zeitgeist about female appetite—who should have, who should receive. These can be hard to release from our cell structures. Awareness is always the first step—but we must release these internalized messages if we are to be powerful in negotiation.

One day, at a summer picnic in a small upstate New York country town, I sat next to a young, good-looking White man in his thirties. He wore a golf cap on his head that said St. Barts (a fancy Caribbean playground for the rich and famous). He had just landed a new job and was bragging about the great perks and salary. When I mentioned something about gender, he assured me that he got what he got because he had asked for it. "Women don't ask," he said.

He was smug, and annoying. And I could feel how much our culture likes to pay these types of guys. Money just flows to them naturally like a moth to a flame. While there is some truth to his comment, it also defies the subtle and not so subtle cultural coding that is passed on to all of us about who has permission to ask, and is able to receive.[2]

I am not proud to admit that over the years of parenting my two kids—a daughter and a son—there was a subtle way that I was inclined to give more to my son than to my daughter. When I noticed this, I stopped aghast. There is absolutely no reason he deserves more than they do; it was just my deep conditioning that I should give more money to the guy so he could take care of things.

Do not fool yourself. How much food gets put on your plate has much to do with your salary, your ability to ask for a promotion, your sense of self-worth. We each need to look at our inner programming and rewrite the script. Plenty of women succeed in bucking the cultural narrative. Oprah is an amazing example. But way too many of us are still swimming against the tide.

Linda Babcock, a researcher in the field of women in negotiation, did some research with men and women about twenty years ago using the game Boggle.[3] Basically, the idea was that everybody who came to play would get $3. They were told they could get from $3 to $10, but then everybody, after they played, were given $3. Afterward, eight times more men said, "Hey, can I have more? Why didn't I get $10? How come I only got $3?" And the researchers immediately gave that person the $10. The women did not question what they had been given. This experiment inspired more research to look at what women's choices about even negotiating in the first place were about. Babcock updated her research, by again interviewing men and women. This time she asked them whether they negotiated their first job offer, and only 7 percent of women did and 57 percent of men did.[4]

The conclusion? Women need to ask. But let's not just blame the victim. Women have been trained to accept what we are given and not ask for too much. I remember once getting "a look" from the matronly gatekeeper whose job it was to set our rates at the firm where I was working. I had asked for "too much" and she looked at me with scorn. Many of us have been punished for asking. We can get our wrists slapped.

There's also research that suggests that even when women do ask, we often do not receive.[5] There can be backlash. At times women are penalized when we ask for "too much." Let's face it: We have often been, and remain, cheap labor. We need to be aware of this hex and claim our power around money.

In the spirit of "We can't change anyone else but ourselves," I find it helpful to look at patterns that undermine us with money, some that I have observed in myself and see in other women. See if any of them look familiar.

- Asking (or manipulating) men to take care of us . . . and being controlled as a result.
- Staying childlike around money.
- Not claiming value that is rightfully ours and not allowing ourselves to receive it when it comes our way.
- Being unwilling to "bite the hand that feeds us."
- Overgiving. Serving. Being the slave.
- Staying foggy-headed and in "learned helplessness."
- Enabling men: allowing them to remain falsely empowered.
- Failing to know and realize our equal value.

Reflections on Our Patterns with Money

- *Do you depend on a man (or others) for your financial well-being? If yes, how do you feel about that?*

- *Do you get foggy-headed about money? What might you do to change this?*
- *Do you ask men (or others) to manage money for you when you are capable of doing it for yourself?*
- *Have you failed to claim value because it felt "unladylike" or you didn't want to upset a male ego? Did you figure you would be more liked if you didn't assert yourself around finances? How did this ultimately impact you?*
- *If you are experiencing financial difficulties, who or what do you fantasize might rescue you?*

Build Your Money BATNA

Does money give you power? What do you think?

"It's not the money that's going to give us power," says money expert Barbara Stanny. "I don't believe that money gives you power. Money has no power. It's the process of who we have to become to be good stewards of our money. We have to become a powerful woman . . . Dispelling the Prince Charming myth is the most important financial decision you will ever make. But rest assured, it's the myth, not the man, that has to go. You can have your prince. You just need to change the job description. He's no longer your rescuer or your savior."[6] So very true and well-said. A man is not a plan. Relying on men for our survival sets us up for an age-old dynamic among women of scratching and clawing to make sure you get the best guy and that some "bitch" doesn't take him away from you.

It is true that our internal money hex can hold us back. But there are also external realities. My daughter shared with me this definition of a feminist from transgender lawyer and activist, Chase Strangio, that is profound: "To me a feminist is someone who works to destabilize the ways in which systems of gender operate to inequitably distribute survival opportunities for different individuals and groups. Critical to this project is recognizing that gender does not just operate on individuals but is inextricable from systems of governance."[7]

Money gives us power because it gives us options. To a large extent money is our BATNA. The person who has the most power in a negotiation is the one who is least dependent on its outcome. If we are not overly dependent on the outcome, we have more power in the negotiation and can walk away.

In job and salary negotiation, we need to have our alternatives at the ready. We need to know that if a situation doesn't work out, we'll find another. Don't give up your alternatives too early—"Oh, I like that offer; I'll stick with that"—and stop negotiating with others. Nope. I have always marveled at my highly successful friend Sarah who has been a master of keeping many irons in the fire throughout her stellar journalism career. She moves from one great job to another because she always keeps her alternatives alive.

Maria told me that she wanted another $10,000 when she was negotiating her annual salary, but she could only take the $7,000 she was offered because she didn't have any other options. That's just real, and sometimes we just need to play the best game we can with the hand we have.

Many women are stuck in relationships because they don't have the money to leave. This is especially true for women that are on a lower rung of the global money hierarchy created by a PWC. Money gives us the ability to leave, the power to walk away from situations that don't serve us. But money isn't our only alternative support; a powerful community or group of friends as well as voting for policies that support our well-being can provide us with an important social safety net. To negotiate with power and pull the plug on situations that no longer serve us, we need to build up our financial, social, and political resources.

So, think about it, do you have a money BATNA? What will you do if things don't work out and you need to walk away from either a personal or professional situation? Knowing your answer to this will give you power as you proceed with any given negotiation.

Negotiate Money

For many women, negotiations around money will always feel like a "difficult conversation." But, in the end, these conversations are just negotiations. All the same principles apply.

What are your interests? What are theirs? What can you offer them (chips) that will meet their interests? (Having great chips in negotiation gives you power to influence.) What can they offer you that will meet your needs? Are your values aligned? Can you work with them? What are your options if this negotiation doesn't work out? What are theirs?

One of the things that can make money negotiations so difficult is that we can be so crazy about money. Many of us tie money to our self-esteem. I once heard Gloria Steinem say that she would like to go to Harvard Business School and let them know that money is boring. It's not all that it's cracked up to be! As usual, go Gloria.[8]

Here are some tips for engaging in negotiations over money.

Do Your Homework Beforehand

What is the standard in the industry for the type of work you are doing? What are others getting paid for similar work? Luckily, in many venues, increasingly there is pay transparency. Advocate for this. It disrupts bias.

Allow Yourself to Receive

We need to allow value in. To receive. This counters the deep indoctrination that our role is to serve and provide emotional labor, sex, and so on. Women tend to give and so very often overgive.

Ask for More

A mom recounted to me, "My daughter got a job offer, and after she got the offer her existing employer gave her a raise. So, she went back to the prospective employer and said, 'Oh by the way, they've given me a raise; will you match it?' That's it," the mom said. "I just think that's amazing." She went on to tell me that, although the prospective employer didn't match it, the mom was gobsmacked that her daughter had "stood up for herself and asked for the raise." She then went on to tell me about herself. "In my situation, as a nearly sixty-seven-year-old woman, I have never negotiated on my own behalf for a salary. I have never said 'no,' or 'hold on, let me think.' Now I need to negotiate some new terms, and I'm aware of my tendencies and I'm committed to not approaching this in the habitual way I have approached this in the past."

And Keep Practicing Asking for More

Most of us ladies (you know who you are) need to keep practicing asking for more. When my ex was a political media consultant, he would come up with his proposed number and then double it. He usually got what he wanted. I wasn't capable of doing that at the time. Now I make sure the number feels fair and meets my needs.

Know Your Value and Don't Underestimate It

One of my blog subscribers was inspired, after reading one of my posts about asking for more and said:

> I read yesterday's post on the way to work where I had a meeting w/ senior ppl . . . about the impossible overlap facing me this summer with (two) projects. Your newsletter talked about knowing your value, and being prepared to walk away, and in the middle of the meeting I said: "guys, my plate is full now and I'm not in a place in my life to add more so I need to figure out the right support. I have a toddler, I don't work after 5, it will be summer and I will need to take a few weeks off and she starts school in September. So, if I'm overwhelmed and am jeopardizing my life, I will walk away from one of these projects in a minute. You could hear a pin drop and then they thanked me for my honesty. It completely changed the dialogue. In a follow up meeting (the senior person modified my assignments) "The goal," she announced, "is for ___ to be able to do her best work."

Talk to a Woman Mentor

Another woman, a colleague in the field, wrote this:

> I realized, at a certain point, that I was great at negotiating for other people, but I still struggled to do it for myself. I've talked to a lot of professional women who have felt the same way. Then something happened to me; for the first time ever I went in to negotiate my salary. I was super nervous, and then their number came in above what I thought! I kept my face neutral, told them I'd run the numbers, and left. Then I called a senior woman in the field and I said, "What do I do?" She told me, "Go in and ask for more, because when you do you teach someone how to value you. You teach them how to value all of us. So, if you're not going to do it for yourself, I want you to go in and do it for the woman who's coming after you . . . think of it as doing community service."[9]

Ask for 10 Percent More

Another women similarly responding to my suggestion to ask for more said: "As I told you, I was accepted to (very competitive graduate program) with a scholarship. (Your post) gave me the courage to ask to be considered for more funding from the program."

And, I took my own advice. As I was writing that post, I was in the process of giving a quote to a long-standing client and added 10 percent to the contract, which I got.

Focus on Your Target, Not Your "Bottom Line"

Your target is your ideal number; your bottom line is what you will settle for.

Too many people focus on their bottom line. Big mistake. Here is counsel from Diana, a seasoned woman lawyer:

> Ask for the range (it might be advertised). Don't get pinned down on what is the minimum you will accept. There's no reason to accept the minimum. Say to them, "I'm certainly hoping you will view me based on my experience, my expertise, my reputation, and my references, as being worthy of the top of your range. And if you don't give me the number that is based on my experience, I'm hoping that you will share with me how you feel I fall short of the top of the range. And assuming you hire me, perhaps we could discuss how I could develop the skills that you feel that I lack in the next six months."

In General, Don't Reveal Your BATNA or Urgency

When you are in an "arm's-length" negotiation (a transaction where parties are independent of each other) involving money, be thoughtful about revealing your alternatives or your urgency about making the deal.[10] If your BATNA is weak, your counterpart might push for terms that are less favorable to you. If your BATNA is strong, the other side might become less motivated to negotiate.

Know What Is Enough for You

There is no objective "good" or "bad" outcome in a negotiation. The question is: Did you get your needs met? Are you satisfied? Did you build a good relationship with your counterpart in the process? I am lucky to have both an excellent therapist and an excellent financial advisor. Both could charge a lot more for their services, but they don't, because they want to make themselves accessible to people and neither is greedy. Just because you charge a lot, or you make a lot of money, doesn't make you some kind of superstar. Charging big bucks all the time for everything is a byproduct of the PWC.

In the end, the best negotiation outcomes involve maximizing needs satisfaction for both you and your counterpart. Build relationships; enjoy the process. Think generosity and abundance. Split the difference in the end if you can as that always has a great feel to it. Relax. Show up whole-bodied with confidence, integrity, and a touch of divine force energy.

Reflections on Messages about Money

- *Where did the messages you received about money come from?*
- *How would you like to rewrite them?*
- *What are your inner obstacles with money?*

Putting into Practice

Practice asking.

Practice asking for more. Add 10 percent.

Let's Step into Our Global Money Power and Change the World

Look at who owns the world. A few (mostly White) men own the bulk of it. From Elon Musk, to Jeff Bezos and Putin, the Bolsonaros, the Obregons, the "Davos Man," you can see that domination is profitable.[11] That's why patriarchy persists.

Money flows to men on this planet like an ingrained neural pathway in our collective human brain. It's deep in our global cultural conditioning, a deep psychic or magnetic vortex as old as patriarchy itself, that men should have the money, manage it, decide about it, and, as women, we should let them do so, especially if they have lighter skin. There are, of course, exceptions to this, but this is the basic current global money pattern.

As the currency of patriarchy with its one-up, one-down worldview, money is currently revered in so many parts of the world, most especially in my country. There is almost godlike status given to the relatively small number of megabillionaires on the planet and somehow an assumption that their brilliance and superiority, rather than rigged systems, false empowerment, and greed, have gotten them where they are and entitle them to control political systems and over-consume, especially when it comes to our rapidly diminishing carbon budget and planetary resources.

A justifying narrative persists that there are the "makers" (often White men) who produce value that trickles down to the rest of us. Unless we decide to put this idea to bed, it will continue to have big consequences for women's dependence on men, democracy, and the health of our planet. For example, Trump's win in 2024 was a clear demonstration of the billionaire power of the PWC—from his billionaire and fossil fuel–endorsing cabinet picks to the selection of the richest man in the world, Elon Musk, as his unelected sidekick, to his agenda to pressure women back to their traditional roles.

But what if we as women, half of humanity, say no?

What would it be like if we as women fully stepped into our money power? Can you imagine a world where women hold the same money power as men and are no longer held captive by men's money? And while we're imagining, can you envision an equitable distribution of planetary wealth in general?

It's impossible to have real democracy with deep income inequality, and impossible to have true gender equality without democracy. Deep income inequality creates a lot of instability because people's needs aren't being met which, as we know, creates conflict. So much comes down to who is going to get resourced in the world. How will resources flow? Who will get supported? Who will not? That's what the big battles are about. And the big negotiations.

How we spend our money says a lot about what we value as humanity. There is no reason that women shouldn't be making half the decisions about how our planetary resources are spent—indeed, perhaps we should have control of even more than half given the fact that the world needs our sensibilities and tendency to care.

Recent research has shown that, in the coming decades, there is consensus among financial analysts that women will increasingly control a larger share of planetary wealth due to factors like inheritance, longevity, and increasing financial independence. In the United States, for instance, the data shows that as much as 70 percent of all wealth will be transferred to women in the twenty-first century.[12] There also is evidence that women make different choices around spending than men. Says finance expert Barbara Stanny:

> Unlike men once we are financially stable, women are rarely motivated by more money. What drives us is knowing we can use our money to improve the quality of life for ourselves and for others. Women will yawn and glaze over when it's just about money for money's sake but get more fired up when we begin to see the power of helping our families and communities.[13]

Men often spend money on status-related items and appear to be more comfortable spending money on the military, guns, and violence. Donald Trump, for instance, has made deals to sell arms to Saudi men and Wahhabists, the most patriarchal men on the planet who use those arms to drop bombs on innocent people.[14]

It's time for women to pay full attention to what we really want to do here. It's time for us to take charge and claim access to money in ways that reflect our different choices in how to spend it. Do we agree with how our planetary resources are being spent? How are we contributing to a PWC that doesn't serve us; for instance, how many dollars are each of us spending on the beauty industry itself?[15] And how much of that goes directly to lining the pockets of (mostly) men? Why are we willing to spend anything and everything on creams, powders, potions, and treatments to look young and firm and ageless? Why are we willing, particularly in the West, to be "good consumers" in spite of what that is doing to our planet?

I heard a story about a Medicine man from the Achuar, an indigenous region in the Amazon rainforest of Ecuador, who had come to the United States to learn about Western culture. After some months, he called his US host and asked, "Where are your women?" After observing what he saw going on in the United States, he said that he thought American women should stop American men from building such huge houses and cities. "That's what men do," he said. In his culture, he said, it is the women who say, "Enough. We have enough canoes. Stop cutting down trees."[16]

So, what is enough? How do we as women answer this very critical question?

The US war system is hugely profitable to some and very costly to all other people and life—approximately $2.5 trillion a year.[17] Women stepping into our power is key to building peace on this planet. Because money is the currency of power, getting smart about money goes hand in glove. How we earn and spend our money matters. There's a big difference, for example, between making money from empowering women versus selling automatic weapons. Women and especially Western women have a great deal of power when it comes to building a more peaceful and sustainable planet. We can invest in ourselves, invest in the feminine, and no longer sit it out on the sidelines.

When enough financially independent women reach critical mass, we'll have the resources, values, vision, and sensitivity to heal this planet and change this world.

Time is of the essence.

Reflections on Stepping into Our Money Power

- *What can you do to strengthen your money power?*
- *Do you feel confident about managing your finances?*

- *Do you have a money BATNA?*
- *Do you believe that women in leadership will generally make different choices about how to spend resources?*
- *If you had all the money in the world, how would you spend it?*
- *What is enough? What is adequacy?*
- *What are your internal obstacles to having the money that you need and want?*
- *What are the external obstacles that you experience?*
- *What has worked for you in negotiating your compensation for your work?*
- *What are your recommendations for other women?*

CHAPTER 11

Reclaim Your Body

> *For women, there is an ocean of sadness for all of us . . . every single one of our bodies remembers in some way, shape, or form that five thousand years ago, before patriarchy, we knew a worthiness in our own bones, we knew a rightness in our own skin, we had a sexual power and a spiritual power that had not been taken from us, every female body remembers that intrinsically . . . it has been thousands of years since any woman on the planet was allowed to live with that kind of power and greatness.*
>
> —Layla Martin, Jade Pleasure, 2020

I was a strong little kid. Athletic. Well-coordinated. I could win any race, beat up any boy, do anything that a boy could do. This fundamental sense of myself in my body gave me the confidence to do the work I do in the world today—but later, when I began to feel inferior for not meeting a certain "feminine" standard, it was the reason I shut myself down.

By the time I was fifteen, I was anorexic and bulimic, and by the time I was sixteen, at a prep school for high-achieving girls, I was down to skin and bones. I thought I looked terrific.

I was leaving behind childhood and entering the world of being "a woman." In this new grown-up world of the culture of that time, my good brain was an asset, sure, but what was far more important was how my body looked in the world of men. It was supposed to be slight, dainty, anorexic. In other words, without power.

My brother made sure I understood that message. Throughout my childhood, if I was slightly chubby, he would call me "thunder thighs." I swallowed a stereotype that his debutante girlfriend, who became my sister-in-law, was the precise standard of beauty that I was not and felt ashamed.

My childhood home on Long Island was right next door to the private and very elite Rockaway Hunting Club (RHC). RHC didn't allow either Jews or Black people, and it preferred its women to be coiffed, blond, and thin. The Jewish club was a few miles away. The Black country club didn't even exist, at least in my awareness.

Like most country clubs, tennis and golf were big features. My mom played tennis, and so did I.

RHC was the kind of place where everyone had to wear white, and everyone was White. It had exquisite grass tennis courts, so nice that the US Open contestants always came to have a warm-up tournament with us before going on to Forest Hills for the real deal. I got to be the ball girl at those events, crouching way behind the back line at the mesh fence, or at midcourt by the net pole and relaying the balls back to the players.

My mother and her friends played a lot of doubles, all nice ladies in their whites, and sometimes it was mixed doubles (men and women), and often I played too.

I have good memories for the most part.

But over time, my awareness grew about the nature of the club next door. The fact that it didn't allow Jews or Black people began to offend me. During this same time, my awareness grew about the war raging in southeast Asia—the horrors being regularly broadcast on the nightly news of bodies, napalm, little kids whose skin had been scorched off. As early as twelve, I remember sneaking up in the early morning hours with trepidation to put a peace sign on the RHC front door.

In 1970, at the age of fifteen, I went away to boarding school, where I played on the high school tennis team. By the time I got to Hampshire College, a school that was dedicated to gender equality, global transformation, and change, I didn't really want to have anything more to do with tennis. It represented something I didn't feel comfortable being part of anymore, like country clubs in general, or having my name in the Social Register, a special phone book for elites so they could stay in touch. I was alienated from that world. Turned off.

Little did I know, while I was letting that world slip through my fingers, two Black sisters, Venus and Serena Williams, who would never have been allowed at the RHC except as the help, were coming up behind me to profoundly transform the world of tennis and all the things I didn't like about it. Both Venus and her younger sister Serena broke all records of what people thought was possible, especially from two Black girls from the low-income neighborhood of Compton, California. While both their stories are incredible, I will focus on Serena here.

In 1998, Serena Williams won her first US Open. She violated just about all of the protocol for women at the RHC. First, she had thick arms and thick legs. She loved her body and she showed it off to the stuffy world of tennis. Instead of the dainty white skirts my mother wore, she wore a black cat-suit with diamond navel insignias. She looked like she was going to a Janet Jackson concert. She put weaves in her black hair and brought a lot of Black culture to the world of tennis and didn't apologize for it. She made a lot of White people very uncomfortable.

The staid world of tennis didn't know what to do with Serena Williams or that kind of Black power. Her body was a thing of authority. And she let her emotions rip. The world of tennis expected her to be "ladylike," to withhold emotion. In their worldview, she behaved like a man, which was not allowed. She was constantly accused of disrespecting the sport.

But for all the Black and Brown people, especially little girls watching, she opened up a world of the possible. And she was healing me and the ways that the cultural metaphor of anorexia was still telling me to stay small, not have, and not receive.

I am so grateful to Serena Williams for being in agreement with herself, and for her amazing manifestation of what is feminine and what is power. And I am so grateful to her, and others like her, for blowing the lid off of White patriarchy and the ways it limits so many of us of any skin color, for modeling liberty in who each of us can become as women—strong, embodied, capable, unstoppable.[1]

The Body Does Not Lie

It makes sense for the last chapter in this book to be about the body because that's where it all begins. Everything begins with the body; everything is the body. The body does not lie, and it does not lie in negotiation.

Dogs are great role models. My dog, Jocelyn, can be fierce and has an outsized bark. She can get into ferocious fights with other dogs and has been known to nip a person or two. While some of this behavior is due to the poor guidance of her owner, some is just because of the wild soul she is. Jocelyn can sense pretty much immediately whether someone feels confident or like a victim. Unfortunately (and noteworthy for negotiation), she barks more aggressively at people who are scared, and she settles down quickly at the ones who are confident.

One weekend, a young guy who didn't know either me or Jocelyn, but who was coming to stay as a guest, arrived at my door. He gave a brief knock and good-naturedly opened the unlocked door before I had time to answer. At the sound of the knocking, Jocelyn went ballistic (as she always does), but in two seconds, the guest was down on his knees, and Jocelyn was licking him in the face. "Unbelievable!" I said. "You are lucky. She can be pretty fierce."

"I love dogs," he said with a big smile.

Dogs know it. Our own sense of confidence and calm communicates powerfully to dogs.

Negotiation books and other management literature recommend various body postures that demonstrate embodied power to help you increase your impact. Cross your arms or don't, put your arms behind your head, strike power poses, stand up with your arms outstretched, use this stance or that. Some of this advice is worthwhile. I have used some of it myself. But no tool or technique can take the place of a deep knowing of your own worthiness and confidence in your bones. Nothing. My dog is a great reminder that most of us can intuitively spot whether someone is in their confidence or not. Whether we want to or not, we transmit our core state just about—instantly.

We can't talk about negotiation without talking about the body. If we don't know inside of ourselves that we can get what we are after, that we deserve it, and that we can receive it if we get it, our body will give us away. Every time. Many aspects of the ways we have internalized patriarchy and believe in our secondary status won't be immediately obvious, but the body communicates it quickly.

Negotiation, especially for women, is an embodied experience. Connecting with the animal of the body, our voices, speaking our truth, and standing boldly in our sexuality and understanding the strength of our motivations and focused intention all speak volumes nonverbally. The more integrated we are with our bodies the more powerful we can and will be as negotiators.

Studies show that approximately 90 percent of communication is nonverbal. In high-context cultures, where people pay as much attention to who is speaking, tone of voice, context, and body language, it is more like 100 percent. In low-context groups, where people are not as attuned to nonverbal communication (e.g., White men), it might be significantly lower.[2] But no matter how good an actor you are, a simple move of your body, even a slight grimace, can reveal your inner state.

I once delivered a negotiation training in Lisbon with a Portuguese colleague named José Calisto Santos. I don't speak Portuguese, but José is a native. We were going back and forth between the two languages, and during an exercise I noticed a group negotiating exclusively in Portuguese. Though I was familiar with the material and could follow a bit because I speak Spanish, I was able to get the gist of what was going on mostly by listening to tone and watching nonverbal body language. I could see when there was conflict and I could see when there was agreement. After the exercise, they affirmed that my interpretation of what I saw was correct.

Women the world over have received messaging that we should be demure, defer, accommodate, apologize, make space for men, be tentative—and all of this shows up in our bodies. While we need to be kind to ourselves about this, we need to recognize it. It takes time to undo deep conditioning, but undo it we must. The mind can change fast, the heart more slowly, and the body the slowest of all.

In my early thirties, after years of dieting and inflicting other various forms of body-hatred on myself, I said to my therapist, "I no longer want to spend so much of my valuable life energy thinking about food." While this was the culmination of a long journey, the decision came to me one day while I was walking down the street in New York City and had heard what women passing by were talking about. Food, weight, and diets were high on the list. Then I read *Fat Is a Feminist Issue*, by Susie Orbach, which helped me transform.[3]

What does it mean to somatically decolonize our bodies, get all that we have absorbed from a PWC out of our cell structures? What does it mean to no longer collude with the "might makes right" of a dominator worldview? What does it mean to own the tremendous power of our sexuality and our life-force energy for ourselves? What does it look like to show up full-bodied and whole, to own the totality of our presence for our own desires and preferences, for our own command of the world, for our own pleasure, and not just for the male gaze? What would it mean to know with certainty for ourselves and the women around us the rightness, beauty, and power of our physical selves, whatever body shape we are or desire to be? What would it mean for our power as we negotiate and lead?

Mother Nature Has Anointed Us Powerful—Let's Own It

We can understand a lot about human life by looking at how nature has structured the "more-than-human" world. First and foremost, reproduction is central to plants, fish, bears, and insects. Nature is pro-life, pro-creation, and pro-female with strong messages about how powerful and critical women are. Everything in nature is all about reproduction and the female of all species is central to this endeavor.

Our bodies as women are first and foremost about creation. We are the egg producers. Our uteri and birth canals are the center of the human form and central to human existence. We have breasts to nurse our young, wide hips to birth them, and more oxytocin to have patience with them. As V (formerly Eve Ensler), the author of *The Vagina Monologues*, says, "My vagina is right in the center of my body and right in the center of the world and it's the one thing that no one in the world talks about."[4]

Everything starts as XX, female, and the original human form is female. The fact that the clitoris is the only human organ that appears to have no other purpose than pleasure with our eight thousand nerve endings to the male's four thousand is a strong message from nature about how things should be ordered—for the pleasure of the female, so that we will want to reproduce life.

Women can reproduce without men with more ease than men can reproduce without women (perhaps a core reason for why authoritarian men want to restrict our reproductive freedom). Nonetheless, despite women's inherent and rising power, there is a crisis of self-confidence among women all over the planet. When Jacinda Ardern, former prime minister of New Zealand, was asked what most stood out to her about women and leadership she commented, "The pervasive lack of self-confidence."[5] There is also a boatload of body shame among us women. These two things—shame and our feelings that our bodies are somehow secondary—are connected. But how can this be so?

Our dear Sigmund Freud, the grandfather of modern psychology, believed that women were inferior men, humans without penises. He saw women's bodies as somehow deformed versions of a man's body.[6] In my life, I can certainly attest to the oh-so-many cultural messages I've received that the penis is of central importance and to be revered, especially in the act of sex, which itself is often an act of negotiation. I grew up looking at the phallic Washington and Bennington monuments to wars. I did not see any monuments that corresponded to female anatomy, which was often unmentionable and a source of shame. All things related to female genitalia were considered dirty. My mother called menstruation "the curse." My ex-husband couldn't bring himself to say the word "menopause." As feminist author Adrienne Rich said, "I know of no woman . . . for whom the body is not a fundamental problem."

As Mama Gena recounts in her book *Pussy: A Reclamation*:

> One of the greatest pieces of unconscious conditioning we have . . . is that we do not teach our children the name of the source of our feminine power. Ask my students . . . what they were taught to call their genitals as a child, and you'll get a parade of colloquialisms: Wickie, Cuckoo, Privates, Down There, Pooter, Pee Wee, the fine China, Name and Address, Venus, Noonie, Miss Kitty, Purse . . . Those who were often

> taught a more direct word were often taught to call it "vagina," a clinical term that is also physiologically incorrect. But what's worse, the majority of women were taught to call it nothing at all. When we have no common language to describe that which is most essentially feminine about us, we have no way to locate and own our power as women.[7]

In spite of our epidemic of self-critique, the fact that female sexual pleasure has so often been ignored in the PWC, the primacy the penis is given, women are not humans without a penis as Freud might have had us believe. Indeed, we are not missing a thing. Self-hatred and the critique of our bodies are just more of the patriarchal hex.

I like to start my day by grounding myself in my body. I use a routine called The Five Tibetan Rites, a system of exercises reported to be more than twenty-five hundred years old.[8] I do this naked looking out at the forest. The first pose is standing arms outstretched, left hand facing down, right hand up in preparation for circling (clockwise in the Northern Hemisphere). When I get into this pose, I always feel like the essential human, kind of like the *Vitruvian Man,* painted by Leonardo da Vinci, but I think "Vitruvian woman."[9] My female form, with my breasts and hips, is like the first human on the planet, which would be especially true if my skin were black.

How do we embody power, feel the rightness of our female form? The breath is always our first entry point. And there are all of our centers of intelligence—our head, our heart, our gut, our pussy. All of these brain centers give us critical information. We need to trust them, trust the whole of us to rely on our full-bodied "yes," and our full-bodied "no," to guide us in life and in negotiation.

Reflections on Our Bodies and Power

- *In what ways does patriarchal conditioning show up in your experience of your body?*
- *How do you embody your power?*
- *Does your sexuality/life-force energy support you when you negotiate? How so?*
- *Have you been ashamed about your sexuality and erotic power? Is your erotic power your own?*
- *Do you insist on your orgasm and pleasure when you have sex? Can you see how this might be connected to your power in negotiation?*
- *What are some ways you can more deeply incorporate knowledge of your sovereignty and worthiness in your body when you negotiate on your own behalf or for others?*

Putting into Practice

Stand at a mirror naked and look at yourself. What's your experience? Do you approve of what you see?

Scan your whole body, feet to crown. Do this slowly. Breathe. Can you feel the power of your body?

Rape Is Not Part of the Bargain

Les Moonves was chairman and CEO of CBS Corporation and one of the most powerful men in the US media industry from 2003 until his resignation in September 2018 following numerous allegations of sexual harassment, sexual assault, and abuse. Illeana Douglas, an actress and writer and one of six women who publicly accused him, recounted what happened to her to Ronan Farrow of the *New Yorker*, who wrote one of the major stories to break open the #metoo movement.

> When Douglas met with Moonves at his office, she began to raise concerns about the "Queens" script, but Moonves, she recalled, cut her off. "He interrupts me to ask me am I single," she said. Douglas, whose nearly decade-long relationship with Scorsese was coming to an end, was caught off guard. "I didn't know what to say at that point," she told me. "I was, like, 'I'm single, yes, no, maybe.' " She began talking about the script, but Moonves interjected, asking to kiss her. According to Douglas, he said that they didn't have to tell her manager: "It'll just be between you and me. Come on, you're not some nubile virgin."
>
> As Douglas attempted to turn the focus back to work, Moonves, she said, grabbed her. "In a millisecond, he's got one arm over me, pinning me," she said. Moonves was "violently kissing" her, holding her down on the couch with her arms above her head. "What it feels like to have someone hold you down—you can't breathe, you can't move," she said. "The physicality of it was horrendous." She recalled lying limp and unresponsive

beneath him. "You sort of black out," she told me. "You think, How long is this going to go on? I was just looking at this nice picture of his family and his kids.[10]

I couldn't get him off me." She said it was only when Moonves, aroused, pulled up her skirt and began to thrust against her that her fear overcame her paralysis. She told herself that she had to do something to stop him. "At that point, you're a trapped animal," she told me. "Your life is flashing before your eyes." Moonves, in what Douglas assumed was an effort to be seductive, paused and asked, "So, what do you think?" Douglas told me (Farrow), "My decision was to get out of it by joking my way out, so he feels flattered." Thinking that reminding Moonves that he was her boss might discourage him, she told him, "Yes, for the head of a network you're some good kisser." Moonves frowned and got up. She scrambled to find her briefcase. "Well, this has been great. Thanks," she recalled saying, moving toward the door. "I've got to go now."

Moonves, she said, followed her to the door and blocked her path. He backed her up to the wall, pressing against her, with his face close to hers. "It was physically scary," Douglas told me. "He says, 'We're going to keep this between you and me, right?' " Attempting to put him off with a joke, she replied, "No, sir, we won't tell anyone that you're a good kisser." Moonves released her and, without looking at her, walked away. "It was so invasive," she said of the threatening encounter.[11]

As #metoo demonstrated, this is just one instance of a huge problem that women need to contend with when we assert ourselves at home, at work, and in the world. In spite of the fact that we are living in the twenty-first century, the instances of women being forced to provide sex as part of the bargain are rampant. With #metoo, record numbers of very powerful men lost their jobs. But at the time of this writing, there has been a backlash most publicly realized by the 2024 election of Donald Trump, a convicted felon who brags about grabbing women by the pussy and appoints sexual predators to his cabinet.[12]

My shorthand for the fundamental paradigm of a PWC is "rape culture," the objective of which is domination, control, and extraction for value. It's an old story. The "prey" have been Black people, Indigenous cultures, poor people, nature, the nonhuman world. Ground zero of this paradigm has been men over women.

Rape culture "noise" is in the backdrop of every negotiation large and small for women. Few of us miss the essential message of rape. Rape is about power-over. It says, "You are weaker, so follow, serve, accept your secondary status, or suffer the consequences." As we have seen in Bosnia, Rwanda, Vietnam, and more, rape is also modern warfare—"quiet, cheap, and scarily efficient."[13] Business as usual. We should just accept it as normal collateral damage.

So many of us see the world through our assumptions about gender and power, and very often even the experts are unaware of this lens. Recently, I was at a workshop with trauma specialist Bessel van der Kolk, author of *The Body Keeps the Score*, along with sixty other participants, mostly younger women. In his presentation, van der Kolk showed a film clip of his work.[14] Then, without warning, he showed a clip of a woman entering her apartment followed by two men who did not have a key and, presumably because they were well-dressed, were allowed in the door. As she went up the stairs, the men assaulted her with their arms around her throat. The footage fast-forwarded, and we didn't get to see what happened next. Then, without commenting on the scene, van der Kolk continued with his talk. But I felt sick. Women all around me in the theater audibly groaned and sighed. Van der Kolk, a trauma expert, didn't appear to notice. He was more interested in demonstrating his acclaimed intervention techniques and bragging about his work with groups. I was furious. I raised my hand to tell him so. "You needed to warn us before showing a scene like that. Ninety-five percent of your audience here are women." He dismissed me. Shaking, I left the room. Dozens of women followed me outside to express appreciation for my courage in letting the "big guy" know.

When patriarchy started to take hold thousands of years ago, we moved from a world where the erotic and women's sexuality were celebrated to one where we had to cover up and be ashamed. As Rabia Roberts recounted in my podcast:

> Goddess cultures were highly sexual. Spirituality and sexuality for a couple thousand years seemed to go together everywhere from Turkey to Egypt. You see it in paintings and in architecture . . . it wasn't only the Goddess that the patriarchy wanted to get rid of, it was sexuality. As patriarchy gained force, it created imagined orders, hierarchies, narratives in which women became less than and the property of men. [15]

It can be maddeningly hard to free ourselves from all the ways the PWC is baked into our relationship with our bodies. I have always understood that the very word "woman" comes from the phrase "womb of the man" and that vagina means "sheath for a sword" and was named as such by Julius Caesar. Whether this is accurate, untangling the implications of that lexicon for anyone interested in creating a more feminist, collaborative, and peaceful world is deep work. The landscape of our bodies has left so many scars—from foot binding in China to brutal female circumcision practices and unwanted pelvic exams when under anesthesia worldwide. I have a foggy memory of going to the male doctor in high school and him fondling me. I didn't have the awareness or the courage at the time to tell him that this was not OK. Many of us carry different variations of these stories.

"Women are objects of sexual desire rather than subjects of sexual pleasure," writes sex educator Emily Nagoski, PhD, "where sex is used as a weapon against women; and where women believe their bodies are broken, simply because those bodies are not male." The hymen and the metaphor of "breaking it," for example, she says, has nothing to do with biology and everything to do with controlling women.[16]

Negotiation in an ideal sense is about giving and receiving, but in a PWC, it is often about male supremacy. Take the metaphor of heteronormative sex. If males are more valuable, who gives pleasure, who receives it? When I was an adolescent and learning about sexuality the dominant message was "You must please the guy" and "Don't leave him sexually frustrated or give him 'blue balls.'" I was taught that women did not have the same kind of wants and needs that men had and that women were not as sexual as men. And so on. These were powerful messages that went to the deepest level of my being. I was conditioned as a woman to give, to serve, to focus on male pleasure rather than my own.

A male sex therapist told me that some men get aroused by the idea of "bloodying a pussy because their cock is their sword." His words reminded me of a scene in Stanley Kubrick's film *Full Metal Jacket* (1987) when US Marine recruits parade with their weapons doing a chant of, "This is my rifle, this is my gun, this (seizing their gun) is for fighting, this (seizing their crotch) is for fun."

Much of the degradation of the feminine is far more subtle than outright abuse. Examples include being made to feel uncomfortable breast-feeding our baby in public, being afraid to look and feel sensual for fear that we will attract unwanted attention (and then be blamed for it). It is also at the heart of how we can dim ourselves down in negotiation.

The lucky among us don't go through life consciously thinking of living in a "rape culture," but if we look, we can see signs all around us, with women, the less powerful, not to mention the natural world. To create a world where a New Negotiation is fully possible for all women and girls, we need to say a collective no to rape culture. It is not an acceptable use of influence or persuasion in a new world order.

Reflections on Sexual Violence and Rape Culture (Please Be Gentle with Yourself Here)

- *How has sexual violence impacted you?*
- *Was your body safe in your family of origin? In your intimate partnerships? Is it safe now?*

- *In what ways has "rape culture" impacted you or women around you in your/their ability to negotiate?*
- *What do you need most to heal?*

Reclaim Our Bodies for a New Negotiation

In April 2020, the evening before I released a podcast called "Reclaiming Our Bodies for Negotiation," I wrote the following in my blog:

> The topic of the relationship between negotiation skills for women and the body evokes a lot in me, enough to wake up at three a.m. before recording this podcast, to write down these thoughts.

- First (as my last guest, mystic Thomas Hübl, suggested), the feminine is the body;
- My body didn't belong to me for a lot of my life;
- My sexuality also didn't belong to me until I did the work to reclaim it;
- Regarding the phrases "I want" and "I need," which are so important in negotiation, I was taught that I was not supposed to have wants, and I'm not sure about needs either. As a girl in my family, I was supposed to serve, and I was supposed to accommodate;
- It was hard for me to have a clear connection to my "yes" and particularly to my "no." And, if we are not connected to our "no," it can be difficult to walk away from a negotiation—which is fundamental to power;

- I didn't feel safe claiming value—a popular negotiation concept—because I was taught so deeply that I was supposed to let a man do that;
- Although I have cleared out a lot of unhelpful acculturation throughout the course of my life, I'm aware of the depth with which these ideas still live in my body.

Martha Eddy, a dance therapist specialist who works with women and their bodies, said, "I'm not aware of cultures that really uplift the strength of the female, and the value of the female, such that the female body, or our experience as females in a body, comes forth as power just automatically. It's climbing uphill, it's swimming upstream to reclaim it."[17]

Trauma expert Thomas Hübl refers to patriarchy as a "frozen trauma structure" in our bodies until we are able to release it. It's like a process of "chimney cleaning." The more we do it, the cleaner we get, the less reactivity we experience, the more we are able to come fully into the present, no longer triggered by unseen ghosts in our being.[18]

So how do we do this?

How do we release ourselves from the ripples of patriarchy and come forth as powerful, sexy, fully present beings who know how to negotiate with presence, collaborative force, and leadership? While there are no shortcuts to putting in the time and doing the work, here are a number of ideas and practices I have found useful.

Use Your Triggers as Guides for Healing

Whenever I feel triggered, I feel into what I need to heal. This puts me in the driver's seat and keeps the focus on what

I can control. Presence is fundamentally a state of having cleared out trauma. We disassociate when we experience a trauma trigger. When we have cleared it, we are more able to show up and stay present and whole-bodied with the pride and knowing that we belong. We are not imposters; this is our planet!

Let me give you a relatively small and subtle example from my own life. I was in Panama getting ready to facilitate a high-level meeting of UN representatives. I had been dating a guy who wasn't emotionally available. He reminded me a lot of my brother—a sure setup for triggering old trauma. But he had recently put things on hold in order to return to his old girlfriend. Nonetheless, he called me in Panama.

I was thrilled to hear from him. In my love-addicted swoon, I ignored the fact that the reason he called was to tell me that he and his old girlfriend had had a fight. What the f—? Why should I want to know that?

Later, while relaxing on a remote island in San Blas off the coast of Colombia, I read *Educated*, the powerful memoir by Tara Westover (2018) about her life growing up in a fundamentalist Mormon family in rural Idaho where the father rules and women submit. As a kid, one of the ways my older brother would torture me was to get on top of me, tickle me to make me laugh, and then spit in my mouth. Just like Tara, who told a similar story, I didn't feel I had the power to say "no" to my brother. While reading the book I realized that if had I learned to say "no" then and had been backed up by my family and culture, it would have been easy for me to tell this current guy to bug off. In my bones, I would have known not to accept such stupid crumbs. It has been years of inner work to get my brother's abuse out of my body, but I have mostly done it. We can collectively clear this kind of harm and as we do, we will become increasingly formidable.

Feed Yourself

Anorexia and dieting are just two ways that women internalize the patriarchy and crush their own sense of self-worth. My life journey has been largely one of moving from anorexia to self-love. My body has led the way. Owning our full-embodied selves is fundamental to our self-confidence and critical for our power to influence. If we are always "just in our heads," we lose a lot.

Allow me to return to a moment at the end of 2017 when I was with a group of about twenty women, all of us naked before a great roaring fire. One at a time, we stated our intentions for the year to come. Mine was to "rid myself of my codependence on men and my anorexia around money," which were inextricably linked.

Flash back a few years prior to that when I was sitting in one of my Gestalt groups. One of the group members gave me a beautiful compliment. "Susan, you have so much compassion for the world," she said. I tried to skip over it quickly, but then Veronica, the facilitator extraordinaire, slowed the process to a crawl. "Where do you feel the compliment in your body?" she asked. "About midchest," I said, pointing. She asked me to take it all the way down into my belly and to truly absorb it. It seemed so simple, but it was a very powerful moment, a great healing to my anorexia. I no longer was a dieter in any way by then, but I was still challenged with receiving.

When my daughter was a teenager, and anorexia was running rampant around the girls in their high school, I said,

"You must feed yourself, honey. You must feed yourself." There's a cultural prohibition against female appetite. Women have been taught to take care of everyone else, not to desire, not to have. Standing for what we want begins with knowing what we desire and following through on it. How can we claim value for ourselves and others if we are not supposed to desire, want, or have in the first place? Receiving what we have negotiated for begins with connecting to our desires and being able to receive them when they come to us.

Pay Attention to Your Pleasure

Have great orgasms! No kidding! Do hip circles. Look at yourself in the mirror and see how beautiful you are. Connect to your life-force energy. Ignite yourself. Dance!

To negotiate with power, we must first be aware of our power and the erotic is its greatest source. It lives inside us; it is there for the taking. The self-described Black, lesbian, mother, warrior poet Audre Lorde provides some guidance in her famous piece "The Power of the Erotic" (which she points out is opposite of the pornographic).

> THERE ARE MANY kinds of power, used and unused, acknowledged or otherwise. The erotic is a resource within each of us that lies in a deeply female and spiritual plane, firmly rooted in the power of our unexpressed or unrecognized feeling . . .
>
> As women, we have come to distrust that power which rises from our deepest and non-rational knowledge . . . [19]

Take Up Space

One day, while I was working on this book at the library, three White men came in and started talking loudly. They were clearly friends. I looked over at them and tried to communicate with my eyes that it would be helpful if they lowered their voices. They acted like they owned the place (which they probably did). They kept up for a long time until the librarian came and asked them to be quiet.

When I worked as a young lawyer, an older White, male rich banker once told me that the way he navigates the crowded streets of New York City is to simply put his head down and walk, because others move out of his way. He was trying to be nice and coach me on how the Wall Streeters do it. I remembered this teaching when I came across a humorous article titled "Walking like a Man," authored by a female reporter who had observed the walking patterns of men and women on NYC streets:[20]

> What happened was that women got out of the way. What happened was that I realized something: Women had always gotten out of the way. Without even making eye contact, we'd automatically rotated around the sidewalk like two repelled magnets. What happened was that men ran into me. Not all of them! Not most! But in every crash, it was a gentleman charting the collision course. Suited ones, mostly. Ages 30 to 50. Sometimes they were on their phones, sometimes they weren't. Sometimes they registered my presence, sometimes not. And then—well, I can't explain it any other way, they ran into me at full speed. They'd apparently expected, via decades of

experience, that I'd move, and so it never occurred to them to.

Dress for You, Your Pleasure, and Confidence

When I worked as a litigation associate at the corporate firm in New York City, I had to wear professional business attire that, at the time, mostly looked like a female version of what my father had worn in all his years practicing law on Wall Street. Over the four years, I amassed the right kind of stuff—Paul Taylor and Brooks Brothers suits, Ferragamo shoes—to match my well-dressed male colleagues. Eventually, I quit this job, went back to school, got married, and ultimately moved to where I live now. No longer vibing with those clothes, I stored them away in a closet.

Eckhart Tolle, a spiritual teacher, talks about the importance of noticing "signposts" on our life journey. One signpost in my life said it all: When I went back one day to look through all those expensive suits stored in the closet, they had been eaten by moths. All of them had to be thrown away. The image served as a good metaphor for what needed to happen with my professional transformation, and perhaps it's a good metaphor for all women as our presence transforms the world of work. Man-mode is over. It is time to step into the feminine and explore what that really means for all of us. What would work look like if it was made up of our voices, our sensibilities, our instincts and values, our leadership? That moment with the suits signaled my time to find out. It would take many years to do so—and it's still a work in process.

Fast-forward to the Roosevelt Hotel 2018. I found myself in the very spot of a large ballroom in which I had taken the

Bar Exam in 1983. But this time I was wearing pink hot pants, fishnet stockings, and a T-shirt that said, "8000 nerve endings at your service." I was part of "Team Pleasure," the volunteer group for Mama Gena's Mastery program and daydreaming about how to build a world beyond patriarchy.

I see so many professional women now dressing in fantastic ways. It's awesome. I used to dress for others. Now I dress for myself, to keep my self-esteem, confidence, and life-force energy high. Of course, I pay attention to what works with a particular client or setting, but first and foremost, I pay attention to what works for me.

Create a "Room of One's Own"

One of the greatest acts of self-care can be providing yourself with a safe space to retreat to as needed. In her memoir *Just As I Am* (2021), the American actress Cicely Tyson remembers how important keeping her apartment was for her sense of serenity in her relationship with the wonderful but chaotic and addicted Miles Davis. This, of course, takes financial resources, which many of us don't have, but the concept still applies. In negotiation language, it is making sure we have a BATNA. We need to have a place, especially in our negotiations with our intimate partners, where we can walk away. A simple corollary to this is to take time for ourselves, take care of ourselves, and "put the mask on our own face first," as they say on the airplane. When we take care of ourselves, it shows up when we negotiate.

Reclaim Your Body for a New Negotiation

"I remember attending an African feminist conference," recounts Nobel Peace activist Leymah Gbowee,

> where high-powered women sat in a circle and were each asked to name our private parts in our native language. Most of us couldn't—we had been taught through our socialization that we shouldn't touch that area or talk about it. As someone who has spent all of these years doing this kind of work with women, I realized that subconsciously I still didn't have that kind of authority over my own body. We have to make sure that we don't pass these taboos along to the next generation.[21]

Our bodies and our sexuality have not belonged to us and for many that is still the case. We might be well-educated, we might have been taught excellent business, legal, and negotiation skills, but if we do not own our sovereignty, it will transmit in negotiation—like a dog who can sense who is vulnerable. This is why we need to reclaim our bodies. We must know them, own them, and cherish them. It is time to transcend the cultural narrative that has left many of us self-abandoning and ashamed.

Reflections on Reclaiming your Body for Negotiation

- *Describe where your confidence and power reside in your body.*

- *What steps might help you further reclaim your body for yourself and your power?*
- *How does how you dress impact your ability to negotiate?*
- *How practiced are you at articulating your desires, the ones that come out of your body, not just your head? How free do you feel in your body to negotiate for what you want?*
- *Ask your sexual partner for something that you have not asked for and that would turn you on. If you don't have a partner, do this for yourself.*
- *How do your feelings about your body impact your ability to negotiate and lead?*

EPILOGUE

A Way Forward

> *I sat at a lunch table with a professor of pre-monotheistic spirituality, plus several women from some of the tribes in this state that has more Native Americans than any other. All agreed that the paradigm of human organization had been the circle, not the pyramid or hierarchy—and it could be again. I'd never known there was a paradigm that linked instead of ranked. It was as if I'd been assuming opposition—and suddenly found myself in a welcoming world; like putting one's foot down for a steep stair and discovering level ground.*
> —Gloria Steinem, *Ms. Magazine,* 1986

Here are two snapshots from my professional past.

In the first, I am in my early thirties, a corporate litigation associate at a firm at Rockefeller Center in New York City. I am sitting around a darkish boardroom in a man-mode suit but with an ear cuff on my ear. I am the only woman in the room, with a dozen or so men. A number of them are smoking cigars. As I observe them taking long puffs, I am wondering if the cigars aren't actually making them a little high.

The second image is an amalgam of hundreds of circles I have facilitated or attended over the last number of decades around the world. My clothing is flowy. My man-mode suits are gone. I am in New York City, I am in South Sudan, I am in Colombia, I am in Afghanistan, I am at the UN, I am with family businesses, Gestalt groups, community activists.

In the first snapshot, I am part of a process that is more masculine—rights, rules, and power-over. I am a gladiator of sorts. In the second, I am facilitating processes that embody the feminine—a focus on needs, contact, connection, deeper listening, and relationship-building.

In the first, the shape is a pyramid; in the second, it is a circle. It is more of the circle, the feminine, that we need to urgently build and grow now.

Alexander Calder, an artist, became famous for his mobiles and he inspired me. I was obsessed with mobiles as a child. I made them out of everything—from chestnuts that had fallen off nearby trees, from yarn and two sticks, and even from dyed eggshells. The ceiling of my bedroom was covered with them. I would lie on my bed and watch them rotate and swirl delicately and in balance with each other. Later, when I became interested in psychology, I came across the work of Virginia Satir, who emphasized the importance of understanding families as systems and compared them to mobiles—when one part moves, it affects every other part of the system. During my professional evolution I learned that to negotiate and resolve conflict well, we need to open up the process and think systemically. We need to get "the whole system" (see notes, Introduction) in the room, if we can, to work the issue. The adversary system that I learned in law school and practiced for a short time, us against them, two poles, is too simplistic, too binary, and nowhere near as effective at reaching common ground.

I began this book scanning the world with a systems lens[1] so it is fitting that I now end it with that focus. It's easier to resolve conflict, to negotiate, when we are thinking systems, circles, and more holistically.

In the early 2000s, I was forced to apply more of a systems lens to negotiation when I was asked to provide collaborative negotiation and mediation skills training to political representatives from Iraqi Kurdistan as part of a larger capacity-building initiative funded by the US State Department. The participants would be representatives of the PUK and the KDP, the two main political factions competing for political control, which had resulted in armed conflict.[2]

The task I was given was to design and deliver a five-day skills training in negotiation and mediation to build an atmosphere of collaboration between the two sides that would serve as a force against Saddam Hussein, who was still in power at that time. None of the participants spoke English and I did not speak Kurdish or Arabic.

When you hear "training," think school. Training is like that, a teacher in front of the room, the students (ideally) attentive in chairs. I knew the limits of training from a systems perspective: that the focus of change is on each individual participant more than the group. I suspected it wouldn't be enough; we needed a whole group shift. A training modality would also require all communication to go through me and the translator. Necessity is the mother of invention and, as I sat with the conundrum of how to design this, I landed on the idea of using a process called Open Space Technology ("OST").[3] I had heard many great things about OST but had never facilitated or been part of one. But my intuition told me that this process would allow participants to have direct and safe contact with each other, in other words, to negotiate directly in a way that could possibly create transformation and change.

OST, a highly collaborative process, allows participants in conflict to self-organize and create their own agenda. It can be done with groups from five to two thousand. While it is not called "negotiation" or conflict resolution, that is, in fact, what is happening. Participants are in full control of their experience and are trying to directly influence or persuade their counterparts as part of a large group conversation.

When the participants arrived in New York from Ankara, Turkey, the atmosphere was more than chilly. People sat on opposite sides of the room and avoided eye contact and all conversation. Group members had lost family in the war between these two sides. For these representatives, this was a paid trip to New York, an opportunity to go to Columbia University, but a passion for reconciliation was not in the air.

We started the intervention in negotiation training mode with direct translation and covered many of the ideas I have discussed in this book including, critically for these participants, an understanding that collaboration makes much more sense when there is interdependence. The group had a strong eureka in that moment: They realized that collaboration made much more sense for them rather than the armed and adversarial conflict they had been engaged in.

The training mode was useful initially in that it allowed us to mix up the two sides in seemingly arbitrary and face-saving ways to resolve simple conflict issues that had nothing to do with their current reality. It helped to de-escalate the polarizing tone. People laughed and got playful with training type games. We gradually increased the complexity and heat of the issues, ending by role-playing PUK/KDP real-life issues. Participants began to see that what they had been experiencing in Kurdistan was largely the same as what people experience everywhere in conflict—whether it is interpersonal conflict or intergroup. The predictable recurring phenomenon of adversarial conflict was normalized.

On day four, we "opened the space," and got out of training mode. Participants were introduced to the theme we proposed for the dialogue, which was "Exploring and Expanding Areas of Cooperation Among Us."

To our surprise and concern, most of the participants took us literally when we said, "We have breakout spaces, but you are free to go anywhere you like." Indeed, they left and rode the subway from 125th to Macy's at 34th to shop, which caused us, me especially, a great deal of anxiety. But eventually everyone returned, packages in hand, and seemed ready to talk to each other. The good news is that everyone had taken us at our word when we said, "Wherever you are, whatever you are doing, be here at 4:30 for 'evening news.'" That's when things started cooking. One by one, participants summoned up the courage to hold our "talking stone," and share about how the Kurdistan issues were weighing on them. The stone, they said, often a weapon of war in Kurdistan, was now a symbol of peace.

The momentum continued through "morning announcements" on day five to various topic discussions to an exciting action planning session on ways they could work together. Day five ended with hugs, tears, and the singing of Kurdish songs. In the following months and years, a joint conflict resolution center was formed and more OST processes were convened to further the work. The tangible outcome was the creation of a bilateral conflict resolution center that supported on-the-ground collaboration in many ways. The less tangible but no less profound outcome is the way our program design continues to ripple throughout Iraq and other places.[4]

I am proud of this piece of work. It inspired me to launch my podcast, *The Peacebuilding Podcast*, a few years later in which I emphasize the use of large-group, whole-system processes to expand direct negotiation to build common ground and resolve conflict. Since that time, OST (and many other similar whole-system processes) have been used in just about every country on earth by thousands of practitioners.[5] It is simple, cheap, and most of the time successful in helping people directly negotiate with each other and arrive at a way forward with seemingly irreconcilable differences. OST and processes like it are to adversarial dispute processes what solar and wind energy are to fossil fuel. In both cases, a PWC pushes back on ways that can help us create a cheaper, better, more democratic world quickly.

We need to think systems and circles. Just look at the natural world. When I first learned about the work of Suzanne Simard, a forest ecologist, I was listening to a conversation with her on a podcast and taking a walk in the woods behind my house where I have gone thousands of times.[6] As I was listening to her speak, I started to cry. It was as if for the first time, I truly saw the community of trees around me that I had seen so many hundreds of times before. I noticed my human-centricity and felt shame. It was as if I'd been living as though if something wasn't on my radar, it didn't exist.

Listening to Simard I learned that trees help each other

and talk to each other. They use underground networks to communicate and cooperate with each other (which is a very different understanding compared to what scientists previously thought about nature). Trees send resources back and forth (carbon, nitrogen, water, and even defense signals) and send resources to trees that might be struggling under stress. And just like the case with negotiation theory, until recently forests in much of the world have been managed on a competition/individualism model with the assumption that each tree is an individual competing for resources. Simard found that while there is some competition going on, trees are all connected—kind of like a "hive-mind" that shares resources. The bigger and older the tree, the more connected it is to others. These are the "mother trees" in aboriginal cultures. Young seedlings regenerate from mother trees. When a mother tree gets ready to die it deliberately passes its resources onto its "children"—shoveling carbon toward them. I find this so moving.

This is the feminine.

When asked about how we might use collaboration in the midst of what seems to be mounting polarization in the climate crisis, Christiana Figueres, a Costa Rican diplomat who led the global negotiation process that culminated in the 2015 Paris Agreement, said:

> The irony is that collaboration is the natural state of affairs. If you look at nature, that's the way nature operates in any ecosystem . . . And, if it's true for nature, it's true for us because we are nature. . . and so if we get in touch with that which is our natural state of operating, then collaboration is what we would

do . . . Everything else is what we have learned either during our lifetime, or . . . handed down and inherited. And that's very unfortunate. But it is clear that in the past twelve thousand years, what we have done is disassociated ourselves from nature and from our own natural state. Starting with the agricultural revolution when we went from being hunters and gatherers to . . . putting picket fences around property, and around women that also became property, (this) allowed us to extend our presence throughout the entire planet with the exception of Antarctica and to . . . give birth to what we today call modern civilization. There have been positive attributes to this of course . . . The issue is though that the price that we (have) paid is to disassociate ourselves from nature instead of having a collaborative inclusive state of mind (that is) in alignment with nature. We . . . began to develop much more of an extractive mindset where we got used to extracting either fossil fuels or minerals or metals or wood from the forest . . . the origin of the extractive society that has led to climate change today . . . I think it is important to question whether an extractive mentality is truly who we are. I don't think so. I think it is learned behavior . . . either consciously or unconsciously, and so in order to get back to our natural state of thinking and acting, we have to unlearn it . . . Collaboration is the way that is more natural to us, so for me it's not a huge reach, "oh my gosh," we are being confrontational now we have to change and be collaborative . . . I think it's about pausing, looking very deep, and really asking ourselves: What is the nature of our interaction with

> ourselves, with others, and with nature? . . . We are deeply rooted in collaboration, (and) it's about getting back to who we really are.[7]

In 2002, I decided to enroll in the "Organization and Systems Development" program, "Gestalt OSD," at the Gestalt Institute of Cleveland. My husband at the time was not happy about this at all. Indeed, he said to me on a number of occasions, "If you do this program, it's going to ruin our marriage." Even though I didn't believe him, I did the program anyway, and it was, as he predicted, the beginning of the end of our marriage. Gestalt OSD strengthened me, helped me get way more powerful in our family system and be able to stand up to him. One of the scariest moments in our marriage's dissolution was doing a well-orchestrated whole-family addiction intervention with a skilled facilitator from an alcohol recovery institute. The point of the intervention was for my ex to hear from his kids, his friends, and me about the destructive impact of his drinking and behavior on all of us and get him into treatment. As the experts say, addiction is a family, systemic disease. He refused and instead was irate, furious, told us all to go to hell, and took off burning rubber out of the driveway.

Fast-forward to a few years later, after my divorce: I found myself in a war zone, at a UN peacekeeping mission. Things were imploding at the mission because of a dysfunctional leader, falsely empowered, very much like my ex. He was making everyone crazy—from the top of the system to the bottom. I orchestrated an intervention with all parts of the mission that included negotiation and mediation training, mediation and coaching of a few important individuals who were fighting, and large systems change work. But the work that I did with the leader was very much like what my family had done with my ex. Even though the language and setting were different, we were essentially doing the same thing—speaking truth to false and dysfunctional power to a guy who ultimately did not have the emotional maturity to be in the position that he was in.

I felt very confident in what I was doing. I would never have been able to do it had I not first experienced my family intervention. What you can do at one "level of system," you can do at another. I've repeated this kind of professional intervention in many places over the years—Gabon, Washington, DC, the Central African Republic, and elsewhere.

When we think conflict and we use negotiation, we need to think systemically. Our families and our workplaces, schools, and international organizations are the building blocks of our world and as we transform them to become more collaborative and feminine-infused, with all the conflicts that occur in them, we transform our world, from home, to work, to world.

Feminist academic Valerie Hudson has said home is the "first political order."[8] Children learn what they live.[9] Family systems become organization systems, which become world systems. Home is where children learn about gender roles and how, or how not to, negotiate and resolve conflict. If children learn a basic message of the equality of all humans and the need to respect and care for each other, they will bring that message with them out into the world. If they learn the rule of the father as patriarchy dictates, that women are somehow secondary, or a one-up, one-down worldview, they will bring that with them as well. The home is where kids get their first instruction about influence, domination, and about fairness. Whatever we learn there, we take with us into our intimate partnerships, our parenting, our workplaces, and into our global politics. We will repeat what doesn't work to the extent we have not reflected on it, done the inner work, made different choices, and created new behaviors and cultures. Notably, study after study shows that more egalitarian marriages—which often involve dual careers and always encompass shared housework and decision-making—unequivocally lead to higher rates of marital satisfaction than do "traditional" marriages.[10] Similarly, studies show that a key to a successful marriage or intimate partnership is negotiating and resolving conflict well, using a collaborative strategy which seeks commitment, not compliance, coercion, or submission.[11]

In our workplaces, in the last fifty years or so, women have left home and entered the workforce in droves which has arguably been the largest change to organizational life in this time period.[12] We have succeeded mightily. But, as #metoo revealed, many of our organizations are not always so welcoming to women. Many of us struggle with imposter syndrome as if it were a pathology, but to a large extent, we are imposters. The world of work was developed by men to "bring home the bacon" to their families. Work was designed by men, for men and it's not surprising that work culture is still largely masculine. As management consultant Peter Hawkins put it to me, "Modern organizations were designed for twentieth-century White men, not twenty-first-century human beings."[13] But luckily things keep moving forward in spite of relentless regressive pushback.

What's auspicious about organizations is that they commonly have an internal education and training function that can shift culture and awareness with greater facility than what often happens behind the privacy of a family (although, of course, "DEI" (diversity, equity, and inclusion) is under attack in many quarters). Women who need and want to work, and the men who support our inclusion, are faced with making workplaces work for us. What are our needs when it comes to work? Should we take on the challenge of transforming the cultures of established organizations, what some call the "brotopia"? Or, should we just start from scratch, like I see women doing now in record numbers, and create our own thing because "the master's tools will never dismantle the master's house."[14]

Whether we work from the inside or the outside, what does it mean to create a postpatriarchal workplace? What does it mean to "bring the feminine to work"? And how does this impact how we resolve conflict, and negotiate in our work lives? This is a "negotiation" of large-scale proportions. Using a needs assessment lens can guide our efforts including, for instance, the need for childcare, flex time, a balanced, humane schedule, and so on. Much of the pushback against DEI happens from people whose narrative is win-lose, zero-sum, "women will take good jobs away from family men," women need to stay in the home, and blah, blah, blah. Let's not go down that rabbit hole.

And on the world stage? In the words of Kristina Lunz, founder of the Centre for Feminist Foreign Policy, "The most significant factor toward whether a country is peaceful, within its own borders or toward other countries, is the level of gender equality. So, it's pretty easy; it just means that there won't be any peace without feminism."[15]

Ninety-nine percent of our time on earth, there was no evidence of war and men and women lived together in harmony. Now, it is clear that modern warfare is not solving any of our problems, but is only creating them, and making a small few (men) very wealthy. It can be a stretch for many to believe, but an active peace is possible in our lifetimes. Empowering women across the planet, with the deeper democracy that comes with it, is the single most important way to get there. It is possible we can return to the gender balance of the masculine and feminine in humanity's prepatriarchal times.

Conventional wisdom has it that war is inevitable but it is not. As negotiation specialist William Ury has said, "I believe peace is entirely an achievable goal. I've been involved in wars and conflicts for thirty-five years and every one of them, if you thought about it, was predictable; there were signs and it was preventable."[16] We have research-based evidence that indicates that preventing war is not difficult, says Dr. Scilla Elworthy:

> We know what we can do and we know what we shouldn't be doing in order to get war to stop—we just haven't done it. The first thing we need to stop doing is spending $1,686 billion annually on militarization. $30 billion would eliminate starvation worldwide and $10 billion would bring clean water to every child on the planet. Many people haven't noticed how enormous this spending really is and how much it is costing society.[17]

The Dalai Lama has spoken often about the power and potential of women as peacemakers.[18] Are we? Is this our nature? I believe the majority of us are uniquely designed for this mission. As we realize the power of our voices, we need to recognize our natural power, we need to see it, own it, and claim it.

We are the ones to say a collective and firm no to violence on this planet. Females in many species, elephants, whales, insects, keep male violence in check. Female elephants kick males out of the herd when they are violent.[19] Similarly, Ury tells a story from our close primate cousins—the bonobos—about the power of what he calls "a winning coalition:" "When the male bonobo gets aggressive with a female, I have often observed the other females responding by building a coalition. The females will line up shoulder to shoulder like linebackers on a football team and slowly back the offending male away. It's as if they are saying, 'Back off, big guy. You've gone too far. Now behave!'"[20] Women as half of humanity can do the same. We can cross the lines of tribe, color, and culture and stand together to create a world beyond war.

While popular culture has it that Mother's Day in the United States is simply a Hallmark holiday to buy cards for our mothers, the original Mothers' Day was started by Boston reformer Julia Ward Howe in the 1870s when she created it to bring women together to end war.[21] In 2000, the United Nations adopted Resolution 1325, which emphasizes the importance of women's participation in peace and security efforts. It recognizes that women are often disproportionately affected by conflict, and that our inclusion in peace processes can lead to more sustainable peace agreements.

In Dr. Elworthy's words:

> A balance of women in negotiating teams has been shown to help reach a peace deal that lasts longer. A statistical analysis of 182 signed peace agreements between 1989 and 2011 revealed that peace agreements

where women are involved are 35 percent more likely to last for fifteen years.

- women are not usually instigators of cycles of violence
- use intuition to enable parties to understand what's needed in the moment
- do not have the male need for revenge
- have an ability to speak truth to power, without provoking hostility and violence.[22]

In other words, we are essential to stop wars and violent conflict. But we need to be at the table. In Ury's (2024) book *Possible: How to Survive and Thrive in an Age of Conflict*, he recounts countless stories of the skillful interventions in the most publicized conflicts of the last number of decades—from Venezuela to North Korea, to Colombia and more of which he has been a part over the last decades. The players in his stories are, with a few small exceptions, powerful men—powerful men in conflict, powerful men negotiating possible resolutions. The absence of women as primary actors in those conversations is glaring and calls for evolutionary change.

The word "peace" can be soporific, but moving to a more peaceful world is anything but. Peace is both "active and passive" and it can come in many different forms: quiet, communion, creativity, innovation, positive containers for conflict, dialogue, nonviolent negotiations or, in the words of a Feminist Foreign Policy, "an inclusive, visionary policy for the twenty-first century, one where security and prosperity, health and climate justice are possible—in other words: where peace is possible for everyone, everywhere."[23]

Moving to a more peaceful world is moving from ego to

eco-consciousness and dismantling patriarchy. Empowering women through how we negotiate is central to this mission.

Family therapist Terry Real says, "Whenever I have a woman who's in trouble in a couple, my first move is to empower the woman, and whenever I have a man in trouble in the couple, my first move is to empower the woman. Women's voices are the voices that will be the wedge into patriarchy. Men will catch up, but women will lead the charge."[24]

Patriarchy, war systems, and an extractive energy system are parallels of the same thing. The reason they persist is because they are profitable for a small few, but very costly for the rest of the human and more-than-human world. They are about domination, not partnership. We don't need them anymore. And they are killing us.

Let's move on.

In 2015, I was more than lucky to get two tickets to the Broadway show *Hamilton*. I knew only enough about it to know that it was great, with the rough theme of rethinking race, especially as it related to the founding of the United States. I figured my then twenty-three-year-old daughter, who was deeply involved in race relations, would really enjoy it. I had no idea that it would become a major Broadway sensation and how totally impossible and expensive it would be to get tickets in the future.

My daughter, Ava, had heard nothing about *Hamilton*. *Hamilton* is a hip-hop opera and a retelling of the founding of the United States with the roles of key historical figures, all White men, being performed by Black and Brown men.

In the darkened theater, I periodically glanced over at my then often surly daughter whom I was intent on pleasing after my messy divorce with their father, and saw them begin to light up as things unfolded. They were delighted: The show was magnificent as was reviewed. While watching, I got to thinking about a sequel where all the main players were not Black men, but founding "mothers" of all stripes. Could we even conceive of such a thing? How that would mess with our heads about who rules, decides, governs, and leads? I would venture, and history bears me out, that it's a bigger stretch to see the United States and a lot of other nations formed and led by women of all tribes than even men of color.

Ironically, probably only a thousand years back, in the very same location as the theater in which we were sitting, this is exactly how things went down in Manhattan, then Manahatta among the Lenape tribe, who inhabited what is now the current city of New York.[25] If you had asked me when I was younger, gifted with an elite education, I would have told you that the US Constitution was inspired by the Greeks and the French Revolution. I had read *The Federalist Papers* in school, the treatise written by Alexander Hamilton. I had never read anything about the Iroquois Confederacy which it turns out had a huge influence on Ben Franklin and other key founding fathers of my country about how to form our democracy:

> The Constitution of the US was modeled after the treaty of the great nations of the Iroquois, a north-eastern forest Native American tribe that runs along what is now the New York State Thruway. This connected the Senecas, the Onondagas, the finger lakes group all through into the Mohawks. The Iroquois lived in relative peace for apparently one thousand years because they had this great treaty. The Iroquois

> were neither matriarchal or patriarchal, but balanced. And what the treaty said, the final decision, yea or nay, about whatever affected the tribe in a big way had to be run by the council of grandmothers.[26]

Now when the founding fathers wrote the Constitution, they left out the part about the grandmothers because we women had little clout. We (at least the White women) were essentially the property of our husbands. And women of color? Chattel slaves for all time.

I certainly did not learn this in my expensive private school education, nor was it pointed out to us kids in the United States that the founding fathers were all propertied White men, and that by "democracy," it meant democracy that really was equality for all of them. Indeed, even though I come from one of those very early American families, I know a lot about what the men were up to, but the women were essentially silent. We had no voice, really, except in the home and perhaps not even there.[27]

The world and especially my country is going through some major "birthing pains," a long-overdue reckoning where we are coming to grips with our beginnings. Democracy is a work in progress and its latest forms are struggling to appear.

If there is any group that can model true global partnership and collaboration, and midwife us into the future, it is women. Dismantling patriarchy is the key to dismantling identity group, adversarial conflict. When patriarchy changes everything changes. Collaborative hardball, a force big enough to match patriarchy, can get us there. No more "might-makes-right," dominion, rape culture, and we're not taking no for an answer. A colleague said at a workshop I was attending on feminine intelligence, "Perhaps the patriarchy is just this little experiment that we're all now realizing didn't quite work out and now we're coming back to wholeness . . ."[28]

"Crisis is opportunity" and our climate crisis is putting us on a trajectory for a change that is a pressure cooker. We must heed the call. In his "mountaintop" speech addressing racial and economic injustice, Dr. Martin Luther King said, "We have been forced to a point where we are going to have to grapple with the problems that men have been trying to grapple with throughout history but the demands didn't force them to it. Survival demands that we grapple with them."[29] The climate crisis and a PWC are forcing us to just such a point right now. We are on a knife's edge but we are evolving and will create something even more beautiful.

A final personal vision . . .

It is 2075, exactly one hundred years after I took my journey as a young woman to Mexico City on a train. I am no longer here, of course, but I can see them walking along a path, laughing, skipping stones. There are multiple children, some dogs. There is still snow on the ground. The earth is vibrant and the air is cool. Birds are singing. The earth is waking up after a cooling winter. The destruction from fossil fuels, predatory extraction, and its corresponding authoritarian PWC and greed is distant in their memory and understanding. So too is the idea that they would be anything other than equal beings in spite of their gender, or the color of their skin. They live in a world of connection, caring, and community—to each other, and to the world around them. Nature is breathing again. Humanity is breathing again. A lanky, tall kid with long strawberry-blond hair puts their bronze arm around their littler sibling. They are wearing a pink dress, with an elastic waist and a bandana to keep their hair pulled back. Affection and playfulness emanates between them. The older asks the younger, "By the way, did you ever read the book that our great-grandmother wrote?"

It is a new earth. A new world.

The End

ACKNOWLEDGMENTS

There are certain people without whom this book would never have been written. In no particular order, they are Terry Real, Scilla Elworthy, William Ury, Rabia Roberts, Debbie Bern, Ellen Raider, Regena Tomashauer, Riane Eisler, and John Carter.

- Terry, you so inspired me with the courage of your unequivocal statement: "We will move beyond patriarchy or we will die; it's that simple." You told me someone once summarized your family therapy work as "dismantling patriarchy one couple at a time," and I thought, *Aha! That's it. This book is about dismantling patriarchy one negotiation at a time.* As you will see, your ideas are all over this book. Thank you.
- Rabia, thank you for all the time and effort you put into researching "Herstory," which you call "a huge empowering story of the evolution of *homo sapiens* most especially from the perspective of women." I'm sorry that health issues have gotten in the way of your completing your work and getting it out there more formally before your physical decline. The path you've laid, your chutzpah, irreverence, and keen intelligence have been a North Star.

- Scilla, thank you for standing unequivocally for the idea that war is an anachronism and clearly stating—and documenting—your resolve that we can move beyond it. A world beyond war, an *active peace,* is possible. You have put such groundbreaking work into the world and set an inspiring bar for so many of us.
- William, thank you for the "Getting to Yes" movement you launched (along with Roger Fisher and Bruce Patton), but even more for your book *Getting to Peace*. You told me was it was a "labor of love," but it was an epiphany for me. You've laid the foundation for this book and my work and have been a steady source of inspiration to me, as to so many, everywhere.
- Regena, you profoundly changed my life with the School of Womanly Arts (SWA), as you have for so many tens of thousands of women around the world. I concur with your declaration that the education you provided—"a PhD in pussy," as you and all of us SWA graduates often refer to it—has been more transformational than many of the elite degrees I have earned. Thank you.
- Debbie, I'm not sure what I would have done without our "conversations." Your help—first in navigating my disintegrating marriage with strength, compassion, and clarity, and then your steady stream of insight, irreverence, laughter, and wisdom—has been amazing. Thank you.
- Ellen, meeting you was a star-crossed moment. Thank you for your chutzpah and showing me how to be a social change entrepreneur. Thank you also for bringing me into the International Center for

Cooperation and Conflict Resolution ("ICCCR") at Columbia University, connecting me with Mort Deutsch, and the "Camelot" we created there for a time—which influenced so many around the world.

- Riane, reading *The Chalice and the Blade* was an early life-shifting moment. Your framing of human history into "models of partnership and domination" offered a paradigm that made deep sense and helped me integrate my education in US imperialism in Latin America, my own psychological healing, and appreciation for collaboration. Thank you.
- John Carter—you helped me think big in how to intervene in complex systems, get stronger, and make a difference with my presence. You were a bit like a matador but your poking and prodding and willingness to stir things up grew my confidence and ability to navigate all kinds of big conflict and challenging group dynamics. Thank you.

There are a few other individuals I don't know personally but whose thinking and writing has been fundamental to me. Gloria Steinem—your activism, and the things you wrote at the time that you wrote them, and continue to write, just amaze me! Bill McKibben, your passion for the natural world and your willingness to fight and write for it have been a role model to me. Long ago, the image of you driving around in a beat-up car—in contrast to our consumer society and your fame—was an inspiration. Heather Cox Richardson, your passion for democracy and your willingness to selflessly show up, day after day, as our country fights off a fascist onslaught has been incredible. Thank you.

From earlier decades of my life, thank you to Lee Zevy, my "red diaper baby" therapist who "reparented" me in stark contrast to my 5th Avenue mom, and to Carollee Bengelsdorf, my college advisor, for teaching me about imperialism and first connecting me to the wonders and excitement of Latin America.

There are also organizations that have laid a foundation for this book (again in no particular order): the United Nations, the School of Womanly Arts, the ICCCR, Hampshire College, the Program on Negotiation at Harvard Law School (PON), and the Gestalt Institute of Cleveland.

Thank you to the United Nations and all of the people who helped create it—and who articulated a vision for a better world order though the Universal Declaration of Human Rights. I know you're not perfect but, just like good governmental institutions, we need you, now more than ever before. Thank you to the founders of Hampshire College who stood by the motto *non satis scire* ("to know is not enough") and envisioned as early as 1955 when the college was first conceptualized how we needed to live on this planet. Thank you to Mort Deutsch, the founder of the ICCCR, whose thinking shaped so much of my work. Thank you to the School of Womanly Arts, and the "sister goddess" community especially in the Hudson Valley where we continue to take ourselves higher and have extremely good potluck dinners. Thank you to the PON for providing me an "off-ramp" from the world of litigation and for your steadfast efforts to educate the world about interest-based negotiation. And thank you to the Gestalt Institute of Cleveland (www.gestaltosd.org) which, like the SWA, provided an education that far surpassed a degree.

I'm not sure how often people thank their dog, but in this instance, it is warranted. My dog Jocelyn has been a constant companion, a regular source of delight, and always a connection to the wild world. She has witnessed me—with enthusiasm and tail wagging—through countless dance breaks from writing.

Throughout the time that I've been writing this book, I've been blessed to be surrounded by a more-than-human community of birds, trees, and other critters. At one point, I felt isolated by this project, but then I became aware that you were all around me and seemed to know exactly who I am and where I fit in the order of things. Thank you. I also acknowledge that this beautiful piece of land I live on is located within the ancestral homelands of the Lenape (Munsee) and Wappinger peoples, whose spirits only whisper to me here now. Thank you. I am grateful to all the enlightened people over time who have made it possible for me to live on this land as an independent woman. It is so unusual, really, for a woman to have this kind of space and freedom. I am aware that, as recently as a few decades ago, it was illegal to convey land here in Philipstown to a person who was not of European descent, or to a single woman. Thank you.

Thank you to my parents who both modeled such basic integrity and decency to me, who lived through some of the complexity I describe in these stories, and who left this world way too soon. I'm especially grateful to my mother for her inspiration and her subtle (and not-so-subtle) messaging about the need for social justice and fairness in the world, her global thinking, and the need to move beyond patriarchy—even though she didn't call it that. Also thank you, Mom, for your keen intelligence and letting me go to Colombia, in spite of all of your friends' warnings that I would be kidnapped.

Thank you to Amplify Publishing Group, especially Will Wolfslau and Jack Callahan, and to Naren Aryal, Eric

Schurenberg, Lauren Magnussen, and the rest of the team. You have been such a pleasure to work with.

Thank you to Haven Iverson, my editor extraordinaire, who had such a hand in shaping this book and making it readable for everyone.

And Alison Anthoine—wow! What a wing woman. I could never have gotten this done without you: our regular "mastermind" dinners, your steady stream of great articles, legal support, intelligent assistance, and friendship. Thank you.

Thank you too to Marva Allen, also a part of our "mastermind," for all your smarts and advice on writing and publishing, and to Peggy Holman, Jade Silverstein, and Gayle Irvin for your savvy comments and generous support.

Thank you to John Dubberstein for your love, companionship, self-mastery, depth, sense of adventure, fun, and patient support throughout this project. It would have been a much heavier lift without you.

And finally, to my daughter, Ava, and my son, Jack—you have been the best teachers about love and the future.

NOTES

Introduction

1 The Doomsday Clock is a symbol that represents the estimated likelihood of a human-made global catastrophe, in the opinion of the members of the Bulletin of the Atomic Scientists. See https://thebulletin.org/doomsday-clock/.

2 Artificial Intelligence ("AI") also stands out to me as a potentially huge challenge. In the brief time I have been writing this book, AI has rapidly appeared on the landscape without much accountability or oversight and with the profits most likely going to a few male tech billionaires. The jury is still out on its impact on our climate, nature, and human relations but indisputably, it is here to stay.

3 Feminism has evolved in waves. The first "wave" was from the late nineteenth to the early twentieth century and secured basic legal rights for women, particularly the right to vote. The second was in the 1960s to 1980s with the focus on equality and liberation, e.g. bra burning. The third spanned from the 1990s to early 2000s with increased awareness that gender, race, class, sexual orientation, and other identities intersect and create unique experiences of oppression. Fourth-wave feminism is generally considered to have started around **2012**. It builds on the gains of earlier feminist movements but uses **digital tools and platforms** to fight for gender equality, challenge misogyny, and amplify marginalized voices.

4 Halla Tómasdóttir, president of Iceland, quoted in *"Is Iceland the Gender-Equality Haven for Women It Seems to Be?"* BBC World Service, December 10, 2024, https://www.bbc.com/worldservice.

5 School of Womanly Arts, https://mamagenas.com/.

6 "Zero-sum" is a common phrase used to describe a purely distributive negotiation, i.e., for every $1 I gain, you lose $1 and vice versa.

7 In organizational consulting, "getting the whole system into the room" refers to a process of engaging all relevant stakeholders, or key players, in a discussion or decision-making process. The idea is to involve representatives from different levels, departments, and functions within an organization to ensure that all perspectives are considered and that everyone who is impacted by or has an influence on the outcome is included.

Chapter 1

Epigraphs

Barbara Stanny (Huson), interview by Susan Coleman, *The Peacebuilding Podcast*, Episode 35, "Becoming Your Own Prince Charming – Women, Money, Power & Peace," released November 2019, https://www.susancoleman.global/the-peacebuilding-podcast.

Kascia Urbaniak, *Unbound: A Woman's Guide to Power* (New York, Harper Wave, 2021).

Belle Abzug. "Keynote Address at the National Women's Conference." National Women's Conference, Houston, Texas, 1977.

1 I believe that the nonhuman world communicates with us and tries to influence us in many ways, see e.g., *The Botany of Desire*, by science writer Michael Pollen, or the strong messages nature is sending us now about our current climate catastrophe.

2 Thanks to Zack Metz and my colleagues at Consensus for this chart. https://consensusgroup.com/.

3 See chapter 3 of this book, subheading "Women and Conflict" and corresponding notes.

4 Thanks to Heather Cox Richardson for this image and idea. Letters from an American, https://heathercoxrichardson.substack.com/, May 1, 2023, "The Myth of the Cowboy."

5 Dr. Martin Luther King Jr., "Power and Love," delivered February 4, 1968, at the Southern Christian Leadership Conference, Atlanta, Georgia.

6 Carol Gilligan, *In a Different Voice* (Cambridge, MA: Harvard University Press, 1982).

7 A widely circulated quote attributed to Alice Walker, American author.

8 I heard him say this, and see Erica Chenoweth and Zoe Marks, "Revenge of the Patriarchs: Why Autocrats Fear Women," Foreign Affairs, March/April 2022.

9 Jane Smith, "LeBron James Threatens to Boycott NBA Games in Protest of Police Violence," PBS NewsHour, August 27, 2020, https://www.pbs.org/newshour/sports/lebron-james-threatens-boycott-nba.

10 Roger Fisher, William Ury, and Bruce Patton, *Getting to Yes: Negotiating Agreement Without Giving In* (Boston: Houghton Mifflin, 1981).

11 I believe this to be from the Belarus Women's Foundation, January 27, 2021, https://www.facebook.com/watch/?v=748625209141492.

12 See e.g., Iceland, "Foreign Minister Addresses United Nations General Debate, 79th Session, UN General Assembly," speech, United Nations General Assembly, New York, September 25, 2024.

13 Donald J. Trump and Tony Schwartz's *The Art of the Deal* (New York: Ballantine Books, 1987) was written by the ghostwriter, Schwartz, who now calls it a fiction (New Yorker, 2016). Similarly, the makers of The Apprentice, a movie about Donald Trump and his TV show of the same name, talk about the fiction and smoke and mirrors of that show; and both creators of the TV show have expressed regret for "creating a monster." See The Apprentice movie (https://en.wikipedia.org/wiki/The_Apprentice_(2024_film). Furthermore, Trump's negotiation

models come from being a real estate developer where his zero-sum mindset made some sense because, in general or as the theory goes, there isn't as much interdependence between people, i.e., you don't see the person again. (In reality, though, that is shortsighted. In my own experience when my ex and I purchased our home, the deal was not exclusively zero-sum. It mattered greatly to the sellers that we were a young family and that's who they wanted to see in their house.) As Angela Merkel commented on the flight home after her first talks with Trump, a deflated Merkel concluded that Trump "looked at everything like the real estate developer he was before he entered politics"—as a zero-sum game. "For him, all countries were rivals in which the success of one meant the failure of another. He didn't think that prosperity could be increased for all through cooperation." The Guardian on Merkel: "I Mistook Trump for 'Someone Completely Normal,'" November, 22, 2024.

14 Nelson Mandela, *Long Walk to Freedom: The Autobiography of Nelson Mandela* (Little, Brown and Co. (1994).

Chapter 2

Epigraphs

Gloria Steinem, "The Full Circle," *The Glorias*, directed by Julie Taymor (Roadside Attractions, 2020), for in theaters and video on demand.

1 Steinem, *The Full Circle*.

2 Elizabeth Lesser, *Cassandra Speaks: When Women Are the Storytellers, the Human Story Changes*. Kindle ed. (New York: Random House, 2020).

3 Rabia Roberts, interview by Susan Coleman, Zoom, on *The Peacebuilding Podcast*, "Herstory," Episode 47, https://www.susancoleman.global/the-peacebuilding-podcast.

4 Ibid.

5 James Gorman, "Ancient Remains in Peru Reveal Young, Female Big-Game Hunter," New York Times, November 4, 2020, www.nytimes.com.

6 William Ury, *Getting to Peace: Transforming Conflict at Home, at Work, and in the World* (New York: Penguin Publishing Group 1999), p. 35.

7 Ibid, p. 33.

8 Ibid, p 37.

9 See also, the work of Maria Gimbutas, an influential archaeologist and anthropologist who conducted extensive research on prehistoric cultures. She is best known for her work on Goddess cultures and matriarchal societies in Europe, focusing on the Neolithic and early Bronze Age periods. *The Civilization of the Goddess: The World of Old Europe* (San Francisco: HarperSanFrancisco, 1991).

10 Douglas Fry, PhD, interview by Susan Coleman, *The Peacebuilding Podcast*, Episode 41, https://www.susancoleman.global/the-peacebuilding-podcast.

When I interviewed Doug Fry, a renowned peace anthropologist at University of North Carolina, here's what he had to say about his surprise that humans have not always been violent. "Back in the 90s . . . I (believed as) the majority of Americans (did), that there always has been war; there always will be war; because that's just what we learned in our culture. It is just part of our human nature. And one of my colleagues, now retired from University of Hawaii, Les Sponsel, wrote an article, which was a very interesting overview of this topic. And he said, you know, for most of human existence, there's not been war. And I read that, and I remember thinking, Les Sponsel has just gone off the deep end, oh, my God, oh Les, how can you write something so ridiculous? And it took me a couple of weeks really, as I . . . reflected on Les and this really crazy idea he had, and so on, and then all of a sudden, could he be right? And that was a key event, mid 90s, late 90s , . . it just focused me to start investigating myself as to how old is warfare, and when did war really come in. And what we find, very interestingly, as often happens, you get cultural beliefs and cultural narratives that just evolve . . . that these narratives are just incredibly important in shaping how we will view the world . . . *these types of domination societies come in very late, or to put it another way, very recently . . .*

11 Bettany Hughes, "The Ancient Mysteries of the Minoans," *Absolute History*. https://youtu.be/nJUpw_wd-7I.

12 Riane Eisler. *The Chalice and the Blade: Our History, Our Future* (New York: Harper and Row, 1987).

13 See e.g., Raymond Faure, *The Secret of the Labyrinth*.

14 See e.g., Joseph F. Kelly, *The Origins of Christmas* (Collegeville, MN: Liturgical Press, 2004).

15 See Sheela na Gig. Wikipedia. https://en.wikipedia.org/wiki/Sheela_na_Gig.

16 Roberts, "Herstory."

17 Ury, *Getting to Peace*, p. 67.

18 Michael Moore. *Rumble with Michael Moore*, Episode 250: "Popes of Genocides Past and Present." Podcast. https://rumble.media.

19 Eckhart Tolle, *A New Earth: Awakening to Your Life's Purpose (*New York: Penguin Group, 2005).

20 Thank you to Layla Martin, laylamartin.com. "Why we Call Ourselves Witches," https://www.youtube.com/watch?v=Yhi4AaMpiSw. I can't confirm all of this, but I know Layla to be a trustworthy source. I also know that the PWC has altered, buried, and changed many meanings. See also https://www.etymonline.com/word/hag.

21 *"Hex,"* Merriam-Webster.com, Dictionary, accessed April 12, 2025, https://www.merriam-webster.com/dictionary/hex.

22 Remarks made by Senator Rick Santorum during the 2012 Republican presidential primary campaign. He made this statement in an interview on *ABC News* on February 28, 2012, while discussing environmental issues and the role of humans in relation to the earth.

23 For the nonbinary in nature, see e.g. https://www.nature.org/en-us/about-us/where-we-work/united-states/washington/stories-in-washington/natures-non-binary-fluidity-in-our-

global-oceans/; https://www.spiralnature.com/spirituality/honouring-queer-non-binary-forms-nature/.

24 Emily Nagoski, *Come as You Are: The Surprising New Science that Will Transform Your Sex Life* (New York, Simon and Schuster, 2015).

25 Ibid.

26 Joseph Campbell, *The Power of Myth* (New York: Doubleday, 1988).

27 Regena Tomashauer, Terry Real, Carl Jung, personal communications with friends, family, and colleagues.

28 Alok Vaid-Menon, *Beyond the Gender Binary* (New York: TarcherPerigee, 2020).

29 Political patriarchy is discrimination based on sex, the oppression of women by men.

30 Terry Real, interview by Susan Coleman, *The Peacebuilding Podcast*, Episode 34, "Building Peace from the Intimate to the Global." 2019. https://www.susancoleman.global/the-peacebuilding-podcast, and from multiple lectures and online workshops with Terry Real.

31 Ibid.

32 Ibid.

33 The *Washington Post* reported that all but 3 of the 165 mass shootings that have occurred have been committed by men. The article went on to say that most of these men carry a "triple cultural entitlement;" in other words, they are heterosexual, male, and White—and they are angry that they are losing their privileged status. John Woodrow Cox, "More Deadly Mass Shootings: Trends in America," *Washington Post*, August 5, 2019.

34 Terry Real, *I Don't Want to Talk About It: Overcoming the Secret Legacy of Male Depression* (New York: Scribner, 1997). See also Michael Kimmel and Lisa Wade, "Toxic Masculinity," *Signs Journal*. https://signsjournal.org/kimmel-wade-toxic-masculinity/.

35 Stuyvesant was the last Director-General of New Netherland, which was a Dutch colony, and served as its leader from 1647 to 1664 until the English seized it and renamed it New York.

Encyclopedia Britannica. https://www.britannica.com/biography/Peter-Stuyvesant.

36 EMDR (Eye Movement Desensitization and Reprocessing) is a type of psychotherapy designed to help people process and heal from trauma and distressing life experiences. It was developed by Francine Shapiro in the late 1980s. Francine Shapiro. *EMDR: The Breakthrough Therapy for Overcoming Anxiety, Stress, and Trauma* (New York: Basic Books, 1997).

37 Conversations with Hilary Heyl, MSW, and Debbie Bern, MSW, clinicians specializing in EMDR and trauma therapies. See Janina Fisher, https://janinafisher.com/.

38 Thomas Hübl, interview by Susan Coleman. *The Peacebuilding Podcast*, Episode 43, "Healing Collective Trauma," https://www.susancoleman.global/the-peacebuilding-podcast. See also https://thomashuebl.com/.

39 There is some evidence that Einstein's work was also attributable (though not credited) to his very brilliant wife, Mileva Marić, an accomplished physicist in her own right. Allen Esterson and David C. Cassidy. *Einstein's Wife: The Real Story of Mileva Marić* (Cambridge, MA: MIT Press, 2019).

40 Thanks to Dr. Nicole Lepera, https://theholisticpsychologist.com/, for this definition.

41 The term "codependency" originates from the addiction field. "AA" or Alcoholics Anonymous was formed in 1935 in Akron, Ohio by the now famous Bill W. with the focus at that time largely on male alcoholics. Al Anon developed shortly thereafter by Lois W., Bill W.'s codependent wife, to address the spouses, largely women, who enabled their husband's destructive drinking. Al-Anon became the earliest of the twelve-step programs to address codependence with its core message to codependents to "keep the focus on yourself." The addict/codependent relationship parallels the addictive and exploitive nature of patriarchy and the ways that women have been complicit with it.

42 Anaïs Nin, *The Diary of Anaïs Nin, Volume One: 1931–1934* (New York: Harcourt Brace Jovanovich, 1966).

43 See e.g., Heinrich Kramer and Jacob Sprenger, **"The Malleus Maleficarum"** (also known as **"The Hammer of Witches"**), 1487. Translated by Montague Summers (New York: Dover Publications, 1971). This infamous treatise played a central role in inciting witch hunts in Europe and includes details on the methods of torture and execution, including burning at the stake. Various of my colleagues, from both Asia and Africa, have told me that witch burnings have also happened on those continents. To the best of my knowledge, persecution of witches continues in various parts of the world.

44 Conversation with Hilary Heyl, MSW, 2024. (Heyl points out that there are non-Western cultures that have not been so patriarchal and thus women living in them don't experience that patriarchy as traumatic.)

45 Conversation with Debbie Bern, MSW, 2024.

Chapter 3

1 Conversation with Dr. Scilla Elworthy, 2024. In 2013, Scilla also cofounded Rising Women, Rising World and Femme Q (2016) establishing the qualities of feminine intelligence for women and men as essential in building a safer world.

2 William Ury, *Possible: How We Survive (and Thrive) in an Age of Conflict* (New York: HarperCollins, 2024), Kindle edition, p. 7.

3 This is not a direct quote but reflects key ideas from Lewin. See e.g., Lewin, Kurt, Ronald Lippitt, and Ralph K. White. "Patterns of Aggressive Behavior in Experimentally Created Social Climates," *Journal of Social Psychology* 10 (1939): 271–299; or Kurt Lewin, *Field Theory in Social Science: Selected Theoretical Papers*, ed. Dorwin Cartwright (New York: Harper & Row, 1951).

4 Morton Deutsch, *The Resolution of Conflict: Constructive and Destructive Processes* (New Haven: Yale University Press, 1973).

5 Dean G. Pruitt and Peter J. Carnevale, *Negotiation in Social Conflict*, 2nd ed. (Pacific Grove, CA: Brooks/Cole Publishing Company, 1993).

6 Susan Coleman and Dorothy Weaver, "Women and Negotiation: Tips from the Field." *Dispute Resolution Magazine*, Spring 2012.

7 Joslyn N. Barnhart, et al. "The Suffragist Peace," paper presented at the American Political Science Association Annual Meeting, 2018; later published in *International Organization* in 2020.

8 Gloria Steinem, "Sex, Lies and the Supermarket," *Ms. Magazine*, 1983. In the essay, she referred to a "codependent woman" as a "well-adjusted female."

9 Christopher Rugaber and Josh Boak, "Biden Warns That an Oligarchy Is Taking Hold in America. There Is Data to Back Him Up," *MarketWatch*, January 16, 2025.

10 The Weather Underground formed in opposition to the Vietnam War. While Students for a Democratic Society (SDS) protested nonviolently above ground, the Weather Underground and similar groups engaged in direct action, including the destruction of munitions plants. (Linda, meanwhile, was babysitting their children.)

11 Linda Coleman, *Radical Descent: The Cultivation of an American Revolutionary: A Memoir* (Wainscott, Pushcart Press, 2014).

Chapter 4

Epigraphs

Mary Parker Follett, *The New State: Group Organization the Solution of Popular Government* (New York: Longmans, Green and Co., 1924).

Jane Fonda, statement made during an interview at the *Film Society of Lincoln Center* in New York City, in October 2017. She was discussing her career, her experiences in Hollywood, and the personal growth she underwent throughout her life, especially when it came to asserting herself and her boundaries in her work.

1 A small, but growing percentage of lawyers are women, and thankfully, a number of them are doing excellent work to create a different rules-based order that supports gender equality.

2 Carol Gilligan, *In a Different Voice: Psychological Theory and Women's Development* (Cambridge, MA: Harvard University Press, 1982). Gilligan drew on research and case studies to illustrate her points, including the idea that when boys get into conflicts, they tend to focus on fairness and rules, often following a "justice" perspective. This contrasts with girls who, according to Gilligan's interpretation, may prioritize maintaining relationships and harmony, adopting a "care" perspective that could lead them to abandon the rules in favor of preserving relationships.

3 Abraham H. Maslow, *Motivation and Personality* (New York: Harper & Row, 1954).

4 Maslow spent six weeks in 1938 at the Siksika Nation's Blackfoot reservation in Gleichen, Alberta, Canada. His experiences there had a profound impact on him and influenced his work, including his theory of motivation, the Hierarchy of Needs. See e.g. Teju Ravilochan, "Could the Blackfoot Wisdom that Inspired Maslow Guide Us Now?" April 4, 2021. Contributing editors: Vidya Ravilochan and Colette Kessler; or see Cindy Blackstock, *The Emergence of the Breath of Life Theory*. BCcampus Open Publishing, 2011.

5 Apparently, Maslow's last category of need, "Transcendence," was one that Maslow was beginning to articulate and was only identified by his wife posthumously in his notes.

6 Mary Parker Follett (The New State) is often now referred to as "an unsung hero" in the field of management and organizational theory. While she was a pioneering thinker in the early twentieth century, her contributions have historically been overshadowed by those of her male contemporaries, such as Frederick Taylor and Henri Fayol. Follett's ideas on leadership, conflict resolution, and the importance of human relations in organizations were revolutionary for her time. She introduced concepts like "power-with" rather than "power-over" and emphasized the importance of collaboration and shared authority. Despite her forward-thinking theories, her work was not widely recognized during her lifetime, and it took many years before scholars began to fully appreciate her impact.

7 Fisher, Ury, and Patton, *Getting to Yes*, p. 38.

8 Gloria Steinem, *PBS NewsHour*, August 18, 2020.

9 Mahatma Gandhi, *The Story of My Experiments with Truth*. Translated by Mahadev Desai. Ahmedabad: Navajivan Publishing House, 1940. *(Note: Quote attribution uncertain; this is the primary text referenced for similar ideas.)*

Chapter 5

1 *Get Me Roger Stone*, directed by Morgan Pehme. Netflix, 2017.

2 Adapted from the film about Donald Trump. *The Apprentice*. Directed by Ali Abbasi. Netflix, 2024.

3 "Permission structure" is a term that originally came from the marketing world and then moved into politics. It means creating an environment that makes it easier for people to do things they would ordinarily shun.

4 See e.g., "Body Choice Emboldened Far-Right Men." Yahoo News. Accessed April 12, 2025. https://www.yahoo.com/news/body-choice-emboldened-far-men-191536054.html?fr=yhssrp_catchall.

5 Elizabeth Lesser keynote, *Do Power Differently Conference*, Omega Institute, Rhinebeck, NY. Used with permission. See https://susancoleman.substack.com/p/doingpowerdifferently?r=3dv5v.

6 Shelley E. Taylor, *The Tending Instinct: How Nurturing Is Essential to Who We Are and How We Live* (New York: Dutton, 2017).

7 In American English, tabling in negotiation means to take something off the table, postpone. In British English it means to put it on the table, start talking about it.

8 Sandra Janoff, *Don't Just Do Something, Stand There: A Guide for Leaders in the Helping Professions* (San Francisco: Jossey-Bass, 2004).

9 Oprah Winfrey, acceptance speech, Cecil B. DeMille Award, Golden Globe Awards, January 7, 2018. In her speech, she

emphasized the importance of women sharing their personal stories and standing up against injustice.

10 Conversation with Scilla Elworthy, November 2024. Used with permission.

11 Lesser. Used with permission. https://susancoleman.substack.com/p/doingpowerdifferently?r=3dv5v.

12 Riya Yuyada. Used with permission.

Chapter 6

1 Mama Gena said this on multiple occasions over the six years I was in programs with her.

2 Kim Anami, remarks from a private workshop, 2020.

3 Daniel Goleman, *Emotional Intelligence: Why It Can Matter More Than IQ* (New York: Bantam Books, 1995).

4 Ibid.

5 Thanks to my colleague, Bill Woodson, for this model, https://www.linkedin.com/in/forwardmotion/.

6 The "**fundamental attribution error**" is a cognitive bias where people tend to attribute others' actions or behaviors to their personality or character rather than considering external factors that might have influenced the situation. In other words, when someone does something wrong or behaves in a way we don't like, we are more likely to assume that it's due to their internal traits (e.g., they're lazy, rude, or selfish), rather than thinking about situational factors that might have played a role (e.g., they were stressed, tired, or facing difficulties). This bias often leads to misjudgments about others' intentions and can contribute to misunderstandings in social interactions. It's called "fundamental" because it is a pervasive and common error in how we think about others.

7 Jean-Paul Sartre, *No Exit (Huis Clos).* First performed in 1944.

8 Andrew Weil, *Spontaneous Healing* (New York: Alfred A. Knopf, 1995). See also www.drweil.com.

9 See https://mamagenas.com/wp3/wp-content/uploads/m18/MA18_Booklet_1_18-20.pdf.

10 See Peter Coleman, "The Power of Walking Together," TEDx, 2020, https://www.ted.com/ or Peter Coleman, *The Way Out* (Divided We Fall, 2025), https://dividedwefall.org/the-way-out/.

11 Gilligan, *In a Different Voice* (1982). The "tyranny of the kind and nice" refers to the social pressure placed on women to always be kind, considerate, and self-sacrificing, often at the expense of their own needs or desires.

12 Leymah Gbowee, *Unlocking the Power of Women for Peace*, TED talk, February 2012, https://www.ted.com/talks/leymah_gbowee_unlocking_the_power_of_women_for_peace.

Chapter 7

1 Geert Hofstede, *Culture's Consequences: International Differences in Work-Related Values* (Beverly Hills: Sage Publications, 1980).

2 Anaïs Nin, *The Diary of Anaïs Nin*, Vol. 5 (New York: Harcourt Brace Jovanovich, 1974).

3 Going International, Part 2: *Managing the Overseas Assignment*, Griggs Production (1998).

4 Oscar Wile, *The English Renaissance*. 1887.

5 See e.g., Edward T. Hall, *The Silent Language* (New York: Doubleday, 1959).

6 *Pirkei Avot* 1:14. The full passage reads: "If I am not for myself, who will be for me? But if I am only for myself, who am I? And if not now, when?"

7 Emma Watson, speech, United Nations Headquarters, New York, 2014.

8 Program on Negotiation, Harvard Law School, PON Staff, "Negotiation, Gender and Status at the Bargaining Table," August 20, 2020.

9 Melinda French Gates. Interview with Bill Gates and Michelle Obama. *The National Geographic Presents: The Women's Leadership Series*, 2019.

Chapter 8

1 Pablo Restrep Saenz. This is something I have heard him say often. https://www.linkedin.com/in/pablorestrepo/.

2 Terry Real. I have heard him say this many times. This specific phrase has been highlighted in his books and in workshops, particularly in his approach to helping couples communicate more effectively. See more at: https://terryreal.com/.

3 Thanks to my colleague, Pablo Restrepo, for this story which we used many times when we trained together. Medellín, Colombia's second largest city, was founded in the 1600s by Spanish Conquistadores and later populated during one of the final Spanish diasporas, largely by Jewish and Basque immigrants. The city's conquest was difficult due to the mountainous terrain, dense jungles, and its location in the coffee-growing region. Medellín thrived for a time, with a strong middle class and an ethos of hard work and community collaboration. A deep sense of social responsibility was widespread. Paradoxically, the city also became the origin of some of Colombia's most violent gangs. Many of these gangs, particularly in Las Comunas, were formed by internally displaced people who had fled rural areas for the cities.

4 See *Rodrigo D. No Futuro*, Directed by Victor Gaviria, Compañía de Fomento Cinematográfico (Focine), 1990.

5 Whatever figure is introduced first into a negotiation—even if arbitrary or unfair—serves as a powerful anchor that pulls the discussion in its direction. For women this can be a challenge when negotiating salary, for example, because the most obvious anchor is our current salary and we are so often underpaid. It makes sense, therefore, to try to locate other data that would be advantageous like job postings and information from industry. See e.g., https://

www.pon.harvard.edu/daily/negotiation-skills-daily/in-negotiation-are-two-anchors-better-than-one-nb/.

Chapter 9

1 *Pray the Devil Back to Hell*, directed by Gini Reticker, produced by Abigail Disney, 2008. The quote is words of Leymah Gbowee in the very opening of the film.

2 Leymah Gbowee, *Mighty Be Our Powers: How Sisterhood, Prayer, and Sex Changed a Nation at War* (Beast Books, 2011).

3 *Pray the Devil Back to Hell*, directed by Gini Reticker.

4 Joanna Kenty, "Lysistrata in Liberia," Medium, July 27, 2015, https://eidolon.pub/lysistrata-in-liberia-25fa4adf138b.

5 PBS NewsHour, "No Sex. No Dating. No Marriage. No Children. Interest Grows in '4B' Movement to Swear Off Men," https://www.pbs.org/newshour/politics/no-sex-no-dating-no-marriage-no-children-interest-grows-in-4b-movement-to-swear-off-men.

6 Contrary to a male-centric view of reproduction, a recent study shows that the human egg takes a proactive role in selecting which sperm it will allow in to fertilize it. There is "a conversation" apparently between the egg and the sperm, but she gets the final word. John L. Fitzpatrick, Charlotte Willis, Alessandro Devigili, Amy Young, Michael Carroll, Helen R. Hunter, and Daniel R. Brison, "Chemical Signals from Eggs Facilitate Cryptic Female Choice in Humans." *Proceedings of the Royal Society B: Biological Sciences* 287, no. 1930 (2020): 20200805. https://doi.org/10.1098/rspb.2020.0805. So much for right-wing jibes of "her body, my choice."

7 Real, interview by Coleman, "From the Intimate to the Global."

8 Timothy Snyder, *On Tyranny: Twenty Lessons from the Twentieth Century* (New York: Tim Duggan Books, 2017).

9 Alexandria Ocasio-Cortez, remarks on the floor of the US House of Representatives, July 22, 2020.

10 Gloria Steinem made this statement at a National Women's Political Caucus event in 1977 and see https://theconversation.

com/home-is-the-most-dangerous-place-for-women-but-private-and-public-violence-are-connected-171348.

11 The Wall of Dolls, or "Muro delle Bambole," is an art installation and memorial initiated in 2014 by singer-songwriter Jo Squillo in Milan, Italy, dedicated to honoring female victims of violence. The wall features numerous dolls—many bearing the names of victims—suspended on a metal grid. Similarly, Turkish artist Vahit Tuna created an installation aimed to raise public awareness about the issue of femicide in Turkey by hanging 440 pairs of high heels on a building's facade. Each pair symbolized a woman murdered by domestic or sexual violence in Turkey during 2018.

12 *Tina*, directed by Dan Lindsay and T. J. Martin, HBO, 2021.

13 Peter Coleman, PhD, "To Support Violence or Nonviolence – That is the Question," October 28, 2024, Medium, https://pc84.medium.com/to-support-violence-or-nonviolence-that-is-the-question-894e39fca05a.

14 See e.g., Carl Sagan, "On Existence of God," https://www.youtube.com/watch?v=ML4kiFCKZGo.

15 Mahatma Gandhi, paraphrased statement.

Chapter 10

Epigraphs

From *Becoming Warren Buffett*, directed by Joe Berlinger, HBO, 2017.

1 Paraphrase of Bob Marley, *Redemption Song*.

2 Linda Babcock and Sara Laschever, *Women Don't Ask: Negotiation and the Gender Divide* (New York: Bantam Books, 2003).

3 Ibid.

4 Linda Babcock and Sara J. Correll, "What Works for Women in Negotiation: The Role of Gender in Negotiating the Job Offer." *Negotiation Journal* 33, no. 4 (2017): 391–407; Linda Babcock and Sara J. Correll, *Ask for It: How Women Can Use the Power of*

Negotiation to Get What They Really Want (New York: Bantam Books, 2008).

5 Laura Kray, "A study by Berkeley Haas Professor Laura Kray found that professional women now negotiate their salaries more frequently than men, but they are more likely to have their requests denied," *Berkeley Haas*. Similarly, a study by Vanderbilt Business revealed that women with MBA degrees are more likely to negotiate higher pay than their male peers. However, despite these efforts, women often receive less favorable outcomes, suggesting that factors beyond the act of negotiating, such as potential biases, may contribute to the persistent gender pay gap. These findings challenge the notion that women don't negotiate and highlight the need to address systemic issues that hinder women's success in salary negotiations.

6 Barbara Stanny (Huson), interview by Susan Coleman, *The Peacebuilding Podcast*, Episode 35, "Becoming Your Own Prince Charming – Women, Money, Power & Peace," released November 2019, https://www.susancoleman.global/the-peacebuilding-podcast.

7 Chase Strangio, interview by *The New Inquiry*. 2019.

8 Gloria Steinem, talk at Cardozo Law School, March 29, 2023.

9 Alexandra Carter, *Ask for More: The Power of Questions to Open Doors, Uncover Solutions, and Spark Change* (New York: Simon & Schuster, 2021).

10 An "arms-length" transaction refers to a deal or transaction between two parties who are independent and have no relationship with each other that might influence the terms of the agreement. In such a transaction, both parties act in their own self-interest, with each striving to get the best possible deal without any pressure or bias from the other.

11 The Davos Man, World Economic Forum. *Global Gender Gap Report 2020*. World Economic Forum, 2020. https://www.weforum.org/reports/gender-gap-2020-report-100-years-pay-equality or see https://www.npr.org/2022/01/20/1074378185/davos-man-is-an-angry-powerful-look-at-economic-inequality.

12 See https://www.mckinsey.com/industries/financial-services/our-insights/women-as-the-next-wave-of-growth-in-us-wealth-management; https://www.newser.com/story/352898/a-horizontal-wealth-transfer-is-coming-in-the-us.html.

13 Barbara Stanny (Huson), interview by Susan Coleman, "Becoming Your Own Prince Charming – Women, Money, Power & Peace."

14 During his first presidency, Donald Trump oversaw significant arms sales to Saudi Arabia, which became a focal point of both domestic and international controversy. In 2017, the Trump administration brokered a landmark $110 billion arms deal with Saudi Arabia, which included various weapons systems such as fighter jets, helicopters, air defense systems, and naval systems which was part of a broader $350 billion package that was framed as a means to strengthen the US–Saudi alliance.

15 In 2022, the global beauty industry generated approximately $528.6 billion in revenue, with projections reaching $579.2 billion in 2023. *ChatGPT* (GPT-4).

16 John Perkins, phone interview. May 24, 2024. https://johnperkins.org/.

17 In 2023, global military expenditure reached approximately $2.443 trillion, marking a 6.8% increase from the previous year. These are the largest: United States: $916 billion (3.4% of GDP), China: $296 billion (1.7% of GDP), Russia: $109 billion (5.9% of GDP), India: $83.6 billion (2.4% of GDP), Saudi Arabia: $75.8 billion (7.1% of GDP), United Kingdom: $74.9 billion (2.3% of GDP), Germany: $66.8 billion (1.5% of GDP), Ukraine: $64.8 billion (37.0% of GDP), France: $61.3 billion (2.1% of GDP), Japan: $50.2 billion. *ChatGPT* (GPT-4).

Chapter 11

1 Thanks to the NY Times podcast, *The Daily,* "Serena Williams's Final Run," September 12, 2022, for inspiration on this.

2 See Chapter 7: Important Worldview Differences That Can Impact Us When We Negotiate.

3 Susie Orbach, *Fat Is a Feminist Issue* (1978).

4 Eve Ensler, "Happiness in Body and Soul," *TEDxWomen* (TEDx, December 1, 2010). https://www.ted.com/talks/eve_ensler_happiness_in_body_and_soul.

5 *Live to Lead*, directed by Liz Garbus. Higher Ground Productions, 2022. Featuring Jacinda Ardern, https://www.netflix.com/title/81096509.

6 Sigmund Freud, *Three Essays on the Theory of Sexuality*, ed. and trans. James Strachey, vol. 7 of *The Standard Edition of the Complete Psychological Works of Sigmund Freud*, 123–246 (London: Hogarth Press, 1905).

7 Regena Tomashauer, *Pussy: A Reclamation* (New York: Penguin Life, 2020).

8 See e.g, https://t5t.com/5-tibetan-rites.

9 https://en.wikipedia.org/wiki/Vitruvian_Man.

10 Ronan Farrow, "Les Moonves and CBS: The Case of the Censored Story," *The New Yorker*, September 10, 2018.

11 Ibid.

12 See e.g. "Trump Is Filling His White House With Men Accused of Sexual Misconduct," *HuffPost*, accessed [insert date], https://www.huffpost.com/entry/trump-is-filling-his-white-house-with-men-accused-of-sexual-misconduct_n_673cb647e4b024dbac5b82c2.

13 Kristine Grønhaug, "Rape as Modern Warfare: 'Quiet, Cheap, and Scarily Efficient,'" *The Guardian*, November 28, 2018, https://www.theguardian.com/global-development/2018/nov/28/rape-modern-warfare-quiet-cheap-efficient.

14 Bessel van der Kolk, *The Body Keeps the Score: Brain, Mind, and Body in the Healing of Trauma* (New York: Viking, 2014).

15 Roberts, interview by Susan Coleman, Zoom, on *The Peacebuilding Podcast*, "Herstory."

16 Emily Nagoski, *Come as You Are: The Surprising New Science That Will Transform Your Sex Life*.

17 Martha Eddy, interview by Susan Coleman, Zoom, on *The Peacebuilding Podcast*, "Reclaiming the Female Body for Power in Negotiation," Episode 44, https://www.susancoleman.global/the-peacebuilding-podcast.

18 Thomas Hübl, interview by Susan Coleman, Zoom, on *The Peacebuilding Podcast*, "Healing Collective Trauma," Episode 43, https://www.susancoleman.global/the-peacebuilding-podcast.

19 Audre Lorde, "The Erotic as Power," in *Sister Outsider: Essays and Speeches* (1984; reprint, Berkeley: Crossing Press, 2007), 56.

20 Monica Hesse, "Walking Like a Man," *The Washington Post*, November 2019.

21 Leymah Gbowee, "The Ms. Q&A: How Leymah Gbowee Turned Anger Into Action," *Ms. Magazine*, June 24, 2019, https://msmagazine.com/2019/06/24/the-ms-qa-how-leymah-gbowee-turned-anger-into-action/.

Epilogue

1 Having a "systems lens" means approaching problems, situations, or processes by looking at the whole system rather than focusing on individual components in isolation. It's about understanding the relationships, patterns, and interdependencies between different elements that make up a system. This approach is often used in fields like systems thinking, systems theory, in disciplines like business, ecology, engineering, and social sciences. When you apply a systems lens, you consider how changes in one part of a system can affect the other parts and the system as a whole.

2 The PUK (Patriotic Union of Kurdistan) and KDP (Kurdistan Democratic Party) are two prominent Kurdish political parties in the Kurdistan Region of Iraq.

3 https://openspaceworld.org/wp2/.

4 Excerpts of this story were first published in Peggy Holman, ed., *The Change Handbook: The Definitive Resource on Today's Best-Run Change Processes*, 2nd ed. (San Francisco: Berrett-Koehler

Publishers, 2010). My colleague, Zach Metz, especially ran with our design and rolled it out in many war-torn parts of the world. See https://www.susancoleman.global/sn008-zachary-metz.

5 For example, OST, Future Search (https://futuresearch.net/), World Café, dialogue and facilitation in many forms.

6 "The Secret Language of Trees," *The Best of Our Knowledge*, April 28, 2018, https://www.ttbook.org/show/secret-language-trees.

7 Cristiana Figueres, interview with Kosha Joubert, the Climate Summit, 2024. Used with permission.

8 Hudson, Valerie, *The Hillary Doctrine: Sex and American Foreign Policy* (New York: Columbia University Press, 2015).

9 Sign on the mantle in Terry Real's office.

10 See e.g., J. Lammers, J. I. Stoker, J. Jordan, M. Pollmann, and A. H. Fischer, "Power Increases Infidelity Among Men and Women." *Psychological Science, 22*(9) (2011), 1191–1197 or L. C. Sayer and M. Fine, "Cohabitation, Marriage, and Women's Economic Well-Being." *Journal of Marriage and Family, 73*(1) (2011), 1–14.

11 See e.g, J. M. Gottman and R. W. Levenson, "The timing of divorce: Predicting whether a marriage will survive." *Journal of Marriage and the Family, 62*(3) (2000), 877–888; or H. J. Markman, S. M. Stanley, and S. L. Blumberg, "Fighting for Your Marriage: A Deluxe Revised Edition." Jossey-Bass (2010).

12 Susan Coleman, interview by Ed Hoffman, *Center Stage Podcast*, Project Management Institute, October 2021.

13 Prof. Peter Hawkins, interview by Susan Coleman, Zoom, on *The Peacebuilding Podcast*, "Gender, 'WeQ' and the Urgent Need for Collaborative Intelligence in Organizations", Episode 29, https://www.susancoleman.global/the-peacebuilding-podcast.

14 Audre Lorde, *The Master's Tools Will Never Dismantle the Master's House*, in *Sister Outsider: Essays and Speeches* (Freedom, CA: Crossing Press, 1984); and see e.g. Jennifer L. E. Lee, "The Rise of Female Entrepreneurship: A Global Shift," *Entrepreneurial Women Journal*, vol. 18, no. 4 (2023):

12–17, https://www.entrepreneurialwomenjournal.com/rise-of-female-entrepreneurship.

15 Kristina Lunz, interview by Susan Coleman, Zoom, on *The Peacebuilding Podcast*, "A Feminist Foreign Policy", Episode 45, https://www.susancoleman.global/the-peacebuilding-podcast.

16 William Ury, "Peace is Possible," https://www.youtube.com/watch?v=jsszyyHuPpk&t=5s.

17 Dr. Scilla Elworthy, *The Business Plan for Peace: Building a World Without War* (Peace Direct, 2018).

18 See e.g. Dalai Lama, interview by *The Guardian*, 2009, "Women Have More Sensitivity and Compassion." In this interview, the Dalai Lama stated that "women have more sensitivity and more compassion" and that they are "better peacemakers" because of these inherent qualities. He has suggested that women, because of their nurturing and compassionate nature, could play a vital role in resolving conflicts and fostering peace globally. He has also mentioned that the world might benefit from more female leadership, emphasizing the idea that women's approach to decision-making often tends to be more compassionate and peaceful. In addition, the Dalai Lama has frequently advocated for the empowerment of women in general, stating that women are more likely to bring about lasting peace due to their deep sense of empathy and care for others. These views have been expressed on various occasions, including in talks, writings, and interviews..

19 Rabia Roberts, interview with Susan Coleman.

20 Ury, *Possible*, p. 286.

21 Julia Ward Howe, *Mothers' Day Proclamation*. 1870.

22 See https://susancoleman.substack.com/p/how-women-leaders-stop-wars.

23 https://centreforfeministforeignpolicy.org/.

24 Real, interview by Susan Coleman.

25 "Manahatta" is believed to mean "island of many hills" or "hilly island," referring to the topography of the island at the time.

Over time, the name evolved into "Manhattan" as English-speaking settlers began to use it.

26 Gloria Steinem, *My Life on the Road* (New York: Random House, 2015).

27 While White women were ourselves oppressed by the PWC, we still played significant roles in upholding and benefiting from slavery—especially in the American South. This pattern continues to this day and needs to change.

28 See https://susancoleman.substack.com/p/so-what-is-feminine-intelligence.

29 Martin Luther King Jr., "I've Been to the Mountaintop," delivered April 3, 1968, Mason Temple, Memphis, Tennessee.

While, I have mixed feelings about AI, it has been enormously helpful in compiling these notes, either by helping me backtrack and recover where I came across something, or by making the note more rich. So, thank you, ChatGPT (GPT-4), March 8, 2025, https://chat.openai.com.

ABOUT THE AUTHOR

For over thirty-five years, **Susan Coleman** has worked from war zones to boardrooms teaching people negotiation skills, mediating conflict, and supporting clients in collaborative change initiatives through facilitation and coaching. She has worked with tens of thousands of people in thirty-four countries on just about every continent and with hundreds of organizations, governments, teams, and individuals including the United Nations, NASA, Senior Women Leaders of the Government of Afghanistan, and Columbia University.

Her initiative with the UN ultimately resulted in over one hundred thousand professionals being trained in collaborative, intercultural negotiation, one of the largest peacebuilding initiatives on the planet. She started her professional journey as a litigator in New York City but detoured to the negotiation and conflict resolution field after attending the Kennedy School at Harvard.

Coleman was born into one of the oldest colonial American families, where she has had a front row seat to the ironies of privilege, power, and patriarchy. Throughout her life, she has been an activist for evolutionary social change with a deep respect for both the diversity of humans and the natural world.